Mysticism

MYSTICISM

A Study of its Nature, Cognitive Value and Moral Implications

William J. Wainwright

Professor of Philosophy,
University of Wisconsin-Milwaukee

The University of Wisconsin Press

Published in the United States of America and Canada exclusively, and
elsewhere throughout the world except for the United Kingdom, the former
British Commonwealth, and Europe by

THE UNIVERSITY OF WISCONSIN PRESS
114 NORTH MURRAY STREET
MADISON, WISCONSIN 53715

ISBN 0-299-08910-X

Library of Congress Cataloging in Publication Data

Wainwright, William J.
    Mysticism: a study of its nature, cognitive
value, and moral implications.

    Bibliography: p. 234-42
    Includes index.
    1. Mysticism—Comparative studies.   I. Title.
BL625.W27   291.4′2   81-12922
ISBN 0-299-08910-X   AACR2

Typeset in 11 on 12 Linotron Baskerville
by Redwood Burn Limited, Trowbridge
Printed by The Thetford Press Limited
Thetford, Norfolk

Table of Contents

viii   *Contents*

Acknowledgements

Earlier versions of parts of this book have appeared as articles. I would like to thank the editors and publishers of thé journals concerned for permission to reprint the following material: 'Interpretation, Description, and Mystical Consciousness', *Journal of the American Academy of Religion* XLV (1977), (Supplement); 'Natural Explanations and Religious Experience', *Ratio* 15 (1973); 'Mysticism and Sense Perception', *Religious Studies* 9 (1973); 'Two Theories of Mysticism: Gilson and Maritain', *The Modern Schoolman* LII (1975); 'Morality and Mysticism', *Journal of Religious Ethics* 4 (1976). 'Stace and Mysticism', by W J Wainwright is reprinted from *The Journal of Religion* 50 (1970) by permission of The University of Chicago Press, © 1970 by The University of Chicago.

I would also like to thank Muriel Becker for her patience in preparing the typescript from my manuscript that was often illegible. I am especially grateful to my wife Eleanor for her support and encouragement, and for many tedious hours spent in proof reading.

Introduction

Throughout the course of history, people have had experiences which are commonly called 'mystical'. While returning from an evening with friends, Richard Bucke found himself suddenly 'wrapped around as it were by a flame-coloured cloud. For an instant,' he said:

he thought of fire, some sudden conflagration in the great city; the next, he knew that the light was within himself. Directly afterwards came upon him a sense of exultation, of immense joyousness accompanied or immediately followed by an intellectual illumination quite impossible to describe ... he saw and knew that the Cosmos is not dead matter but a living Presence, that the soul of man is immortal, that ... all things work together for the good of each and all ... The illumination itself continued not more than a few moments, but its affect proved ineffaceable ... neither did he, or could he, ever doubt the truth of what was then presented to his mind.[1]

Karl Joel spoke of an experience in which, as he lay on the seashore, 'Distance and nearness become blurred into one; without and within glide into each other ... the world exhales in the soul and the soul dissolves in the world.'[2] Describing absorption in Brahman, the 'disciple' in Śaṁkara's *Crest Jewel of Discrimination* says:

The ego has disappeared. I have realised my identity with Brahman and so all my desires have melted away. I have arisen above my ignorance and my knowledge of this seeming universe. What is this joy I feel? Who shall measure it? I know nothing but joy, limitless, unbounded! The ocean of Brahman is full of nectar – the joy of the Atman. The treasure I have found there cannot be described in words. The mind cannot conceive of it. My mind fell like a hailstone into that vast expanse of Brahman's ocean. Touching one drop of it, I melted away and became one with Brahman ... Where is this universe? Who took it away? Has it merged into something else? A while ago, I beheld it – now it exists no longer... Here is the ocean of Brahman, full of endless joy... Is there anything apart or distinct from Brahman? Now, finally and clearly, I know that I am the Atman [which in this context, can be identified with Brahman], whose nature is eternal joy. I see nothing, I hear nothing, I know nothing that is separate from me.[3]

Describing 'unification' (tauhīd) Junayd said:

Unification is this, that one should be a figure in the hands of God, a figure over which His decrees pass according as He in His omnipotence determines, and that one should be sunk in the sea of His unity, self-annihilated and dead alike to the call of mankind to him and his answer to them, absorbed by the reality of the divine unity in true proximity, and lost to sense and action, because God fulfills in him what He hath willed of him, namely that his last state become his first state, and that he should be as he was before he existed.[4]

In speaking of the 'sixth mansion' of prayer, Teresa of Avila reported that the soul is sometimes

conscious of having been most delectably wounded... It complains to its Spouse with words of love, and even cries aloud, being unable to help itself, for it realises that He is present but will not manifest Himself in such a way as to allow it to enjoy Him, and this is a great grief, though a sweet and delectable one... So powerful is the effect of this upon the soul that it becomes consumed with desire, yet cannot think what to ask, so clearly conscious is it of the presence of its God.[5]

John of the Cross spoke of a state in which 'the soul lives the life of God'. In this state, its understanding

is now moved and informed by ... the supernatural light of God, and has been changed into the Divine, for its understanding and that of God are now both one. And the will ... has now been changed into the life of Divine love; for it loves after a lofty manner with Divine affection and is moved by the Holy Spirit in Whom it now lives, since its will and His will are now only one... And finally, all the movements and operations which the soul had aforetime ... are now in this union changed into movements of God.[6]

One of the most striking features of these experiences is what William James referred to as their 'noetic' character. Those who have them are usually convinced that they are, for the first time, seeing things as they really are. This may, as in Bucke's case, involve a sense of discovery, an overpowering revelation of something hitherto unknown. In other cases, it involves the conviction that one directly perceives realities which one had previously only heard of, or had accepted on faith. In either case, the mystic believes that, in his experience, he is directly aware of a reality which is normally hidden from us. Cognitive claims, that is claims about the nature of reality, are thus built into the very structure of mystical experiences.

The truth of these claims would have significant implications for our understanding of human nature and the world. For example, mystics typically distinguish the 'true self' from the ordinary empirical self. The latter is roughly identical with a person's body, his ordinary consciousness, and those aspects of his unconscious life which are accessible to psychoanalysis. The empirical self is thus identical with the self as usually understood. Mystics, however, frequently assert that the empirical self is the least important aspect of human personality; and they sometimes assert that our empirical selves are unreal. If their experiences can be trusted, it would seem that what we truly are is something radically unitary and inherently joyful which altogether transcends space and time.

Mystical assertions about the world are equally radical. Some mystics claim to *perceive* that the distinctions which we normally draw between one phenomenal object and another are merely conventional – that suns, trees, birds and stones are one. Others claim that, during their experience, time is somehow *seen* to be unreal. Some maintain that they have experimentally apprehended an undifferentiated unity, or One, which transcends the space-time world, or assert that they have 'felt' or 'touched' the being of God. If these convictions are correct, our ordinary ways of understanding reality are defective. At the very least, any view is mistaken which identifies reality with the world of science and common sense.

The validity of mystical experience would also have significant implications for the theory of knowledge. At least in the West, it has normally been assumed that there are ultimately only three, or possibly four, sources of knowledge – introspection, sense perception, and inductive or deductive reasoning. Some would add an intuitive knowledge of the truth of certain necessary propositions (for example, that a whole is greater than its parts, or that cruelty is *prima facie* wrong). But *perceptual* knowledge, the direct and immediate apprehension of extra-mental things, has usually been restricted to sense perception.[7] If the mystics are correct, this is mistaken, for mystical consciousness provides a quasi-perceptual grasp of realities·inaccessible to our senses. Nor is the mistake trivial, since it is highly probable that views about reality which are based on introspection, sense perception, reasoning, and the intuition of necessary truths will prove to be very different from views about reality which are based on these things *and* mystical consciousness.

The following chapters will investigate the cognitive pretensions of mystical experience. Chapter 1 is preliminary but important. In that chapter we shall attempt to determine whether there are different types of mystical consciousness, and how descriptions of mystical experience are to be distinguished from interpretations of mystical experience. These issues are important because different types of mystical consciousness may incorporate different claims, and because we must be able to distinguish descriptions from interpretations if we are to identify the claims which are built into the structure of the experience itself. Chapter 2 will explore the implications which the existence of an adequate scientific explanation of mystical consciousness would have for its cognitive status. Chapter 3 will examine the contention that mystical experiences are significantly similar to sense experiences, and discuss standard objections to the claim that these experiences have cognitive value. Chapter 4 will examine two important theories of mystical experience – the theory of Walter Stace who argues (among other things) that mystical experience transcends logic and the distinction between subjectivity and objectivity, and certain neo-scholastic theories which maintain that the mystic's awareness of God cannot be direct and immediate. Chapter 5 will attempt to determine whether ethical ideals and convictions are implicitly built into mystical experience, and are thus sound if mystical experience is veridical.

The primary purpose of this book is to show that there are good, if not conclusive, reasons for believing that some mystical experiences are veridical, and that the claims which are built into them are true. Its secondary purpose is to clarify the relevant philosophical issues, and to suggest that their resolution is more difficult than either defenders of mysticism, or its detractors, have sometimes supposed.

Notes

[1] *Cosmic Consciousness*, New York, 1956, pp 9–10.
[2] Quoted in Carl Jung, *Psychology of the Unconscious*, New York, 1947, pp 360–1.
[3] *Shankara's Crest Jewel of Discrimination*, transl and with an intro by Swami Prabhavananda and Christopher Isherwood, New York, 1970, pp 103–104.
[4] Quoted in Annemarie Schimmel, *Mystical Dimensions of Islam*, Chapel Hill, North Carolina, 1975, p 146.
[5] *Interior Castle*, transl and ed E Allison Peers, Garden City, New York, 1961, pp 135–6.
[6] *Living Flame of Love*, transl and ed by E Allison Peers, Garden City, New York, 1962, pp 78–9.
[7] Perception is sometimes construed more broadly, introspection being regarded as a kind of 'internal' perception. But this does not affect the main point, for 'external' perception is restricted to sense perception.

CHAPTER 1

The Nature of Mystical Experience

I

While modern English speakers use 'mystical experience' to refer to a wide variety of praeternatural experiences, scholars have tended to restrict the term to
(1) 'unitary' states which are
(2) noetic, but
(3) lack *specific* empirical content.
In these experiences, the distinctions which are ordinarily drawn between subject and object, between one object and another, and between different places and times are radically transcended. Although they are noetic, or perception-like, they are not experiences of specific items within the phenomenal world but intuitive apprehensions of the (character of) the space-time world as a whole or of something which transcends it.

Mystical experiences should be distinguished from ordinary religious feelings and sentiments, from numinous experiences, and from visions, voices and such occult phenomena as telepathy, clairvoyance, and precognition. None of these experiences is unitary. In addition, voices, visions, and 'occult' intuitions have specific empirical content, while ordinary devotional feelings and sentiments are not noetic. A consideration of these differences will clarify our definition of mysticism, and provide reasons for its adoption.

A
Liturgical activity, prayer, the proclamation and reception of God's word or the contemplation of religious subjects can be the source of deeply affective experiences. In devout people,

1

love, awe, trust, fear, devotion, gratitude and other religious affections and sentiments are habitual both in the sense that they are easily and frequently aroused, and in the sense that they become constituents of their personalities, shaping and influencing their actions and responses. These experiences are undoubtedly essential to any kind of vital piety. Nevertheless, they should not be confused with numinous experience or mystical consciousness, for the latter have a perceptual character and ordinary religious affections and sentiments do not.

The failure to see this may be partially responsible for the view that all people, or at least all believers, are somehow immediately aware of the 'Ground of being'.[1] This failure is not entirely inexcusable for ordinary religious affections and sentiments do have a cognitive dimension.

For example, consider some of the feelings or sentiments associated with theism – a sense of the world's contingency and dependence, the impression that existence is a gift, a sense of the 'beauty and sweetness' of the gospel, or feelings of sinfulness. Three things should be noticed about these affections and sentiments.

(1) These affections are not 'mere' feelings, for they are essentially connected with certain beliefs. For example, the sense of contingency is not just a feeling but a feelingful *conviction*; the *belief* that the world is contingent comes home to us in wonder or dread. In order to feel that existence is a gift, one must at least entertain the proposition that its cause is a person: (for gifts are bestowed by persons.)

(2) It is possible to argue that one cannot appreciate religious claims, see what there is 'in them', or why people take them seriously, if one has never experienced religious feelings and sentiments. Religious affections may be needed if one is to understand religious claims. The sense which the term 'understand' has in the last sentence is the sense it has in 'I did not understand the meaning of romantic love until I read *Tristan and Iseult*,' or 'I did not understand that war was hell until I was sent to Vietnam.' Acquiring this sort of understanding is not a matter of picking up new information. A person who has read *Tristan and Iseult* or spent time in Vietnam is not necessarily able to make any significant true statements about romantic love or war which he was unable to make before.

What then has happened? He now knows what something *is like*. A proposition which he perhaps already believed has come home to him. What has been acquired is a new appreciation of things. It is legitimate to speak of this as a 'new understanding', or to say that one now *sees* something one had formerly missed. (The relevant sense of 'see' is analogous to its sense in 'I now see what you mean by saying that Freud's libido is similar to Plato's appetite.' 'See' could be replaced by 'understand' without loss of meaning.)

(3) Contrary to what is sometimes said, most theists are prepared to offer arguments for their beliefs. (For example, 'the history of Israel shows that God was actively at work,' 'only a divine man could have performed the signs and wonders which Jesus performed,' or 'the world would not be so orderly if there were no designer.') A person's assessment of the force of these arguments appears to be partly determined by his religious affections and sentiments, or lack of them.[2]

Religious affections and sentiments thus have a cognitive dimension. Nevertheless, they are no more like ordinary perceptual experiences (seeing, hearing, tasting, etc.) than entertaining a belief, understanding a proposition, or grasping an argument are like ordinary perceptual experiences. Unlike numinous and mystical experiences, religious affections or sentiments do not involve an intuitive sense of objective presence or reality, and are therefore not genuinely perceptual.[3]

B

In *The Idea of the Holy*,[4] Rudolf Otto described a mode of religious consciousness which he called 'numinous'. Numinous feeling contains five strands or components which are woven together to form one complex experience. The relation between these components is indicated by the following diagram:

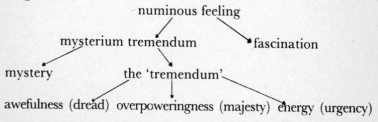

(1) The experience involves 'blank wonder, an astonish-
ment that strikes us dumb, an amazement absolute' (p 26). Its
apparent object is wholly other, irreducibly mysterious.
Gabriel Marcel has distinguished 'problems' from 'mysteries'.
Problems (for example, a chess problem, an engineering
problem, or the problems brought to Sherlock Holmes) have
solutions, although these solutions may never be discovered.
But if and when its solution is discovered, a problem disappears. A mystery, on the other hand, has no solution. No
matter how much we learn about it, it remains uncanny,
mysterious, unfathomable, incomprehensible. Numinous experience includes an impression of being in the presence of
something which is a mystery in this sense.

(2) Religious dread must be distinguished from ordinary
fear. It is more like a fear of ghosts or the dread of haunted
places. It is analogous to feelings which make our flesh creep
and our blood run icy cold. It is the impression of something
eerie, weird, and potentially very dangerous. (But not evil.
Tigers are dangerous but they are not evil or bad.)

(3) One has a sense of 'impotence and general nothingness
as against overpowering might,' or being 'dust and ashes as
against majesty' (p 21).

(4) One has the sense of being in the presence of something
overwhelmingly alive and urgent, something indicated by
terms suggesting 'vitality, passion, emotional temper, will,
force, movement, excitement, activity, impetus' (p 23).

(5) But the numinous is not only mysterious, awful and
overpowering, it is also fascinating, compelling, alluring,
enchanting. One is, so to speak, forced to turn towards it, to
make it one's own, or to be 'covered' by it. One wishes to
possess it, or be possessed by it. For it is a value so great, so
splendid, and so wonderful that all other values pale to insignificance when compared with it.

As this description implies, numinous experiences involve a
'sense of presence' and are thus noetic. They have the character of 'meetings' or 'encounters' with something or someone
both terrifying and wonderful.

Trees (the grove at Dodona), mountains (Olympus), rivers

(the Ganges), artifacts (the ark), places (Mecca), times (the New Year), human beings (Moses, the Buddha) and visionary 'realities' (the throne chariot of Ezekiel) can be objects of numinous feeling. But numinous feeling often lacks specific empirical content. In these cases its object is 'shapeless' and 'formless', an overwhelming reality which cannot be easily identified with any constituent of the phenomenal world.

Some numinous experiences, therefore, satisfy our second and third criteria, but they do not satisfy the first. A sense of unity is at the heart of mystical experience. Distances are annihilated, and distinctions overcome. If the experience has an object, the mystic experiences identity or union with that object. By contrast, a sense of absolute otherness, or distance, or difference is built into the very fabric of numinous experience. The numinous object is fascinating and wonderful, but it is also awful, majestic and overpowering; in its presence one feels empty, stripped of power and value. ('Who can survive before Yahweh the holy God!') Otto believed that mystical experience was a species of numinous experience. However, this difference between numinous experience and the unitary experiences which are usually regarded as mystical appears to be sufficiently striking to justify placing numinous experience in a separate category.[5]

C

Corredo Pensa has convincingly argued that a careful and unbiased examination of Yoga, Buddhism and Neoplatonism shows that while magical and occult powers are not cultivated for their own sake, they are believed to be a sign of increased spiritual power and a means to enlightenment. They are thus, he says, an integral part of these mystical paths.[6] According to Peter Moore, 'visions as a matter of fact have played rather an important role in the lives of many mystics, while in some mystical traditions they have been the focal phenomena and thus deliberately cultivated.'[7]

Pensa and Moore undoubtedly have a point. Occult phenomena are associated with mysticism. The aim of Merkabah mysticism was visionary experience, a perception of God's 'appearance on the throne, as described by Ezekiel, and cognition of the mysteries of the celestial throne-world.'[8] 'Visions of the Bodhisattvas, and of the Buddhas and their Paradises' were deliberately cultivated in Mahāyāna Buddhism.[9] Those who are familiar with the autobiographical writings of Teresa of Avila cannot help but be aware of the important role which visions and auditions played in her spiritual life.

It is not unreasonable to use 'mystical' for any ecstatic experience of transcendent reality. It is thus not unreasonable to apply the term to visions of the divine throne-chariot. Nor is it unreasonable to apply the term to any of the praeternatural experiences which typically occur in the lives of people who, like Teresa, are universally regarded as mystics.

Nevertheless, there are at least two reasons for using 'mysticism' in a more restricted sense. (1) Buddhist and Christian mystics tend to be suspicious of visionary experiences and occult phenomena, and to distinguish them from other more valued experiences. Scholem points out that in Merkabah mysticism, there was not only 'no divine immanence' but 'almost no love of God': that 'throughout there remained an almost exaggerated consciousness of God's *otherness*.'[10] The broader usage tends to blur a genuine distinction between visionary and occult states, and unitary states of consciousness. (2) Most of this century's important work on mysticism has been done by people who were primarily interested in unitary states of consciousness.[11] To alter what has now become a fairly standard usage invites confusion.

I would add that there is a good reason why philosophers should be especially concerned with unitary states of consciousness and numinous experiences. Visionary experiences and some occult phenomena are noetic. Telepathy, clairvoyance, and precognition, for example, are the source of empirically testable claims. However, while not all of these claims can be discounted, many, and perhaps most, of them should. Furthermore, it seems obvious that the content of most visionary experiences is culturally conditioned. (Buddhists seldom have visions of the Virgin Mary, and Christians rarely have visions of Bodhisattvas.) This does not preclude the possibility that the visionary is apprehending Reality through the medium of images which are supplied by his culture or by his own unconscious. Nevertheless, some scepticism is surely in order.

By contrast, since unitary and numinous experiences do not include empirically falsifiable beliefs, they do not include empirically *false* beliefs. Nor is it *obvious* that they are culturally conditioned. There are, therefore, reasons for discounting visions and occult phenomena which do not apply to unitary states of consciousness and numinous experiences. Consequently, the case for the cognitive validity of the latter must be taken more seriously.

D

There are, then, good reasons for distinguishing mystical consciousness from other types of religious experience. However, up to this point, little has been said concerning the nature of mystical experience itself. In the remainder of this chapter, we will (1) examine three influential attempts to characterise and classify various types of mystical experience; (2) discuss arguments which purport to show that no viable distinction can be drawn between the description of a mystical experience and its interpretation, and that a cross-cultural typology of mystical experience is impossible; (3) critically examine criteria which might be used to distinguish descriptions from interpretations and determine whether we are dealing with several experiences or with only one experience; and (4) propose a working typology.

Apart from their intrinsic interest, the problems with which we shall be concerned in the remainder of the chapter are significant for two reasons. In the first place, the typology we adopt will determine the manner in which we approach other problems. For example, Stace's typology of mystical experience has been adopted by a number of social scientists including Walter Pahnke, and Jean Houston and R E L Masters.[12] Their experimental investigations of chemical mysticism are important, and their interpretations of the relation between drug-induced states and mystical consciousness are intelligent and balanced. Nevertheless, because Stace does not recognise the existence of a distinctively theistic type of mystical experience, their use of his typology prevents them from clearly asking whether hallucinogens are capable of inducing theistic mystical consciousness. (One is unlikely to ask if drugs can induce theistic mystical consciousness if one does not believe that there is such a thing as theistic mystical consciousness.)

(2) The problem which we are considering also has important philosophical implications. If mystical experiences are cognitive, and if R C Zæhner is correct in maintaining that there are distinctively theistic forms of mystical experience, mystical experience would appear to provide at least some evidence for theism. If, on the other hand, Walter Stace and Ninian Smart are correct, these experiences are not intrinsically theistic but are only interpreted theistically. In that case, mystical experience does not provide any evidence for theism (as opposed to monism or pantheism). If it is also true, as Stace believes, that the accounts of mystical consciousness provided by Buddhists and Advaitins are freer from interpretation than the accounts of mystical experience provided by theists, then it is at least plausible to suggest that mystical experience provides evidence for the truth of monism and, therefore, for the falsity of theism. In short, if we are to determine the sort of evidence which mystical experience provides for religious claims we must not only determine the cognitive status of these experiences, we must also clarify their nature.

II

A

Walter Stace has drawn a very influential distinction between extrovertive and introvertive mysticism.[13] Extrovertive mystical consciousness is said to exhibit the following characteristics:

(1) All (phenomenal) things are perceived as one. Though the mystic sees trees, people, houses and so on, they appear to be mysteriously identical and/or rooted in some unity which lies behind them.

(2) The world is experienced as alive, or conscious, or as intimately rooted in life and consciousness: it is a 'living presence'.

(3) The experience is characterised by a 'sense of objectivity or reality,' (p 79). It does not seem to be 'a mere inner and subjective state of the soul', but on the contrary appears to have

'objective reference'. (p 67) Those who have the experience cannot help but suppose that it involves a perception of reality.

(4) The mystic enjoys a 'feeling of blessedness, joy, happiness, satisfaction, etc'. (p 79)

(5) He feels 'that what is apprehended is holy, or sacred, or divine'. (p 79)

(6) Paradoxicality is another feature of the experience. The experience and its object are typically described in terms which are, if taken literally, contradictory, and are in any case queer, odd or strained.

(7) The experience and its object are allegedly ineffable. The mystic claims that they cannot be adequately described in words. (Although, as Stace points out, some mystics manage to provide detailed, subtle and apparently accurate accounts of their experiences.)

Introvertive mystical consciousness is also said to exhibit seven characteristics:

(1) It is a unitary consciousness. This involves three things: (a) The mind of the mystic is emptied of ordinary contents. Awareness of the phenomenal world vanishes. The mystic no longer remembers, reasons or imagines. His soul is stripped of abstract thoughts and sensuous images. He does not, however, lapse into sleep or unconsciousness; (b) the mystic experiences a One (a Unity) which may be identified with his transcendent self, with Nirvāna, God, or something else of the kind; (c) the mystic experiences union or identity with this One.

(2) The introvertive mystic ceases to experience space and time.

In addition to these characteristics which distinguish introvertive mysticism from extrovertive mysticism, introvertive mystical consciousness is also said to be characterised by:

(3) The 'sense of objectivity or reality' (p 110);

(4) 'Feelings of blessedness, joy, peace, happiness, etc' (p 110);

(5) The 'feeling that what is apprehended is holy, sacred or divine' (p 110);

(6) Paradoxicality; and

(7) (Alleged) ineffability.

Stace's remarks are open to three minor objections and to one major objection. (1) His characterisation of extrovertive mysticism may not be entirely adequate. (a) It is not clear that the second characteristic which Stace ascribes to extrovertive mystical consciousness is always a feature of it. (The fact that Rudolf Otto does not include this feature in his characterisation of extrovertive mysticism is suggestive.) (b) In any case, there are two other characteristics which Stace does not mention but which seem to have an equal right to be regarded as essential (or at least typical) features of extrovertive mystical consciousness. The first characteristic is the sense of transfiguration. Natural objects become 'transparent, luminous, visionary'.[14] The second characteristic is perhaps more important. Time often appears to stand still for the nature mystic. While things are observed to occur during the experience, they somehow seem to take place timelessly. (A subject who was observing a wasp while under the influence of mescalin said that the wasp 'moved without moving'. (p 72)[15] The extrovertive experience typically involves something of this kind.) (c) There may be several different kinds of extrovertive mystical consciousness. Otto, for example, distinguishes between an experience in which all phenomenal things are seen as one, and another experience in which phenomenal objects are apprehended as rooted in their ground. In the first experience, the mystic, trees, stones, and blades of grass are 'perceived' to be mysteriously identical with one another. Natural objects are transfigured and resplendent, and time stands still. All phenomenal things seem to be one, but there is no thought of a reality over and above these phenomenal objects. In the second experience, the mystic seems to apprehend a power, or depth, or ground which is somehow behind them, which manifests itself through them, and is the source of their being. Phenomenal objects are now perceived to be changing modes or appearances of an underlying unity, or 'One'.[16]

(2) The phenomenal world is not always entirely obliterated during an introvertive mystical experience – a peripheral awareness of nature may remain. Teresa, for example, describes an introvertive state in which one may see letters but be unable to read them, may hear but be unable to understand what one hears, and so on. The senses are affected, but the mind takes little or no cognizance of these affects.[17] It is im-

portant to notice, however, this qualification does not blur the distinction between extrovertive and introvertive states, for while nature is in some sense the *object* of extrovertive mystical experiences, it is not the *object* of introvertive mystical experience even in those cases in which the introvertive mystic remains peripherally aware of it.[18]

(3) It is not clear that mystical experience is genuinely paradoxical. Peter Moore[19] has suggested that we should distinguish between autobiographical accounts of mystical experience (for example, those of Teresa or Suso), 'impersonal accounts' which describe mystical experience in general and abstract terms (for example, the works of John of the Cross, or the anonymous *Cloud of Unknowing*), and theological and speculative accounts of the apparent object of the experience (for example, Plotinus' philosophical works, Eckhart's speculative theology, of Śaṃkara's reflections on the Ātman-Brahman). Impersonal accounts may be partly based upon the author's own mystical states, and traditional lore concerning the nature of spiritual experience. (It is reasonable to suppose that the lore itself is partly based upon the experiences of men and women in the author's tradition.) Theological and speculative accounts of the mystical object do not describe mystical experience, and therefore at best provide only indirect indications of its nature. As Moore points out, it is significant that genuine paradox most frequently occurs in speculative accounts of the object of mystical experience, and only rarely in autobiographical and 'impersonal' accounts of the experience itself.

(4) The major difficulty with Stace's account is, as R C Zæhner insists, its failure to mention love. This is extraordinary in view of the central role which love plays in the accounts of both Eastern and Western theistic mystics. One fears that Zæhner is not being too harsh when he concludes that Stace's 'failure to mention love can only be due to an obvious anti-Christian [or, more accurately, anti-theistic] bias reinforced by a massive ignorance of the whole tradition of love-mysticism within Hinduism itself.'[20]

B

In *Mysticism, Sacred and Profane*,[21] Zæhner distinguishes three different sorts of mysticism.

(1) Nature mysticism or cosmic consciousness is (a) 'panen-henic' (p 28), 'without and within are one'. (p 41) The mystic experiences himself as either containing or being contained by everything else. His soul expands so as to include nature or else it dissolves into nature. In either case there is an 'abdication of the ego' or 'I' of ordinary consciousness (p 102), and (b) space and time are transcended.[22] (p 41) (c) The world which reveals itself to the nature mystic is one of extraordinary and marvellous beauty. (p 99) (d) The experience may be interpreted as a return to Eden (to 'original innocence') or as an experience of the 'natural bliss' of Limbo (pp 99, 200–201), for not only is cosmic consciousness ecstatic, (e) it is a pre-moral vision innocent of the distinction between good and evil.

(2) Soul mysticism or monistic mysticism[23] is an experience of undifferentiated unity which transcends space and time. It involves 'the isolation of the individual spirit ... from the whole psycho-physical complex which is the mortal part of man'. (p 168) The eternal is disentangled from the temporal so that the soul is totally free from desire and aversion and, since this 'detachment means a total indifference to all actions, whether they be good or evil' (p 128), is consequently amoral. The bliss which it experiences is that of the unbaptised infant in Limbo touched neither by actual sin nor by actual virtue.[24] (p 130)[25]

(3) (a) Like the soul mystic, the theistic mystic empties his mind of images and clear concepts, 'annihilates' his empirical ego and detaches himself from space and time, but unlike the soul mystic the theistic mystic does not regard this as an end in itself. On the contrary, it is merely a preparation for the mystical marriage in which the eternal self becomes the bride of God and is '"ravished", "annihilated", "assimilated" into the beloved.' (p 151)[26] (b) The monistic mystic enjoys 'peace' but he does not experience love and the 'ecstacy of union'. (p 172) He experiences a calm or rest of which the best image is deep and dreamless sleep, and which al-Ghazālī said, 'is near to non-existence'. The theistic mystic on the other hand rests in God, not in himself, and his experience is dynamic rather than quietistic, his soul plunging ever more deeply into the depths

of the Godhead. (p 182) (c) Theistic mysticism is further distinguished from monistic mysticism by the fact that theistic
mystics believe that 'it is God Himself who works in them and
makes them fit for union' (p 192), whereas monistic mystics
believe that the emptiness and unity which they achieve is
their own work. (d) Finally, 'the mystic who is genuinely
inspired by the divine love, will show this to the world by the
holiness of his life', (p 193) The amoralism of monistic mysticism contrasts with theistic mysticism's insistence upon the
importance of active charity. (pp 187–8)

The clear distinction between nature mysticism and
monistic mysticism becomes somewhat blurred in Zæhner's
later works.[27] Potentially more significant is the fact that, in
Concordant Discord, Zæhner shifted to the position that there
are *four*, rather than three, types of mystical experience.[28]
These are:

1   Cosmic consciousness, 'the transcending of spacial limitations and the consequent feeling that one is the All.

2   The transcending of temporal limitation and the consequent realisation that one cannot die.' (This experience may
accompany the first but it need not do so.)

'When these two experiences ... combine, they may con-
verge in yet another experience.' viz,

3   'The final denudation, the final stripping away from
spirit of all material, mental, and affective adjuncts, of all
difference and diversity,' 'the intuition of oneness outside
both space and time.' This oneness may be identified with
the Ātman-Brahman of Advaita Vedānta, the isolated puruṣa
of Sāṃkhya-Yoga, or 'the Absolute reflected in finite things,
the "image of God"' of the theistic traditions.

4   'The love of God in the context of pure spirituality
beyond space and time and beyond the "One".'

The last two appear to be indistinguishable from what
Zæhner had earlier identified as monistic mysticism and theistic mysticism respectively, but temporal transcendence is, for
the first time, clearly distinguished from cosmic consciousness
and monistic mysticism and treated as a separate mode of experience.

There are difficulties in Zæhner's new account.

(1) In one of the earlier lectures in *Concordant Discord*,

Zæhner had reasserted his belief that 'there are three types of
mystical experiences. First, there is nature mysticism … it
sees the human self as encompassing all Nature, the subjective
"I" is merged into the cosmic All … Secondly, there is the
mysticism of "isolation" – the isolation of the eternal soul from
all that has its being in space and time … Lastly, there is the
mysticism of the love of God.' (p 59) Zæhner never explains
the shift in his position.[29]

(2) Monistic mysticism cannot be a *combination* or *convergence*
of cosmic consciousness and the transcendence of time, for the
awareness of nature which is essential to cosmic consciousness
is not a feature of the monistic experience.

(3) It is not entirely clear that Zæhner's second kind of experience is a distinct form of mystical consciousness.

There appear to be at least two different sorts of temporal
transcendence – (a) the sense that time stands still, that all is
happening in an 'eternal now', and (b) the sort of temporal
transcendence which occurs when one altogether loses consciousness of the space-time world.[30] The second appears to be
a *property* of soul mysticism and theistic mysticism, and not a
separate mode of mystical consciousness. The first sort of temporal transcendence, on the other hand, may define a unique
type of mystical experience.

To support the claim that temporal transcendence is a
distinct mode of mystical consciousness, Zaehner refers to
Eckhart's concept of the Eternal Now, and quotes from the
Bhagavad-Gītā and Richard Jefferies. The quotations from the
second chapter of the *Gītā* prove nothing.[31] The quotation
from Jefferies is more significant. The experience described by
Jefferies[32] is an experience of nature in which time is transcended; everything takes place in an 'eternal now'. Other features usually associated with cosmic consciousness or nature
mysticism are either absent, or are at least not mentioned. (For
example, there is no mention of the transfiguration or identity
of natural objects, of the expansion of the self, or of nature as a
living presence.) Zæhner is right to this extent: there may be a
distinct form of *extrovertive* mystical consciousness which essentially consists in seeing nature *sub species aeternitatis*.

There are, then, difficulties in Zæhner's later account. It is
important to notice however that Zæhner never modified his

most significant and controversial thesis, viz, that theistic mystical experience is a distinct type of mystical consciousness. Is Zæhner correct?

C

According to Ninian Smart[33] two considerations suggest that Zæhner has failed to show that soul mysticism and theistic mysticism are distinct forms of introvertive mystical consciousness.

(1) If Zæhner is correct, Buddhist mystics, Yogic mystics and Advaitin mystics are all monistic mystics. Nevertheless they *interpret* their experiences in radically different ways. The Buddhist claims that 'there are no eternal selves, but only impermanent' empirical egos which 'go out like a flame' when they pass into Nibbāna. (p 83) According to Yoga, a plurality of eternal selves exists. Each individual can free his own eternal self from its entanglement in nature, and this freedom is liberation. The Advaitins maintain that there is only one eternal self (the Ātman) which is identical with the ground of being (the Brahman). Liberation consists in the recognition of one's identity with the Ātman-Brahman.

If Zæhner is correct, it is a mistake to argue from the difference between these *interpretations* to a difference in the *experiences* which are being interpreted. Is it any less of a mistake to argue that since theistic mystics and monistic mystics provide different accounts of their experiences, the *experience* of the theistic mystic must differ from the *experience* of the monistic mystic? The force of this point is reinforced by the fact that the differences between theistic accounts and Advaitin accounts appear to be no greater than the differences between Advaitin accounts and Buddhist accounts.

(2) Zæhner relies heavily on passages from Ruysbroeck in which the Flemish mystic appears to distinguish between soul mysticism and theistic mysticism *on the basis of his own experience*. Smart quotes two of these passages:

Now observe that whenever man is empty and undistracted in his senses by images, and free and unoccupied in his highest powers, he attains rest by purely natural means. And all men can find and possess this rest in themselves by their mere nature, without the grace of God, if they are able to empty themselves of sensual images and of all action.

Through the natural rest, which they feel and have in themselves in empti-ness, they maintain that they are free, and united with God without mean, and that they are advanced beyond all the exercises of Holy Church, and beyond the commandments of God, and beyond the law, and beyond all the virtuous works which one can in any way practise.[34]

Smart suggests that Ruysbroeck's distinction between mystics who rest in themselves and mystics who rest in God can be easily explained by (a) Ruysbroeck's recognition of the fact that some mystics refuse to subscribe to, and act in accord-ance with, moral and ecclesiastical norms whereas other mystics do not, and (b) by his conviction that while both claim to have experienced God, only the latter are interpreting their experiences correctly. According to Smart there is no need to suppose that Ruysbroeck's distinction is based upon his own experience of two modes of introvertive mystical con-sciousness. Smart could be correct. Whether he has offered the most plausible interpretation of these passages is another matter.

More is at issue than two texts. The most impressive evi-dence for Zæhner's position is provided by the fact that several Eastern and Western theistic mystics (Ruysbroeck, Rāmā-nuja, and possibly Richard of St Victor and al-Junayd)[35] create the impression that they have *themselves* experienced two types of introvertive consciousness, that they know what mon-istic experiences are like because they have had them, but that there is a clearly distinct introvertive experience which is the-istic in character which they have also experienced and which is not to be confused with them.[36] The examination of one or two short passages settles nothing. What is needed is a careful examination of the writings of these mystics, in order to deter-mine whether or not the alleged distinction actually does have a basis in their experience. Familiarity with the relevant texts must be combined with a freedom from theistic or antitheistic bias, a suspension of antecedent assumptions about the unity or diversity of mystical experience, and good judgment. An investigation which meets these standards will not result in a conclusive demonstration that theistic and monistic experiences are or are not the same. Nevertheless, a person who approaches the texts in this manner will find some support for Zæhner's interpretation or at the very least, be forced to conclude that his interpretation is not clearly mistaken.

Smart realises that he has by no means *established* that theistic and monistic experiences are the same, but he believes that what he has said 'is sufficient to cast doubt on the Zæhner analysis' (p 87), and that the following theses are quite possibly true:

(1) Phenomenologically, [introvertive] mysticism is everywhere the same.

(2) Different flavours, however, accrue to the experiences of mystics because of their [different] ways of life and modes of auto-interpretation.[37]

(3) The truth of interpretation depends in large measure on factors extrinsic to the mystical experience itself. [For example, the truth of a theistic interpretation depends upon the truth of theism, and mystical experiences are not the only things relevant to a determination of theism's truth or falsity.] (p 87)

I do not wish to quarrel with Smart's third point. His first two theses, however, appear to be logically incompatible. If the experiences of monistic and theistic mystics actually have different *flavours*, then it is false that these experiences are phenomenologically *identical*. If the second thesis is true (and it appears to be), the experiences of monistic mystics and theistic mystics cannot be exactly the same. Or does Smart only mean to say that all introvertive experiences are alike in *most* respects? Perhaps they are, but *that* they are is compatible with Zæhner's thesis, for experiences can be alike in most respects and not be the same experience. If, for example, we compare Stace's description of extrovertive mystical experience and his description of introvertive mystical experience, we find that most of the features which characterise one also characterise the other. If Stace is correct, extrovertive and introvertive mysticism is alike in most respects. But it does not follow that we are dealing with a single experience. Similarly, the fact (if it is a fact) that all introvertive experiences are alike in most respects does not entitle us to infer that there is only one type of introvertive experience, and that the difference between monistic and theistic mysticism is essentially a difference of interpretation.[38]

III

Stace, Zæhner and Smart assume that a viable distinction can be drawn between the description of mystical experience and its interpretation, and that a cross-cultural typology of mystical experience is possible. This assumption has recently been challenged.[39]

A
Bruce Garside asks us to consider the following argument.

(1) Experience is a joint product of 'set' (the conceptual framework which the subject brings to the experience) and 'setting' (the external stimuli). Therefore,

(2) 'An interpretative framework ... enters into ... experience itself as a constitutive factor.' (From 1) Therefore,

(3) An interpretative framework enters into *mystical* experience as a constitutive factor. (From 2) Therefore,

(4) There is no such thing as 'a mystical experience "undistorted" by any interpretative framework.' (From 3) Therefore,

(5) 'It makes no sense to look for an "authentic" description' of such an experience. (From 4)[40]

It is not entirely clear what Garside means when he says that 'an interpretative framework ... enters into ... experience itself as a constitutive factor.' One's conceptual framework is not normally an object of experience, nor is it some kind of mental act. It is true, however, that beliefs which reflect or depend upon interpretative (conceptual) frameworks are constituents of many experiences including mystical experiences.[41] If (4) does no more than call this to our attention, then (4) is true.

How are we to understand (5)? An authentic description of a mystical experience could be regarded as (a) a description of the 'given', the 'raw data' contributed by the setting; or (b) as a description of the elements common to that experience and the experience which would be enjoyed in a similar setting by someone who belonged to a different religious tradition and thus possessed different conceptual equipment, or by someone who possessed ordinary conceptual equipment (the equipment which is relatively invariant from culture to culture) but did not habitually interpret the world in terms of the categories and concepts of a particular religious tradition;[42] or, more plausibly, (c) as an accurate description of those and only those features which are – whether contributed by setting or set – constitutive of the experience, i.e. of those features which are part of the experience and without which the experience would not be the sort of experience it is.

By contrast, an interpretation would attempt to relate the elements so described to a larger context, that is to beings, qualities, events or states of affairs, the existence of which is supposed to explain or account for the experience and/or its components. Thus, as Garside points out, a psychoanalyst who attempts to explain religious experience by connecting it with childhood traumas, the operation of certain psychic mechanisms, and so on, is interpreting religious experience. Similarly, when a mystic asserts that God is the cause of his experience he is offering an interpretation of it.[43]

If (4) and (5) are understood in the way I have suggested, (4) does not imply (5). That the beliefs which partially constitute mystical experience reflect conceptual structures does not imply that we are unable to give authentic descriptions of mystical experience in any of the three senses of 'authentic description' which have been provided, or that a viable distinction between description and interpretation is impossible.

B

According to Steven Katz, there are no 'pure' or 'unmediated experiences'. Attitudes, expectations, beliefs and intentions shape experience. Since attitudes, expectations, beliefs, and intentions vary from tradition to tradition, mystical experience varies from tradition to tradition. It is thus a mistake to suppose that there are only a few types of mystical experience. On the contrary, there are as many types of mystical experience as there are traditions. A cross-cultural typology of mystical experience is therefore impossible.[44]

Katz's argument is essentially this:

(1) Mystical experience is largely constituted by the tradition within which it occurs.[45] Therefore,

(2) There are as many types of mystical experience as there are traditions. Therefore,

(3) A cross-cultural typology of mystical experience is impossible. The argument is not compelling.

What is Katz' evidence for the first premise? (1) There are, in general, no 'pure' or 'unmediated' experiences. (2) Not only are there great differences between the experiences of (for example) Jewish mystics and Buddhist mystics, there are also differences between the theistic mysticism of the *Bhagavad-Gītā*, Rāmānuja, Teresa, Isaac Luria and al-Hallaj, and between the monism of Śaṁkara, Spinoza, and Eckhart. (3) A person's beliefs, training, intentions and expectations determine the type of experience he will have. It is not an accident that Jewish mystics do not have monistic experiences, and that Buddhist mystics do not have theistic experiences. (4) Lists of characteristics allegedly common to all mystical experience, or to all mystical experience of a certain type, are misleading. They are misleading because the meaning of a term like 'ineffable' or 'nothingness' depends upon the context in which it is uttered, and these contexts vary.

These considerations do not establish Katz' premise. His epistemological assumption is unexplained and unsupported. In any case, that no experience is entirely 'pure' or 'unmediated' does not entail that the nature of mystical experience is significantly determined by the religious tradition to which the mystic belongs. The contribution of the subject's set may be comparatively negligible, and even if it is not, other elements in the subject's set may be more important than his tradition.

The second and third pieces of evidence show that there is a strong correlation between the tradition to which a mystic belongs, and the type of experience he will have. They do not show that the connection is necessary, and thus do not show that the experience is *constituted* by the tradition with which it is correlated.[46] The gastronomic experiences of Eskimos, Parisians, and Vietnamese are quite different. There is a strong correlation between these experiences and their cultures. Nevertheless, it would be absurd to suppose that the connection was anything but contingent, and that a person from a different culture could not have the gastronomic experiences of an Eskimo. Again, an epicure who deliberately seeks the experience associated with a rare fish sauce is more likely to obtain it than a person who does not. It is nonetheless implausible to suppose that his experience is (largely) constituted by his expectations, the steps which he took to secure the experience, and so on.[47]

Katz is correct in maintaining that terms like 'ineffable', 'noetic', and 'blissful' are applied to experiences which are very different from one another. It does not follow that the *meaning* of these terms varies when they are applied to different experiences. (Cats and whales are quite different, but 'mammals' has the same meaning in the sentence 'cats are mammals' and the sentence 'whales are mammals'.) Furthermore, the fact that two experiences can both be ineffable or noetic and still be very different does not imply that two experiences can share *all* of (for example) Zæhner's characteristics of theistic mysticism and be very different, and yet it is the latter which needs to be demonstrated. Nevertheless Katz does have a point. The use of a few similar terms is not sufficient to show that experiences are importantly similar. As he observes, Buddhists, Kabbalists, and Pseudo-Dionysius mean very different things by 'nothingness'. Some Buddhists, for example, use the term to refer to ordinary reality viewed without conceptualisation, and without attachment or aversion. By contrast, Dionysius uses the term to express the absolute difference between God and created being. But the argument is again a non-sequitur. It does not follow that the experience of these Buddhists and the experiences of Dionysius are somehow *constituted* by their respective 'contexts'.

I conclude, then, that the sort of considerations adduced by Katz fail to show that mystical experience is (largely) constituted by the tradition within which it occurs. Considerations of this type do, however, provide some evidence for (2), viz, that there are as many different mystical experiences as there are traditions. Katz therefore does not really need (1).

Unfortunately, (2) does not entail (3). That there are many

diverse mystical experiences does not show that it is unreasonable to classify mystical experiences under a few general head-
ings. All that is necessary is that some of these diverse
experiences sufficiently resemble one another to be grouped
together. Rabbits, bass, grasshoppers, whales and butterflies
are very different from one another. It is nevertheless reasonable to divide the animal kingdom into relatively few categories (mammals, fish, reptiles, etc.). There are differences
between Tristan's love for Iseult, Romeo's love for Juliet, and
Werther's love for Lotte, but it is not a mistake to suppose that
these loves exhibit important similarities, and that the concept
of romantic love is a useful concept with a basis in reality. In
short, *even if* there were as many different mystical experiences
as there are traditions, a cross-cultural typology of mystical
consciousness might still be possible.[48]

C

I do not wish to deny that mystical experiences include beliefs
which reflect conceptual structures which the mystic brings to
his experiences, although I am not convinced that these beliefs
primarily reflect *religious* structures. (The belief that one immediately apprehends an overwhelming non-empirical good
incorporates concepts, but the concepts are not specifically *religious*.) Nor do I wish to deny that the 'colour' or 'taste' of
mystical experience varies from tradition to tradition; that, for
example, Teresa's experiences, and not merely her descriptions, have a Christian flavour. Furthermore, there are undoubtedly cases in which it is plausible to suppose that not
only the 'colour' or 'tone' of an experience but some of its constituents have been contributed by the mystic's religious tradition. As Peter Moore suggests, when a mystic's experience
contains imagery peculiar to his tradition or provides a 'phenomenological analogue' of one of its distinctive beliefs or doctrines, it is reasonable to suppose that his experience is partly
constituted by the traditional material he brought to it.[49]
These points are not at issue. What is at issue is their relevance
for the possibility of a typology.

　　Problems are allegedly created by the fact that the mystical
'given' cannot be abstracted from the other components of
mystical experience. I suggest, however, that (1) it is not clear

that a mystical 'given' can never be abstracted and described, but that (2) even if it cannot, it does not follow that we are unable to abstract a 'common-core' from the mystical experiences of different traditions. Only the latter is needed for a cross-cultural typology.

(1) In the case of visual experience, we can distinguish (1) the external stimulus, (2) raw visual data, that is, conceptually unstructured sense impressions, (3) the phenomenological object, for example, a desk-like surface apprehended from a particular point of view, and (4) the experience's apparent object, for example, a desk. (Unless the experience is delusive, it entitles us to say not only that we see a desk-like surface, but that we see a desk.) When the experience is veridical, (4) (or at least (3)) will actually exist and (4) (or (3)) will coincide with (1). The distinction between (2) and (3) is roughly this: (2) is all that would have been experienced in the circumstances in which (3) was experienced, if the perceiver had (like a new-born child) lacked ordinary conceptual equipment. Raw visual sense data are presumably that part of a visual experience which is uniquely contributed by its setting. What is 'given' in visual experience is these impressions (and, in another sense, the phenomenological object which is presented ('given') to the person who apprehends it). Because the experience's phenomenological object is distinct from its apparent object, the experience provides a warrant for *two* perceptual claims – a claim to have perceived the experience's phenomenological object ('I saw a desk-like surface'), and a claim to have perceived its apparent object ('I saw a desk'). The experience's phenomenological object is a part, or aspect, or mode, or property of its apparent object, and hence, when both perceptual claims are in order, a perception of the first *is* a perception of the second.[50]

The application of these distinctions to mystical experience is problematic. In the case of nature mysticism, the 'raw data' are presumably fairly ordinary visual, auditory, tactual and (sometimes) olfactory sense data, although these may be unusually intense and vivid, and may sometimes include impressions of luminosity. Its phenomenological object often seems to be (surfaces of) certain natural objects (trees, stones, blades of grass) seen as one and transfigured, while its apparent object is nature or the cosmos. Whether these distinctions can be made in the case of monistic consciousness is less clear. Blissful empty consciousness appears to be its phenomenological 'object'. Blissful empty consciousness could also be regarded as the experience's raw data if it were in no way constituted by the concepts which the mystic brings to his experience. Since the experience appears to be non-conceptual (but see chapter 3, II*E*), it is tempting to conclude that it is not, and that blissful empty consciousness is therefore the experience's raw data as well as its phenomenological object. (Its apparent object may be one's puruṣa, Nibbāna, or the Atman-Brahman.)

The phenomenological object of theistic mystical consciousness seems to be (something like) an overwhelming loving presence. Its apparent object may be Yahweh, the necessary and immutable God of classical Christian theism, or Viṣṇu. I am strongly inclined to believe that this phenomenological object is part of the common-core of all theistic mystical experience. I suspect that it is a product of nothing more than the action of an appropriate stimulus and ordinary conceptual equipment. What is not clear to me is that the experience includes anything corresponding to sense data. Theistic mystical experience does include feelings and sensations. For example, it includes a feeling of presence, transports of love, and sensations of delight. But whether these function like sense data is a moot point.[51] Nor is it clear that *anything* would have been experienced if God (or some other appropriate stimulus) had acted upon a consciousness or sensibility that lacked conceptual equipment, in the same manner in which He (allegedly) acted upon Teresa. It is thus not clear that theistic mystical consciousness includes 'raw data'.

Although the details may be mistaken, the thrust of these remarks seems to me to be correct, viz, that while all mystical experiences have a 'given' in the sense that they have some kind of phenomenological 'object' which is 'presented' to the person who has the experience, some mystical experiences do *not* have a 'given' in the sense of raw data which would have been experienced in that setting by a person who lacked ordinary conceptual equipment.[52]

But it is important to notice two things. First, even if some mystical consciousness contains no raw data, it does not follow that it is 'merely subjective'. It is possible for an experience to be partly determined by an external stimulus even though no part of that experience can be isolated and identified as its unique contribution. It is a philosophical superstition to suppose that every experience which is a joint product of set and setting is composed of parts that can be neatly separated into those contributed by the set and those (the raw data) contributed by the setting. Hence, the fact that a separation of this sort is sometimes impossible does not imply that the set is totally, or even primarily, responsible for the character of the experience.

Second, in those cases in which it *is* reasonable to suppose that the experience includes raw data (for example, nature mysticism), there seems to be no reason to suppose that it would be any more difficult to isolate and describe these data than to isolate and describe the sensory data involved in ordinary perception.[53]

(2) A 'common-core' must be distinguished from the 'given' or raw data. Thus, the common-core in our visual perceptions of the cathedral at Chartres includes elements contributed by the subject as well as elements contributed by the setting. The common-core which can be abstracted from the visual experiences of a poor child and a rich child who judge a coin to be larger and smaller respectively, includes more than raw data. (Both children see a *coin*, not just colours and shapes.) Similarly, the person who sees a puzzle picture as a duck and the person who sees it as a rabbit, both see it as a *figure*.

The point of these considerations is this: *even if* mystical experience were principally constituted by what the subject brings to it, and *even if* it were impossible to identify a 'given' by isolating the contribution of the experience's setting, one might still be able to abstract a common-core from the experiences of mystics belonging to different traditions. All that is necessary is that there be significant similarities between their experiences.

D

Our discussion suggests that three mistakes or confusions, in particular, may prevent us from seeing that a cross-cultural typology of mystical experience is possible. The first two confusions are (1) the confusion between interpretations *of* mystical experience, and elements incorporated *within* it which reflect the beliefs, attitudes and expectations which the mystic brings to his experience, and (2) the confusion between the 'given' and the 'common-core'.

Recognising the difficulty of distinguishing those elements of an experience which are contributed by the mystic from those elements which are not, or of isolating an experience's raw data from its other aspects, one concludes that interpretation cannot be distinguished from description, and that typologies which are based upon the assumption that (pure) descriptions of mystical experience *are* possible are inherently flawed.

The error is to assume that a pure description of mystical experience is a description of what is contributed by the setting, or the 'given'.[54] This is an error because what is contributed by the setting, or the 'given', is not the experience itself but, at most, one of its components. Nor can the contribution of the setting, or the 'given', be identified with the common-core shared by mystical experiences from different traditions. A typology would be impossible only if it were impossible to describe the experience as a *whole* (incorporated beliefs, 'given', colouring, and all). A cross-cultural typology would be impossible only if it were impossible to isolate a common-core in experiences from different traditions. Neither of these tasks requires us to identify those elements in the experience or common-core which are 'given' or contributed by the setting. Hence, neither task has been shown to be impossible.

The third confusion is the confusion between 'significantly different' and 'not significantly similar' or 'not of the same type'. Recognising the existence of interesting and sometimes significant dissimilarities between the experiences of mystics in different traditions, one concludes that, because an adequate cross-cultural typology presupposes the existence of significant cross-cultural similarities, an adequate cross-cultural typology is impossible.

The mistake is to suppose that the existence of significant dissimilarities is incompatible with the existence of significant similarities, or that two things which are significantly different (for example, whales and kangaroos) cannot be the same type of thing (for example, mammals).

I therefore conclude that no adequate reasons have been provided for asserting that mystical experiences cannot be described, or that a cross-cultural typology of mystical experience is impossible.

IV

In principle, then, there appears to be no reason why we cannot distinguish interpretations of mystical experience from descriptions of mystical experience, or determine whether we are dealing with several types of mystical consciousness or a single type. In practice, our ability to perform these tasks depends upon the existence of criteria for making these distinctions and determinations. What might these criteria be like? Let us approach the question by asking whether there are reasons for supposing that the differences between introvertive mystics are (Stace and Smart), or are not (Zæhner), largely differences of interpretation.

A
What might lead someone like Zæhner to suppose that while Yogic, Advaitin and Theravādin mystics are each interpreting the *same* experience, Teresa or John of the Cross on the one hand, and these monistic mystics on the other, are interpreting different experiences? The experiences of Yogic, Advaitin and Theravādin mystics clearly exhibit many common characteristics[55] and this is *a* reason for supposing that they are all interpreting the *same* experience. It is also true that the experiences of Teresa and the experiences of the Advaitins exhibit many common characteristics. Why, then, should we suppose that Teresa's experiences differ from those of her Advaitin counterparts? Perhaps, because (1) we can somehow see how a common experience characterised by bliss, peace, an apprehension of undifferentiated unity, and so on, could be interpreted either as an experience of the puruṣa in its isolated purity, or as an experience of the impersonal nirguna Brahman, or as an entry into the transcendent condition or place called

'Nibbāna'. (2) If, on the other hand, Stace and Smart are correct, then either theists have read an impression of loving mutuality into an experience (of blissful emptiness) which simply does not contain it or, alternatively, monistic mystics like Samkara have failed to notice that the passion of love is an integral part of their experience. Both of these alternatives are implausible. These considerations suggest that Zæhner is correct. They are obviously not conclusive.

B

Ninian Smart suggests[56] that whenever we encounter hetero-accounts and the use of highly ramified concepts, it is plausible to conclude that we are dealing with interpretations rather than descriptions.

The belief that there is a genuine distinction between theistic and monistic mysticism is partly based upon the fact that the autobiographical accounts provided by theistic mystics are strikingly different from those provided by monistic mystics.[57] (Monistic mystics do not speak of love,[58] they suppose that the 'object' of their experience is impersonal, etc.) These accounts are, of course, auto-accounts. Nevertheless, because they employ highly ramified concepts, they must, according to Smart, be regarded as interpretations rather than descriptions. Consequently, they do not justify the conclusion that the *experiences* of theistic mystics differ from the *experiences* of monistic mystics. How reliable are Smart's criteria?

An auto-account[59] of an experience is an account provided by the person who had that experience. A hetero-account of an experience is an account which is provided by some other person. Since hetero-accounts are, by definition, secondhand accounts, it is not unreasonable to suspect that they are laden with interpretation. Nevertheless, this test cannot be regarded as conclusive. It is logically possible for a hetero-account to be precise, accurate, and free from interpretation. Nor is this only a logical possibility. Stace and Smart (among others) have suggested that Theravādin Buddhists provide us with a descriptively accurate and relatively interpretation-free account of the nature of *all* introvertive mystical experience. Although I believe that it is mistaken, this contention is not entirely implausible. If it is correct, then a Buddhist's hetero-account of a Christian experience may be freer from interpretation than the auto-account which is offered by the Christian who had the experience.

According to Smart, an account of an experience should be regarded as an interpretation if it includes (many) highly ramified concepts. A ramified concept (for example, 'God', 'electron', 'Brahman', 'Id') is one which 'occurs as part of a doctrinal scheme ... and gains its meaning in part from a range of doctrinal statements taken to be true.' (p 79) A ramified account is an account which employs ramified concepts. The degree of ramification 'can be crudely estimated by asking: How many propositions are presupposed as true by the description' which employs that concept? (pp 79–80)[60] 'The mystic merges with God,' is highly ramified. 'The spirit by the loss of its self consciousness has ... established its abode in this glorious and dazzling obscurity,' is less ramified. 'The experience was bliss,' is still less ramified. (p 79)

Smart appears to be arguing in the following way: (1) The use of highly ramified concepts commits us to the existence of certain problematic entities. Since (2) the pure description of an experience would presumably not commit us to the existence of any problematic entities, (3) any account containing highly ramified concepts is more plausibly regarded as an interpretation than as a description.

In spite of its superficial plausibility this argument is unsound. It is unsound because it ignores the fact that accounts which employ highly ramified concepts do not necessarily commit us to the existence of anything. Thus, if I describe my experience by saying, 'I *seemed* to be in the presence of God,' my description does not commit me to the existence of God or any other problematic entities even though I am employing a highly ramified concept (viz, the concept of God).

All terms are 'theory laden' in the sense that their meaning is articulated by a set of analytic and quasi-analytic statements (a 'theory') in which those terms are employed. We might regard a highly ramified term as one which is embedded in a relatively sophisticated and complex 'theory' or, alternatively, we might regard highly ramified concepts as concepts whose meanings are articulated in more specialised, less

widely employed, or more problematic 'theories'. On the basis
of either criteria, the concepts of witchcraft, nuclear physics,
and Christian theology would be more highly ramified than
colour concepts.

Why should we suppose that the degree of ramification (so
understood) provides any indication of the presence of interpretation?

In an earlier article, Smart asserted that the use of ramified
concepts would involve interpretation because 'one would in a
sense be *explaining* the experience, for one would be putting it
in a certain wider setting and connecting it indirectly with a lot
of other experiences, practices, etc.'[61] Smart apparently supposes that when one employs highly ramified concepts in his
account of an experience, he links that experience to other
things which are supposed to explain it, and that to do this is to
interpret it. (See section IIIA.) This is mistaken. In describing
Teresa's experience, I might say, 'She felt that she was in the
immediate presence of God,' and in so doing I would be
employing a highly ramified concept (viz, the concept of God).
Nevertheless, while that concept is analytically connected
with many other concepts, and while some of these other concepts are problematic, I have not thereby linked the element in
her experience which was picked out by my remark, to any
other entity or event or state of affairs the *existence* of which is
somehow supposed to *explain* her experience. In fact, I have
not offered an explanation of her experience at all. Consequently, I have not offered an interpretation in the sense in
question.[62]

Smart has failed to explain why the use of highly ramified
concepts is a sign of interpretation. The presence of highly
ramified concepts may however *be* a criterion of interpretation.
(Perhaps it is significant that highly ramified concepts seem to
occur with greater frequency in theological and speculative
accounts of the mystical object than in impersonal or autobiographical accounts of mystical experience.) It would be rash to
reject this criterion altogether. Nevertheless, it can hardly be
regarded as conclusive.

Even though Smart's criteria may not be entirely reliable, it
is worth noticing that the results which are obtained by their
application support Zæhner's thesis.

Mystics often provide theistic accounts of their experiences. Hence, as Smart admits, his first criterion is satisfied. It is, of course, true that theistic mystics frequently employ highly ramified concepts when they attempt to communicate their experiences to others. What is crucial, however, is that there are less ramified accounts of the same experiences which theistic mystics would undoubtedly find acceptable, for example, 'the experience appears to involve a union with something which is personal and loving but cannot be seen, heard, smelled, touched, or tasted.' It should be noted that none of the terms employed in this description is theological, abstruse, or specialised. Given that the theistic mystic would find this account accurate (although excessively abstract and incomplete) it can be regarded as a relatively unramified auto-account of his experience.[63] Since it is a relatively unramified auto-account, it should, on the basis of Smart's own criteria, be classified as 'description' and not as 'interpretation'. It is a description, however, which is theistic rather than monistic in its implications. There are, therefore, relatively unramified auto-accounts of the experiences of theistic mystics which have theistic implications. This suggests that Smart is mistaken, and that the *experiences* of these mystics, and not merely their interpretations, are theistic.

C

Mariasusai Dhavamony[64] argues that when the objects of two experiences, the aims of those experiences, and the means to them differ, we may conclude that we are confronted with two different experiences rather than with two different interpretations of what is essentially the same experience.

Although the presence of these differences provides a reason for supposing that experiences differ, it is not conclusive. For example, consider Yoga and Advaita Vedānta.

According to Yoga, the 'object' of a mystic's experience is his puruṣa – one of a *plurality* of pure selves, each of which is eternal and free from impurities – devoid of content, changeless, inactive, and unconcerned. According to Advaita Vedānta, the 'object' of mystical experience is the Ātman-Brahman. The Atman-Brahman is the *unique* ground of both world and self. In the last analysis, it alone is real.

The aim of Yoga is isolation. The purusa is to be freed from its entanglement in 'nature' (prakṛti) in order that it may exist in splendid solitude. The aim of Advaita Vedānta is the intuitive and existential appropriation of the fact that one *is* the Atman-Brahman.

Patanjali's yoga (which includes special postures, breathing exercises, the withdrawal of the senses from the sense object, concentration upon an object of meditation, etc.) provides the means to the isolation of the purusa. The Advaitin believes that he can achieve his object by using jnāna yoga – a study of, and meditation upon, scripture.

If Dhavamony's tests are adequate, we should conclude that Yogic experiences differ from Advaitin experiences, yet it is not clear that this conclusion should be drawn, or that Dhavamony would wish to draw it.

One might argue that the differences between Yoga and Advaita Vedānta (with respect to object, aim, and method) are less extreme than those between either Yoga or Advaita Vedānta on the one hand, and theistic mystical traditions on the other, and that there is, therefore, less reason to suppose that there is a difference between the experiences of the Advaitins and the adherents of Yoga than to suppose that there is a difference between monistic mysticism and theistic mysticism. While I believe that this is true, Dhavamony's tests are clearly inconclusive.

But Dhavamony makes another point. He argues that the experience of the theistic mystic must differ from the experience of the monistic mystic, because the experience of the theistic mystic is primarily a love experience, while the experience of the monistic mystic is primarily a knowledge experience, and love experiences and knowledge experiences are phenomenologically distinct. The proposed criterion can be formulated in this way: if mystical experience A is more like ordinary experience x than it is like ordinary experience y, and if mystical experience B is more like experience y than it is like ordinary experience x, then A $\neq$ B. This criterion is not implausible and, as Dhavamony points out, its application supports the conclusion that the experiences of mystics like John of the Cross and Teresa of Avila are qualitatively distinct from the experiences of mystics like Śaṃkara and Plotinus.

D

It is probably a mistake to insist that the criteria which we use to distinguish interpretation from description and to determine whether we are confronted with different experiences or with a single experience must be logically conclusive, or that we must be able to apply these criteria in a mechanical way in order to produce clear-cut decisions in each instance. If this *is* a mistake, then the criteria which have been examined in this section should not be dismissed too quickly. They may be adequate for practical purposes. Whether they are entirely adequate or not, it is significant that their employment does, on the whole, support the conclusion that Zæhner is correct, and that monistic mysticism must be distinguished from theistic mysticism.[65]

V

What would an adequate typology of mystical experience be like? It must allow for a variety of extrovertive experiences, and recognise the existence of a real distinction between monistic consciousness and theistic mysticism. It is possible that there are other types of introvertive mystical consciousness, but this is not clear.

A

Consider the features which allegedly distinguish nature mysticism or cosmic consciousness from other forms of mystical experience:

(1) A sense of the identity of phenomenal objects (Stace, Otto, Zæhner).

(2) The feeling that 'within' and 'without' are one (Stace, Otto, Zæhner).

(3) A sense of the world as a living presence (Stace, Zæhner).

(4) An impression of the transfiguration and extraordinary beauty of natural objects (Otto, Zæhner).

(5) The feeling that time stands still, that everything exists

in an 'eternal now' (Otto, Zæhner).

None of these features appears to be a necessary condition of extrovertive mystical consciousness. The list does, however, call our attention to a *family* of similar experiences, each of which exhibits *some* of the characteristics on our list.[66]

Although a number of different combinations of those characteristics are possible, I would suggest that three occur with particular frequency:

(1) A sense of the unity of nature, and of one's identity with it. (Characteristics 1 and 2.) This variety of extrovertive mysticism is often accompanied by a sense of transfiguration and/or an impression of timelessness. (Characteristics 4 and 5.)

(2) The sense of nature as a living presence. (Characteristic 3.)

(3) The sense that everything is transpiring in an eternal present. (Characteristic 5.)[67]

There may be a fourth type of extrovertive mysticism which is rather different from these.

Frederick Streng has argued[68] that, in Mādhyamika, one is attempting to arrive at a state in which the world of becoming (the phenomenal world) is viewed as 'empty' (śūnya). The object of this experience is not some permanent substratum, or substance underlying phenomenal things, but the flow of phenomenal reality itself. The world of becoming is not, however, viewed in the ordinary way for it is apprehended without conceptualisation and without attachment. The experience of 'emptiness' is achieved by deliberately cultivating a non-conceptual way of apprehending things. In part, this appears to involve a deliberate reversion to the blooming, buzzing confusion of impressions (roughly, the 'dharmas') which confront an infant who has not yet learned to structure and order his experience. In part, it appears to involve the existential appropriation of an intellectual conviction, viz, that all categories and concepts are invalid, and that the distinctions which we draw between one thing and another are arbitrary and conventional. A consequence of this abandonment of 'views' is that one beholds reality without attachment. (Since our desires and aversions depend upon our opinions concerning the properties and relations of things, we can eliminate our

desires by eliminating our opinions.) It can be argued that this
is also the central experience of Zen. Ch'ing-yüan said,

Before I had studied Zen for thirty years, I saw mountains as mountains,
and waters as waters. When I arrived at a more intimate knowledge, I came
to the point where I saw that mountains are not mountains, and waters are
not waters. But now that I have got to its very substance, I am at rest. For it's
just that I see mountains once again as mountains, and waters once again as
waters.[69]

D T Suzuki was asked what satori was like and replied that it
was just like everyday experience but about two inches off the
ground.[70] In view of Mādhyamika's influence upon Zen, it is
not unreasonable to suppose that these passages refer to an experience of the same type.[71]

The experience of 'emptiness' clearly fits our definition of
'mysticism'. (1) It is a unitary state of consciousness. (Distinctions are dismissed as unreal.) (2) Its content or object is the
(character of) the phenomenal world as a whole. (3) It is
noetic. (According to T R V Murti, it is prajnā pāramitā (the
perfection of wisdom), the immediate non-conceptual intuition of the suchness of things.[72])

Since its 'object' is the phenomenal world, it is reasonable to
regard it as an extrovertive experience. On the other hand, it
should probably be distinguished from other extrovertive
states. (1) Although, its occurrence may be 'sudden', the experience is not spontaneous. On the contrary, it is deliberately
sought (by meditation and arduous intellectual work (Mādhyamika), by the use of Zazen and the Koan (Zen), etc.). The
more familiar extrovertive states tend to occur spontaneously,
that is, without conscious preparation. (2) It is at least not *clear*
that viewing things without distinctions (as an unstructured
flow) is the same as perceiving their identity, or seeing that
they are rooted in some unity or larger life. (3) The other forms
of extrovertive mysticism appear to involve conceptualisation.
For example, when one claims that things are one, or that
nature is a living presence, one is conceptualising reality. (It
should be remembered that a person who employs concepts
metaphorically or paradoxically need not be thinking non-
conceptually. Hegel is a case in point.) (4) Non-attachment is
not characteristic of what is usually called 'nature mysticism'
or 'cosmic consciousness'. On the contrary, the latter typically

involve a joyous new 'attachment' to nature and to the self (the sense of expansion).[73]

I conclude, then, that there are at least four distinct types of extrovertive mysticism which occur with some frequency.[74] Although these experiences differ in many ways, it is reasonable to group them under a common heading ('extrovertive mystical consciousness'). They all have nature (the external world) for their object. They are all noetic, and they all involve a sense of unity or the transcendence of distinctions.[75]

B

Sections II and IV have provided reasons for believing that there are at least two distinct types of introvertive mystical consciousness.

The first is an experience of pure empty consciousness. The mystic withdraws his attention from the external world and empties his mind of concepts and sensuous imagery. Instead of lapsing into unconsciousness as one might expect, the mystic remains conscious – but conscious of nothing. The experience and/or its 'content' is – at least relatively speaking – an undifferentiated unity.[76] Its emotional tone is normally positive. (But not always. J A Symonds was subject to experiences of this type and disliked them.)

The second could be described as the 'naked' and loving awareness of 'God'. The experience is introvertive; the mystic withdraws his attention from the external world, and empties his mind of sensuous imagery and all but the most obscure and general ideas. Unlike the first experience, this experience has a distinct object, although it is an object which is apprehended obscurely and non-sensuously, and which cannot be identified with anything in the space-time world (or with the space-time world as a whole). The experience is thus 'dualistic' rather than 'monistic'. The nature of the relation between the mystic and the object of his experience is indicated by the fact that he typically attempts to express it, by the imagery of mutual love. For example, Christian mystics speak of spiritual marriage, and have interpreted the *Song of Songs* as an allegory of the relation between God and the soul. Bernard referred to the highest union as the 'kiss of the mouth'. Some of the Sufis wrote lyrics which can be read as ordinary love poetry. Hymns and songs from the Indian bhakti traditions provide other examples. It should be emphasised that the imagery in question is the imagery of *mutual* love. Monistic mystics may appropriately use erotic imagery. For example, the One of Plotinus is an object of eros. The mystic desires it and delights in it, and uses the language of love to express his longing for it. Nevertheless, it would be inappropriate for him to use the language of *mutual* love, for while the One is loved, it cannot love.[77] The emotional tone of theistic mystical experience seems to be invariably positive.

In some respects, this experience is similar to numinous experience. Both experiences involve a distinction between subject and object, and are thus 'dualistic'. In both cases, the person who has the experience tends to describe its object by employing concepts and images which suggest personality. (The object of numinous experience is almost invariably described as a Thou which addresses us, a will confronting our own. Theistic mystics typically employ love imagery.)

There are also differences. (1) Theistic mystical consciousness is an introvertive state which is obtained by deliberately emptying the mind of ordinary contents. Having suspended the empirical self, the 'depth' of the soul unites with the 'Ground of Being'. Numinous experiences are typically I-Thou encounters which seem to occur spontaneously. They do not appear to be introvertive, nor do they seem to involve a temporary extinction of the subject's empirical ego. (2) While the lives of theistic mystics include periods in which they are overcome by a sense of sinfulness and distance from God (the dark night of the senses, and the dark night of the soul), these tend to be periods in which the sense of God's presence has either grown dim or altogether disappeared. A sense of distance and otherness does not appear to be an integral part of their illuminative and unitive *experiences*.[78] On the contrary, in these experiences, distance and otherness are transcended.

It would be possible to distinguish theistic mystical experience from monistic consciousness, and classify it as a species of numinous experience in which the 'mysterium tremendum' is relatively insignificant, and fascination especially prominent.

It would be better not to do so. In the first place, the fact that so many knowledgeable and intelligent students of mysticism have believed that theistic mystical consciousness is essentially identical with other introvertive mystical states must be taken seriously. If they have confused monistic and theistic mystical consciousness, they have probably done so because these states really *are* very similar. In the second place, numinous experience has been defined by *two* features (the 'mysterium tremendum' and fascination). Since theistic mystical consciousness tends to lack the first of these characteristics, it is a dubious instance of numinous experience.

C

Any typology should be taken with a grain of salt. Almost invariably, there will be phenomena which seem to fall within the range of phenomena for which the typology was devised but cannot be subsumed under its categories. This can happen in several ways. A phenomenon may be a borderline case displaying many, but not all, of the characteristics of a given type. It may be a hybrid, displaying several characteristics of two or more types. Or it may be a sport displaying few of the characteristics associated with any recognised category. Borderline cases are to be expected with any typology. When they occur infrequently, it is often safe to ignore sports and hybrids. Even if they cannot be ignored, they can sometimes be accommodated by adding new categories. However, if a fairly large proportion of the phenomena falling within the range of phenomena for which the typology was devised are borderline cases, hybrids and sports, the typology is inadequate. If the hybrids and sports cannot be accommodated without major revisions, it may be better to abandon the typology altogether and devise a new one. On the other hand, whatever its inadequacies, it is reasonable to continue to use a typology which is not patently silly or absurd until a more adequate typology is discovered. In thinking about a subject matter, it is impossible to avoid some sort of classification and categorisation. Classification and categorisation are normally unreflective. Because they are also uncritical and frequently confused, it is better consciously to employ the best available typology and recognise its inadequacies than to abandon oneself to pre-reflective typologies, while pretending to respect the richness of phenomena.

What is true of typologies in general, is true of typologies of mystical experience. Borderline cases are to be expected, and some sports and hybrids will occur. Nevertheless, if a typology is adequate, it must accommodate most mystical phenomena.

If the argument of this chapter has been correct, Zæhner's typology is superior to Stace's, and both are superior to a typology which recognises as many principal categories as there are traditions. Nevertheless, none of the existing typologies is entirely satisfactory. I have suggested ways in which they might be amended. In doing so I have sketched the outlines of what I believe is an adequate typology of mystical experience.

Some of its features will be important for the following chapters but others will not. A number of the arguments which I shall develop presuppose a real, if rough, distinction between extrovertive mysticism, monistic mysticism and theistic mysticism. On the other hand, nothing of significance will depend upon the claim that these are the only sorts of experience which ought to be called 'mystical', or upon the claim that these types of mystical experience are *infama species* which cannot themselves be further divided into sub types.

For example, it is possible that there are other types of introvertive mystical experience. There appears to be an introvertive state in which theistic mystics direct their will and affections towards God but do not 'touch' Him. This is distinct from theistic mystical consciousness because it does not involve an experimental perception of God (a sense of divine presence). Since it is not noetic, it does not conform to our definition of 'mysticism', and in fact appears to be no more than a form of concentration. (It would thus be structurally similar to the various types of concentration (on an image, on one's physical and mental processes, etc.) which other traditions use to induce mystical consciousness or enlightenment.) Nevertheless, because it tends to transform itself into theistic mystical consciousness, one might wish to call it 'incipiently mystical'. (For more on this state see chapter 4, IIA.)

There may also be an introvertive experience which is dualistic but which cannot be appropriately expressed by the imagery of mutual love since its object is impersonal. Introvertive mystics sometimes describe an experience in which they seem to apprehend a non-personal One while retaining a residual sense of their own individuality. It is possible that some of these accounts are descriptions of a transitional state which occurs as one moves from ordinary dualistic consciousness to monistic consciousness. Others may be dualistic *interpretations* of monistic consciousness. Some may be descriptions of theistic experiences in which the third feature (mutual love) is relatively inconspicuous. There may, however, be accounts of this type which cannot be disposed of in this fashion. If there are, then a third category of introvertive mysticism should be added to our typology.

Another interesting problem is provided by experiences of the 'mystic light'.[79] These are of various types. Experiences of flames, coloured lights, and so on, should probably be regarded as visionary. There are also experiences in which a particular, natural object appears luminous, and still others in which nature as a whole seems to be imbued with supernatural radiance. This sense of supernatural radiance is sometimes combined with other features of extrovertive mystical consciousness (as in the case of Bucke), but it should probably not be classified as mystical when it occurs in isolation (unaccompanied by a sense of unity). There are, however, experiences of this type which include an impression of being imbued and invaded, permeated, with light, and these should probably be classified as mystical – extrovertive when the light is a light pervading nature, but introvertive when the space-time world is relegated to the margin of consciousness. On the other hand, it is not *certain* that we should do so, for the experiences in question could be regarded as experiences with a specific 'empirical' content – a kind of visionary experience in which the object is light, rather than colours or shapes.[80]

There are, then, reasons for suspecting that the category of introvertive mystical consciousness is richer than I have previously indicated, although the reasons are not conclusive. These and similar issues must be resolved before we can be confident that our typology is fully adequate. Nevertheless, little in the following chapters depends upon their outcome. The resolution of these issues is intrinsically interesting, but philosophically unimportant.

VI

If the argument of this chapter has been sound, the following propositions are true:

(1) Mystical experiences should be distinguished from numinous experiences, from visionary experiences, from occult phenomena, and from ordinary religious affections and sentiments.

(2) The typologies of mystical experience which were devised by Stace and Zæhner are inadequate.

(3) There are no good reasons for believing that interpretations of mystical consciousness cannot be distinguished from descriptions of mystical consciousness, or that it is impossible to construct a cross-cultural typology of mystical experience.

(4) There are rough and ready criteria for distinguishing interpretations of mystical consciousness from descriptions of mystical consciousness, and for determining whether we are dealing with several experiences or a single experience.

(5) The application of these criteria tends to support Zæhner's distinction between monistic mystical experiences and theistic mystical experiences.

(6) Any adequate typology must recognise the existence of several types of extrovertive mystical consciousness, and distinguish monistic mystical experiences from theistic mystical experiences.

Notes

[1] See, for example, Paul Tillich, 'The Two Types of Philosophy of Religion', *Theology and Culture*, New York, 1959; or the works of Friedrich Schleiermacher and Rudolf Otto. This view has been widely held. Historically, it is closely associated with the Romantic reaction to eighteenth century rationalism. Religious feelings and sentiments were said to be as essential to human nature as reason. Given that these feelings and sentiments are valid intuitions of a transcendent order, it was natural to conclude that everyone is (implicitly) aware of the 'Unconditioned'.

[2] What religious affections and sentiments appear to affect is one's assessment of the relative plausibility of certain propositions, and (in the case of

informal arguments) the degree to which an argument's premises support its conclusion. Thus, one can show that, given certain modal assumptions, if God is possible, God exists. One's religious feelings and inclinations (*or lack of them*) will affect one's assessment of the relative plausibility of 'It is impossible that God exists,' and 'God exists,' and thus partly determine whether one will accept the argument's conclusion or deny its premise. Again, while theists and atheists tend to agree that apparent design, religious experience, etc. count for theism, and that suffering counts against it, the relative weight assigned to these considerations by theists and atheists appears to be partly determined by their different affections and sentiments.

3. The devout are sometimes overwhelmed by a feeling of God's presence. The belief in God's (universal) presence comes home to them and, in fear and joy, they realise that, if God is omnipresent, He is present *to them*. This is not an 'experimental perception' of God's presence, although it might be confused with it. The distinction between a feelingful conviction of God's presence and the experimental perception of God is analogous to the distinction between, for example, being aware that someone I love is now thinking of me (perhaps we have arranged to think of one another each day at noon) and seeing her. Both experiences may be intense, but only in the second case is it appropriate to speak of direct acquaintance.

4. Rudolf Otto, *The Idea of the Holy*, New York, 1958. All references in this section are to this work.

5. There are other, less conclusive, differences. (1) There are well established and familiar techniques for obtaining certain types of mystical experience (introvertive experiences), and for obtaining visionary experiences. The type of numinous experience which satisfies the second and third criteria tends to occur spontaneously. Generally speaking, I-Thou encounters are not *deliberately* sought, but are obtained without conscious preparation. (2) Mystics tend to describe the object of their experience in impersonal language ('light', 'fire', 'the dazzling darkness', 'the desert of the God-head', 'the One', 'the Opposite Shore', 'the Island', 'the Refuge', 'Being-itself', 'Emptiness', 'Nothingness', and so on). Those who have had a numinous experience which satisfies the second and third criteria tend to describe its object in personal terms; they regard it as a Will confronting their own; they address it as a Thou. (These differences are not absolute, for nature mysticism tends to occur spontaneously, and theistic mystics typically employ love imagery to express and describe their union with God.)

6. Corrado Pensa, 'On the Purification Concept in Indian Tradition with Special Regard to Yoga', *East and West*, 19 (1969), pp 194–228.

7. Peter Moore, 'Mystical Experience, Mystical Doctrine, Mystical Technique', *Mysticism and Philosophical Analysis*, ed by Steven T Katz, London, 1978, p 119.

8. Gershom Scholem, *Major Trends in Jewish Mysticism*, New York, 1961, p 44.

9. Edward Conze, *Buddhist Meditation*, New York, 1969, p 59f.

10. *Op cit* p 55.

11. For example, Auguste Saudreau, Albert Farges, Auguste Poulain,

Jacques Maritain, Joseph Maréchal, Henri Bergson, Richard Bucke, Friedrich von Hügel, Aldous Huxley, Walter Stace, R C Zæhner, Jean Houston and R E L Masters, Walter Pahnke, William Johnston, Rudolf Otto, Ninian Smart, Evelyn Underhill, D T Suzuki, etc.

[12] Their work will be discussed in chapter 2.

[13] Walter Stace, *Mysticism and Philosophy*, London, Philadelphia and New York, 1960. Page references in this section will be to this work unless otherwise noted.

[14] Rudolf Otto, *Mysticism, East and West*, New York, 1957, p 46.

[15] How are we to understand this? As Jean-Paul Sartre has observed, in the light of our past, we project ourselves towards the future. Our experience of time is integrally bound up with certain mental activities – remembering, regretting, hoping, anticipating, deciding, and so on. During the extrovertive experience, these activities are often suspended. There is no (conscious) recollection, and no (conscious) projection towards the future. One is still, and rests in the present. Not experiencing time in the normal way; the mystic says 'time has stopped'. But sometimes more than this is involved. In some cases, the mystic has the impression that changes and movements, which take only a few seconds of clock-time, last forever. 'Time has stopped', is then an exaggerated way of saying 'time has slowed down'.

[16] See *Mysticism, East and West*, chapters IV and V. Otto distinguishes 'The Inward Way' (roughly introvertive mysticism) from the 'The Way of Unity'. The latter has three stages – the two forms of extrovertive vision I have just described, and a vision of the One 'apart' from the many. In the latter, the many disappears from consciousness and the One appears in naked isolation. It is not clear that there is any phenomenological difference between the *experience* involved in the third stage of Otto's second 'way', and the *experience* of the introvertive mystic. The only difference between them seems to be with respect to the paths by which they have been obtained, the introvertive mystic having obtained his experience by turning inwards rather than by progressing through the three stages of 'The Way of Unity'.

[17] *The Life of Teresa of Jesus*, transl and ed by E Allison Peers, New York, 1960, chapter xviii.

[18] For a detailed discussion of the way in which images, thoughts, external perceptions, etc. can accompany (without constituting) mystical prayer, see Auguste Poulain, *The Graces of Interior Prayer*, St Louis, 1950, pp 124–9 and 180–4.

[19] *Op cit* p 103.

[20] R C Zæhner, *Concordant Discord*, Oxford, 1970, p 200.

[21] R C Zæhner, *Mysticism, Sacred and Profane*, New York, 1961. References in this section will be to this work unless otherwise noted.

[22] Time stands still. Space is transcended in so far as the separation between place and place collapses. ('All things are one.')

[23] These terms refer to a type of experience rather than to a type of interpretation. Soul mystics or monistic mystics may not believe in the reality of soul and they need not be monists. Theravāda mysticism is a case in point.

[24] Is there any *significant* difference between the bliss and innocence of the nature mystic and the bliss and innocence of the soul mystic? (That they *are* different is stated by Zæhner. p 193.) The objects of delight are different (nature, the soul), but are there any other relevant differences?

[25] Soul mysticism should be distinguished from 'integration', the state in which all parts of the self are fully developed and harmoniously balanced. Integration is a source of inner strength, peace and psychological equilibrium; it enables a person to act as a whole being, without hesitation, and without anxiety. According to Zæhner, integration involves the reconciliation of *anima* (the 'feminine' instinctive unconscious) and *animus* (the 'masculine' intellectual ego). In so far as it includes a 'descent' of *animus* into *anima*, i.e. the emergence of the 'collective unconscious' into consciousness, integration includes nature mysticism. (pp 106–18) Zæhner also argues that integration is a prelude to the isolation of the monistic mystic. (pp 150 and 202–203; cf *Concordant Discord*, p 138.) Neither of these claims is clearly true. The first depends upon a controversial theory of nature mysticism which will be discussed in chapter 3. As to the second claim, integration is more often an effect of mystical experience than its prelude. (Although mystical experience is not normally a *sufficient* condition of integration; whether a mystic achieves integration depends upon what he does with his experiences.) Integration is associated with mysticism, but it can be achieved by other means, for example, by evangelical conversion or psychoanalysis. It is not noetic and is therefore not itself a mystical state.

[26] Notice that it is the 'eternal self' which unites with God, not the 'empirical self'. Theistic mystical consciousness does not involve images, visions, voices, sentimental feelings, etc.

[27] In *Mysticism, Sacred and Profane*, Zæhner distinguishes soul mysticism from nature mysticism on the grounds that the latter has nature for its object whereas the monistic mystic has emptied his soul of *all* sensory contents. The monistic mystic experiences his 'own soul as being the Absolute'. He does not 'experience the phenomenal world at all. To say that this is identical with the panenhenic experience, is to say something that is patently and blatantly untrue'. (p 29; cf pp 33 and 145) Zaehner sometimes makes the same distinction in later works (see, for example, *Concordant Discord*, p 67; and *Drugs, Mysticism and Make Believe*, London, 1972, pp 118–19), but the difference between them ceases to be as clear as it once was. Thus, in *Concordant Discord*, he distinguishes between nature or prakṛti or 'primal matter' which is the object of cosmic consciousness, and an 'an eternal mode of being' which is the object of monistic experience. (p 142) But the two are closely related for the monistic mystic '*sees* the eternal shining in and illuminating the whole phenomenal world, all things are [apprehended as being] shot through with one single eternal essence which is Brahman.' (*ibid* p 130) The distinction between cosmic consciousness (experiencing 'the Eternal One as prevading all nature and oneself') and monistic consciousness (entering into the '"dead" essence of this One' and seeing the world and oneself from its point of view) has become at best opaque. As a consequence, in the later work, it is sometimes difficult to

determine whether Zæhner is speaking of monistic mysticism or cosmic consciousness. In discussing Zen and Jung, for example, the distinction blurs and occasionally vanishes. (Another problem is that the relation between soul mysticism, as described in his earlier work, and the apprehension of this 'eternal mode of being' is never made clear. On p 130 of *Concordant Discord*, Zæhner asserts that 'by unifying and integrating one's own spirit, by withdrawing all the faculties into the self within, one realises the unity of the macrocosm *through* the unity of the microcosm,' and on p 304, he considers the suggestion that this eternal mode of being is the collection of all transcendent selves. In an earlier work (*Hindu and Muslim Mysticism*, New York, 1969, pp 79–80), Zæhner had argued that because the essence of each soul (viz, an 'eternal mode of being') is identical, knowing the essence of one's own soul involves knowing the essence of all souls. (Zæhner is explicating Rāmānuja, but with apparent approval.) This is probably what Zæhner has in mind in *Concordant Discord* although it is impossible to be sure.)

[28] The quotations in the text are from *Concordant Discord*, pp 203 and 204. The claim is reasserted in *Drugs, Mysticism and Make Believe*, p 93.

[29] Nor, for that matter, does he anywhere state that his position *has* shifted.

[30] Similarly, there appear to be two forms of spatial transcendence – (1) a sense of the unity of all places, the 'identity' of all phenomenal objects, and (2) the 'falling away' of the whole spatial world. The first is characteristic of nature mysticism. The second is characteristic of soul mysticism and theistic mysticism.

[31] The passage from the *Gītā* teaches the eternity of the self (and perhaps that this eternal self can be consciously experienced – see chapter 2, verse 29) but not that there is a distinct mode of mystical consciousness of the sort which Zæhner calls 'the transcending of temporal limitation'. Eckhart's concept of the Eternal Now is a theological or metaphysical concept. Although it undoubtedly has experiential roots, it is difficult to determine precisely what these are.

[32] Richard Jefferies, *The Story of My Heart*, London, 1947, chapter III.

[33] Ninian Smart, 'Interpretation and Mystical Experience', *Religious Studies* 1 (1965), pp 75–87. References in this section will be to this article.

[34] These passages were originally quoted by Zæhner on pp 170 and 171 of *Mysticism, Sacred and Profane*.

[35] See Jan van Ruysbroeck, *The Adornment of the Spiritual Marriage, etc.*, transl and ed by Evelyn Underhill, London, 1951, p 155ff; and Rāmānuja's commentary on the *Bhagavad Gītā* (*The Gitabhashya of Ramanuja*, transl by M R Sampatkumaran, Mardas, 1969). (Selections from Rāmānuja's commentary are included in Appendix A of Zæhner's *Hindu and Muslim Mysticism*.) For example, it would seem that 2:53, 2:65, 2:69, 2:72, 6:20–23 and 6:29–31 of Rāmānuja's commentary describe monistic mysticism; that 6:47 describes a theistic experience, and that the introduction to 7 and 12:11–12 distinguish between them. See also Richard of St Victor, *Selected Writings on Contemplation*, transl by Clare Kirchberger, London, 1957, pp 122–4. Portions of Junayd's *Kitāb al-Fanā* can be found in Zæhner's *Hindu and Muslim Mysticism*. (Appendix B II, specially pp 223–4.) Cf. Zæhner's

discussion of Junayd on pp 135–53 of the same work.

[36] Or if this is too strong, that within their traditions there are people who have had both, and that those who have had both are convinced they are different.

[37] For an explanation of this term, see section IV*A*.

[38] There are obviously many thorny questions here. For example, how do we count characteristics and, if we cannot count characteristics, what entitles us to say that a pair of experiences have most of their features in common? Should we only pay attention to important or essential characteristics and, if so, how do we determine what is important or essential?

[39] In addition to Garside and Katz, whose arguments will be examined below, see, for example, Ronald Burr ('Wittgenstein's Later Language Philosophy and Some Issues in Philosophy of Mysticism', *International Journal for Philosophy of Religion* VII [1976], pp 261–87); Carl Keller ('Mystical Literature', *Mysticism and Philosophical Analysis, op cit*, pp 75–100); and Peter Moore ('Recent Studies of Mysticism: A Critical Survey', *Religion* 3 (1973), pp 146–56, and 'Mystical Experience, Mystical Doctrine, Mystical Technique', *op cit*). While the thesis of these scholars is roughly the same, their arguments are not. Burr's case rests upon a Wittgensteinian theory of meaning, and especially upon the alleged impossibility of a private language. Keller believes that it is impossible to get behind mystical texts to the experiences they purportedly describe. Moore has a number of useful and judicious things to say concerning the complexity of the relations between interpretation and description, and between doctrine, practice and experience. The most that their arguments establish, however, is that it may be more difficult to disentangle description from interpretation than is sometimes supposed.

[40] Bruce Garside, 'Language and the Interpretation of Mystical Experience', *International Journal for Philosophy of Religion*, III (1972), p 99.

[41] Remember that mystical experience is noetic, involving a sense of objective reality, a conviction that one immediately apprehends or is apprehended by some overwhelming supernatural good, etc.

[42] In order to isolate these elements, one must know what factors are included in the experience's setting. This presents a problem, for unless we know that the experience is delusive, we cannot rule out the possibility that its setting includes relevant supernatural factors. If the operation or presence of these factors is a constant, then all settings include it, and hence all settings are relevantly similar in that respect. Some alleged supernatural factors are constants in this sense (for example, the plurality of puruṣas, Nibbāna, the Ātman-Brahman) but others are not (for example, God's gracious activity). Nevertheless, I believe that an approximation to this set of elements can be obtained by examining cases in which people with different conceptual sets have had similar experiences in empirically similar settings. For example, Yogins, Buddhists practising the jhānas and non-traditional mystics like Tennyson, or Christian love mystics and Indian love mystics. This assumes that those features which an experience has in common with a family of similar experiences occurring to people with different conceptual sets in similar empirical settings roughly co-

incide with those features which an experience has in common with the experiences which people with different conceptual sets would have if they were subjected to the same external stimuli (including supernatural stimuli, if any).

Even if I am correct, we are still faced with the problem of determining when two settings are empirically similar. The notion of the same empirical setting is not as clear as one might like. Nevertheless we are not hopelessly at sea. The mystic's physical environment must be taken into account. One should also take account of physiological facts, techniques of meditation employed by the mystic, and certain aspects of his social environment. (There is a sense in which one's body can be regarded as part of one's environment. To the extent to which techniques can be distinguished from the beliefs, attitudes, and intentions of those who use them, they too should be included in the setting. In so far as a person succeeds in internalising the values and point of view of his culture, his social environment forms part of his set; to the extent to which society's institutions, arrangements and activities are part of his environment, they belong to his setting.) In addition to physiological similarities (similar brain waves, similiarities in body chemistry, etc.), there are similarities between techniques of meditation employed in different religious traditions, and between these and techniques employed by people whose conceptual sets are not specifically religious. For example, consider the experiment in which Arthur Deikman asked his subjects to concentrate on a blue vase. Although Deikman's experimental procedure was consciously 'based on classical descriptions of contemplative meditation', it was employed in a non-religious context. ('Implications of Experimentally Induced Contemplative Meditation', *Psychedelics*, ed by Bernard Aaronson and Humphrey Osmond, Garden City, NY, 1970, p 297. The article originally appeared in the *Journal of Nervous and Mental Disease* 142, (1966), pp 101–16.) Or consider the experiences which Tennyson obtained by repeating his own name. Both techniques are similar to well known traditional techniques (concentration, and the repetition of mantras or some other formula). There are also significant similarities between the physical and social environments of monastics and recluses from different religious traditions, and between these and the physical and social environment of some non-traditional mystics (with respect to such features as physical quiet, solitude and isolation).

[43] 'Account for' and 'explain' must be construed rather broadly. Suppose that someone has a theistic mystical experience and after the fact identifies the object of that experience with Krishna. We would, I think, regard this as an interpretation even though the mystic is not providing a causal account of his experience (unless 'x experiences y' entails 'y causally acts on x'). He is, however, explaining or accounting for his experience. He implies that he had the experience he did, not because he was insane or deluded, but because Krishna was there to be perceived and because he perceived him. He is classifying his experience and relating it to what he believes to be other elements in reality, and he is doing this in an attempt to make sense of it.

[44] Steven T Katz, 'Language, Epistemology, and Mysticism', *Mysticism and Philosophical Analysis* (*op cit*).

[45] The term 'largely' is important. If the tradition's contribution is relatively minor, it is possible that all mystical experience is *essentially* the same.

[46] If these experiences are (partly) constituted by the traditions in which they occur, then components contributed by those traditions are part of the experiences and, hence, essential to them.

[47] His pleasure in the experience may be largely constituted by these things, but that is a different matter.

[48] If (1) the *traditions* were incomparable, i.e. if all judgments such as 'Viśiṣṭādvaita Vedānta and Christianity resemble each other more than either resemble Theravāda Buddhism' were false or nonsense, and if (2) mystical experiences were largely constituted by the traditions within which they occurred, *then* a cross-cultural typology of religious experience would be impossible. But, as we have seen, (2) has not been established, and that traditions are incomparable is hardly obvious.

[49] Peter Moore, 'Mystical Experience, Mystical Doctrine, Mystical Technique', *op cit*, pp 108–109. Moore refers to this as 'incorporated interpretation'. The use of 'interpretation' is misleading. Flavour, doctrinal beliefs or concepts, imagery, and phenomenological analogues are parts or aspects of these mystical experiences, not interpretations of them. If it were legitimate to speak of these things as interpretations, there would have to be something (the 'given' or 'raw data') which they interpret. Unless this is clearly identified, and it is shown that these incorporated elements explain or account for it, it is better to avoid the term 'interpretation'. (To see the problem, ask how the flavour of an experience or incorporated imagery explains the 'raw data'. Incorporated doctrinal elements are a better candidate, but are all incorporated doctrinal elements (e.g. the concept of the Trinity) attempts to *account for*, or *make sense* of, the 'given'? As we shall see in a moment, in some cases it is not even clear that there is a 'given'.)

[50] This should not be confused with the type of mediated perception which will be discussed in chapter 4, II. The phenomenological object of an experience is not some kind of 'sensible species', or sensum, through which an external object is grasped. ((3) must be distinguished from (2).) Nor is it existentially distinct from the experience's apparent object in the way in which a person's facial expression is existentially distinct from his state of mind. Although it is possible for a desk-like surface to exist and for there to be no desk, when both perceptual claims are in order, the desk-like surface belongs to a desk. Hence, even though one only perceives *part* of a desk, viz, its surface, one's perception of the desk is immediate and direct.

[51] Do these feelings *mediate* the phenomenological object? Or are they instead *effects* of the intuition of the phenomenological object? One important attempt to show that the feelings and affections of theistic mystics play the role of sense data will be examined in chapter 4.

[52] My remarks also imply that a distinction can normally be drawn between a mystical experience's phenomenological object (e.g. blissful empty consciousness, or an overwhelming loving presence with which one unites in

ecstasy) and its apparent object (e.g. one's puruṣa, or the God of classical theism). If the claim to have perceived the experience's phenomenological object, and the claim to have perceived its apparent object are both in order, then (e.g.) blissful empty consciousness *is* (an aspect of) one's puruṣa, and the loving presence with which one unites in ecstasy *is* (an aspect or mode of) God, and hence a perception of the first *is* a perception of the second. (While this is normally the case, there may be instances in which no distinction can be drawn between an experience's phenomenological object and its apparent object. Teresa's 'intellectual visions' of Christ, in which she somehow just *knew* that He was present, might be regarded as experiences of this type. However, it is equally plausible to suppose that the phenomenological object of her experience was a localised loving presence which (because of her Christian beliefs) was perceived *as* Christ, i.e. that Christ was the apparent object of her experience, not its phenomenological object.)

53 Of course we cannot describe these data without conceptualising them, but it does not follow that we are unable to abstract the data from the concepts which are incorporated in the experiences which include them. (For one thing, the two sets of concepts are different though related. To describe the sensa involved in an experience of a desk, one need not use the concept of a desk.)

54 Notice that these are not necessarily the same. The setting may help to shape an experience and thus contribute to it, even though no specifiable part or aspect of the experience can be identified as its special contribution. The 'given', on the other hand, corresponds to the sensory data involved in ordinary perception, and is thus in principle specifiable.

55 The Theravādin experiences I have in mind are those associated with the eighth jhāna ('the stage of neither perception nor non-perception'), and with the state of 'cessation' (in which there is a temporary suspension of thought and feeling) that is sometimes said to succeed it.

56 'Interpretation and Mystical Experience', *op cit*. Page references in this section will be to this article unless otherwise noted.

57 It is also based upon the fact that 'impersonal accounts' of theistic mysticism differ from 'impersonal accounts' of monistic mysticism, and upon the fact that some theistic mystics appear to distinguish between the two on the basis of their own experiences.

58 Or at least they do not speak of *mutual* love, of not only loving but *being loved by* the 'object' of their experiences.

59 Smart uses the expressions 'auto-interpretation' and 'hetero-interpretation'. 'Account' is less question-begging than 'interpretation', since an account can be either an interpretation *or* a description.

60 Smart appears to be saying that more highly ramified descriptions entail more propositions than less ramified descriptions. But any proposition entails an indefinitely large number of propositions. (Thus p entails p v q, p v [p v q], etc.) It would follow that no description is any more or any less ramified than any other description. Again, if there are an infinite number of necessary truths, then any proposition entails an infinite number of propositions for any proposition entails all necessary truths.

[61] Ninian Smart, 'Mystical Experience', *Sophia* I (April 1962), p 20.
[62] Smart's remarks might be construed in still another way. Consider the following argument:
    (1) The essential constituents of a religious experience remain invariant from culture to culture.
    (2) Highly ramified concepts are not culturally invariant. Therefore,
    (3) Highly ramified concepts cannot be essential components of a religious experience and, so, when highly ramified concepts occur in the account of an experience we may safely conclude that we are dealing with an interpretation rather than with a description.
It is not clear that Smart has this argument in mind. In any case, it is a bad argument. (1) is trivially true in the sense that any feature which is essential to an experience must belong to that experience whenever and wherever it occurs. However, (2) is true in the sense that highly ramified concepts do not (normally?) occur in all cultures. (Though it is worth noting that theistic and monistic concepts occur in unrelated cultures.) The argument fails because it equivocates on 'culturally invariant'.
[63] For an account to be an auto-account, in any significant sense, all that is necessary is that the mystic endorse it – that he accept it as an accurate account of his experience. It is not necessary that he actually be its author.
[64] Mariasusai Dhavamony, *Love of God According to Śaiva Siddhānta*, Oxford, 1971, Part Five, III.
[65] Smart's first criterion is more reliable than his second. Dhavamony's second test is more reliable than his first. None is conclusive. Nevertheless, when all four point towards the same conclusion, it seems unreasonable to reject it.
[66] Although none of these features is necessary, I would suggest that, with the exception of the fourth, the occurrence of any of these characteristics is a sufficient reason for speaking of an experience as an extrovertive mystical experience. The reason for the exception is this: it has become customary to reserve 'mystical' for experiences which involve some sort of transcendence of distinctions. I have argued (section I) that this custom is justified. If a noetic experience is *only* characterised by a sense of the splendid transfiguration of natural objects, it is not a 'unitary' experience. It is therefore misleading to refer to it as 'mystical'.
[67] The first two more or less coincide with the first and second stages of Otto's 'Way of Unity'. The third roughly corresponds to Zæhner's experience of temporal transcendence. Good examples of the first are provided by the accounts of Karl Joel (included in C G Jung, *Psychology of the Unconscious*, op cit, pp 360–1, and quoted by Zæhner, *Mysticism, Sacred and Profane*, pp 38–9), Forest Reid (*Following Darkness*, London, 1902, p 42, quoted by Zæhner, *ibid*, pp 40–1), and Thomas Traherne (*The Centuries of Meditations*, London, 1927, I: 27–31). Though the *Iśa Upanishad*, and *Chāndogya Upanishad* 7: 24–26, are speculative accounts of a mystical object, it seems reasonable to suppose that they, too, express an experience of this type. The experience recounted by Bucke in the opening pages of *Cosmic Consciousness* appears to be an example of the second. Wordsworth's *Tintern Abbey* may express a less intense form of this type of experience. (Cf. his

Prelude, Book I, lines 357–424.) Examples of the third are provided by Richard Jefferies (*The Story of My Heart*, chapter III) and (combined with a sense of the extraordinary beauty of nature) Thomas Traherne (*The Centuries of Meditations*, III: 1–3).

[68] Frederick Streng, *Emptiness: A Study in Religious Meaning*, Nashville and New York, 1967.

[69] Quoted in Alan Watts, *The Way of Zen*, New York, 1957, p 126.

[70] Or see Seng-t'san, 'On Believing in Mind', (in D T Suzuki, *Manual of Zen Buddhism*, New York, 1960, pp 76–82).

[71] Satori has been interpreted in very different ways. For example, Stace believes that it is the final stage of the mystical path in which one lives in the world while remaining in permanent contact with the undifferentiated One of introvertive mysticism. Zæhner, on the other hand, thinks that satori is merely a form of cosmic consciousness. The fact of the matter may be that 'satori' is used for rather different experiences, and that there is some truth in *each* of these accounts.

[72] T R V Murti, *The Central Philosophy of Buddhism*, London, 1955, pp 218–20.

[73] It is interesting to note that EEG tests performed on Yogis cultivating introversion yield different results from EEG tests performed on Zen meditators. Although there is a preponderance of alpha waves in both cases, the former 'exhibit no response to an external stimulus', while the latter do. In contrast to non-meditators however, the Zen meditators did not become habituated to a repeated stimulus, and 'alpha waves returned quite soon after' each stimulus. (Victor F Emerson, 'Research on Meditation', *What is Meditation?*, ed by John White, Garden City, NY, 1975, pp 234 and 236.)

While Zen meditation is not the same as satori, the two are not entirely dissimilar. Consequently, these results provide some support for the view that satori is not a species of introvertive mysticism as Stace seems to have thought. One suspects that, because cosmic consciousness ('expansion') is a state of enthusiasm or excitement, EEG tests would reveal beta waves indicating 'a state of arousal'. (To my knowledge there is no evidence which either supports or disconfirms this hypothesis. Since cosmic consciousness tends to occur spontaneously, it would be difficult to conduct the appropriate experiments.)

[74] This hypothesis could be tested. To do so one would first select a fair sample of first person accounts of extrovertive mystical experience. He would then perform a content analysis of these reports, isolating their key features (unity, time standing still, beauty, etc.). Finally, he would employ some form of cluster analysis to sort these characteristics into groups. If the groups or clusters coincide with these four types of extrovertive experience, the hypothesis is confirmed. If they fail to do so, it is disconfirmed. Tests of this type would undoubtedly be useful. On the other hand, they should be treated with caution. The sample must be sufficiently wide and sufficiently varied to be genuinely representative. (And notice that one's results will partly depend upon what one initially counts as 'extrovertive'. For example, one's results may be significantly affected by a decision to include or exclude the experience of 'emptiness'.) The

value of the content analysis will depend upon the completeness of the first person reports. Although length does not guarantee completeness, detailed accounts are preferable to brief descriptions. (The latter are likely to mention only one or two especially striking features.) Finally, one should be cognizant of the fact that different types of cluster analysis (Elementary Cluster Analysis, Clustering by Single Linkage, etc.) produce different results. It cannot be employed to yield *the* correct classification. One should also recognise that these techniques provide no help in determining whether a group of characteristics is a reasonable candidate for a mystical 'given', or a 'core' which is common to several traditions. To make these determinations, one must examine the *nature* of the clusters, and the cultural contexts in which they occur.

[75] 'Extrovertive mysticism', 'nature mysticism', and 'cosmic consciousness' are often used interchangeably. On the other hand, Stace asserts that while 'nature mysticism' is sometimes used for extrovertive mysticism, it is also used to refer to a sense of presence in nature (cf. Wordsworth) which does not amount to a fully developed mystical experience. (*Mysticism and Philosophy*, pp 80–1) Otto attempts to distinguish the first two stages of the 'Way of Unity' from something which he calls 'nature mysticism', but his argument is unclear. The difference appears to be that the 'nature mystic' rests in the first stage without progressing beyond it, or is somehow more interested in nature than in the One that appears in (through) it. (*Mysticism, East and West*, pp 73–5) Zæhner borrows the term 'cosmic consciousness' from Bucke and tends to use it interchangeably with 'nature mysticism'. None of these authors was thinking of the experience of 'emptiness' when they spoke of extrovertive mysticism, or nature mysticism, or cosmic consciousness. In view of its history, it might be advisable to reserve the term 'nature mysticism' for experiences that display at least some of the five characteristics listed on page 33f. ('Cosmic consciousness' is perhaps most appropriately applied to the first two 'cluster's on page 34.)

[76] When we discuss Stace's theory of mysticism in chapter 4, we shall see that there are reasons for believing that this unity is not *absolutely* undifferentiated.

[77] It is by no means clear that the imagery of mutual love is *part* of the experience itself. There are some cases in which the mystic's experiences may be partly constituted by this imagery. But in others (for example, some of the experiences described by John of the Cross, or by the anonymous author of *The Cloud of Unknowing*) the experience is not *constituted* by this imagery since the experience is *free* from imagery. It does, however, include an 'obscure touch' which is *best expressed* by the imagery of mutual love. It is this type of experience which I have in mind. (Whether the first type of experience should be classified as an introvertive mystical experience or as a visionary experience depends upon (1) the degree to which the mystic is abstracted from the external world and from ordinary mental contents, and (2) whether the imagery which helps constitute the experience is the *object* of the mystic's experience or only a medium through which he 'experimentally' apprehends some non-sensuous reality. Where the

abstraction is fairly complete and the imagery is merely a medium, it is not unreasonable to regard the experience as a somewhat less fully introverted form of the second type of introvertive mystical consciousness.)

[78] A residual sense of self (the 'feeling of one's own being') is *not* a sense of distance or otherness.

[79] Cf. Mircea Eliade, 'Experiences of the Mystic Light', *The Two and the One*, Mircea Eliade, New York, 1965.

[80] Content analysis and cluster analysis might be helpful in sorting out various types of introvertive (or non-extrovertive) experiences although, as I have pointed out (fn 74), these tools must be used with caution.

CHAPTER 2

Chemical Mysticism and the Scientific Explanation of Religious Experience

Whatever else they may be, mystical experiences are human experiences. Since most human experiences have identifiable natural causes, it is not unreasonable to suppose that mystical experiences, too, have identifiable natural causes. The purpose of this chapter is to determine whether the existence of an adequate natural explanation of mystical experience would preclude its cognitive validity. I shall argue that it would not.

In order to make my discussion more concrete. I shall begin by examining recent attempts to isolate one natural cause of mystical experience, viz, the ingestion of LSD, psilocybin and other hallucinogens.

The philosophical questions which are raised by experiments with hallucinogens are essentially the same as those raised by any empirical investigation of the causes of mystical experience. We might, therefore, have considered psychoanalytic explanations of mystical experience, or investigations of the connections between sensory deprivation or hypnosis and altered states of consciousness. I have chosen to examine studies of chemical mysticism for three reasons. First, because of the extravagance of some of the claims which have been made. For example, after ingesting mescalin, Aldous Huxley claimed that he now 'understood, not on the verbal level, not by inchoate hints or at a distance, but precisely and completely' exactly what the expressions 'beatific vision' and 'satcit-ānanda' (being consciousness-bliss) 'referred to'.[1] Or to take another example, in commenting on Stace's and Huston

54

Smith's claim that psychedelic experiences are the same thing as mystical experiences, Zaehner said 'The reply in both cases is given by Charles Péguy: "A learned fool is a worse fool than an ignorant one." The worst fool of all, one might add, is the learned fool who is also ignorant.'[2] Second, psychoanalytic and other psychological explanations of religious experience tend to incorporate tendentious theoretical claims. A good example is provided by an interesting paper in which Raymond Prince and Charles Savage offer an explanation of mystical experience which rests upon their interpretation of mystical consciousness as a regression to 'very early infancy'.[3] By contrast, the hypothesis that the physiological changes induced by the ingestion of drugs are among the causes of mystical experience is directly based upon observed correlations between the ingestion of hallucinogens and altered states of consciousness, and does not commit one to controversial physiological or psychological theories. Third, the cause which is allegedly isolated by the studies we shall examine is a 'physical' or 'material' cause, and it might seem more likely that causes of this kind would turn out to be incompatible with the validity of mystical consciousness, than causes of a 'psychological' nature.

I

The most significant studies of chemical mysticism have been conducted by Walter N Pahnke, Walter H Clark, and Jean Houston and R E L Masters.[4] These studies are distinguished by the care with which they were conducted, the balance of the investigators, and their familiarity with the nature of religious and mystical experience.

A
The subjects of Pahnke's experiment were twenty Christian theological students who had had no previous experience with hallucinogens. The students were divided into five groups of four 'on the basis of compatibility and friendship'. Each of the five groups were assigned two guides with psychedelic experience. Prior to the session, the subjects were given psychological and medical tests, filled out a 'questionnaire evaluation of

previous religious experience', were interviewed, and attended a group session with their guides which was designed to reduce fear and maximise positive expectations. The preparatory procedures took a total of five hours.[5]

In each group, two of the subjects and one of the guides was given psilocybin. The rest were given a placebo which caused a tingling sensation and a feeling of warmth thus maximising suggestion. Neither the subjects, the guides nor the experimenter knew who were getting the placebo and who were getting the drug. The subjects and guides were then taken to a private chapel where they listened to a two and a half hour Good Friday service consisting of readings, prayers, music and meditation. (The setting of the session was therefore familiar and supportive.) Individual reactions immediately following the service, and a subsequent group discussion, were tape recorded. As soon as possible after the session, each subject wrote a 'phenomenological account of his experience' and, 'within a week', filled out a '147-item questionnaire'. This was used as 'the basis for a ninety-minute tape-recorded interview that followed immediately'. 'Six months later, each subject was interviewed again after completion of a follow-up questionnaire.' The second part of the follow-up questionnaire was essentially a condensation of the first questionnaire. The first part was designed to determine whether the subject had perceived any persistent changes in his attitude and behaviour, and whether he thought them beneficial. The third part was designed to determine whether positive or negative changes had actually occurred. (Implications, pp 191–2)

Mysticism was defined by the following characteristics:

(1) 'Unity'. (Pahnke was clearly aware of the distinction between introvertive ('internal') unity and extrovertive ('external') unity.)

(2) 'Objectivity and reality', i.e. a sense of 'illumination' and 'certainty'.

(3) 'Transcendence of space and time.'

(4) 'Sense of sacredness.'

(5) 'Deeply-felt positive mood,' i.e. 'joy, love, blessedness and peace.'

(6) 'Paradoxicality.'

(7) 'Alleged ineffability.'

(8) 'Transiency.'

(9) 'Positive changes in attitude and/or behaviour', for example, self-acceptance, empathy, self-confidence, and 'vocational commitment'. ('Implications', pp 176–83)

Pahnke's typology was thus essentially identical with the typology of Stace. He simply added 'transiency' (William James), and 'positive changes in attitude and/or behaviour' to the latter's list of characteristics.

The 'phenomenological accounts' were scored by three housewives who had formerly been school teachers. They were ignorant of the genesis of the reports, but had been trained to detect evidence of the presence of Pahnke's nine characteristics. Rankings of strong, moderate, slight, or none were assigned, depending on the degree to which the subject's reports exhibited the characteristics in question.[6] The two questionnaries were also scored numerically – low scores being given when a feature of mystical experience was either not experienced at all, or experienced incompletely. The scores for each category of mystical experience were then averaged. (There were thus three measures – the scores of the first questionnaire, the scores of the follow-up questionnaire, and the scores assigned to the subject's written reports.)

The results were as follows: Nine of the ten subjects who had ingested psilocybin claimed to have had a religious experience. Only one member of the control group did so. The only subject who had received the drug and failed to report a religious experience admitted that he had hoped to show that there was no connection between drugs and religious experience. (Clark, p 77)

A mystical experience was defined as an experience receiving a total score of at least 60 per cent in each category. 'Three or four' in the experimental group reached this level of completeness, but none in the control group. ('LSD', p 67) When the experimental group as a whole was compared with the control group it was discovered that, with respect to internal unity, the experimental group scored 70 per cent of the maximum possible, while the control group scored only 8 per cent. With respect to external unity, the scores were 38 per cent and 2 per cent, respectively.[7] The other percentage scores were: transcendence of space and time, 84 and 6; positive mood, 57 and 23; sacredness, 53 and 28; objectivity, 63 and 18; paradoxicality, 61 and 13; alleged ineffability, 66 and 18; transiency 79 and 8; and persisting positive changes, 51 and 8. ('Contribution', p 637).

Perhaps the most surprising aspect of these results is the high score for internal unity. This score, when taken together with the score for spatio-temporal transcendence, suggests a high incidence of introvertive experiences.

B

In Clark's experiment, LSD was administered to eight normal subjects 'daily over periods up to sixteen days'. Approximately ten months after the conclusion of the experiment, the subjects were given a list of twenty characteristics of mystical and religious experience and asked to rate themselves on a scale from O ('no different from normal') to 5 ('beyond anything over experienced or imagined'). 'All subjects, in varying degrees, reported aspects of religious and particularly mystical experience.' The experience of three subjects were particularly intense, and their scores are given below:

		K	M	W
1	Timelessness	5	4·3	5
2	Spacelessness	5	4	4
3	Unity and Loss of Self	5	4·7	5
4	Unity with Objects and Growing Things	0	2·7	4
5	Unity with People	4	4·7	4·3
6	Ultimate Reality	5	3·3	5
7	Blessedness and Peace	5	5	5
8	The Holy and Divine	5	5	4·7
9	Paradoxicality	5	4·3	5
10	Ineffability	2	3·3	5
11	Fear and Terror	5	5	3
12	Mystery	5	4·3	5
13	Joy	5	4	5
14	Sense of Dying	0	3·3	5
15	Rebirth	1	5	5
16	Presence of God	5	4	5
17	Esthetic Experience	5	5	5
18	Color Intense	5	4·7	5
19	Music Moving	5	3	5
20	Significance of Experience	5	5	5

(Clark, pp 81–3)

C

Houston and Masters discuss their procedures in chapter 5 of
The Varieties of Psychedelic Experience.

The psychedelic session should be conducted by someone
who is not only a psychotherapist, or an anthropologist, or an
historian of religion, but has been trained as a psychedelic
guide. In addition to his specialities he should have a broad
background in the social sciences, arts and humanities, 'be
mentally and emotionally stable and possess the capacity to
stimulate feelings of security and trust in the subjects'. (p 131)[8]
He should also have had psychedelic experience.

The setting must be friendly and supportive, and preferably
one with which the subject is already familiar. A clinical environment should be avoided.[9]

Houston's and Masters' subjects were required to be in
good physical and mental health, to be 'between the ages of
twenty-five and sixty' with 'a minimum IQ of 105', and to
have had two or more years of college education or its equivalent. (p 138)

Preparatory meetings were held 'over a period of several
weeks'. These sessions enabled the guide 'to explore the psychology of the subject', to provide information and clear up
misconceptions, to develop 'rapport' and 'positive expectations', and to 'help the subject to determine the intended goals
of his session'. (In several cases, the goal was religious experience.) In order to prepare himself for the psychedelic session,
the subject was encouraged to practise suspending his usual
way of viewing things – his 'value-judgments, ways of apprehending form and colour ... self image', etc. (p 139).

The guide enters the psychedelic session with a set of goals
and a set of techniques designed to meet these goals, although
both techniques and goals may be modified in the course of the
session if the subject's reactions appear to warrant it. During
the session, the guide leads the subject towards his goals, and
also explores those areas in which, as a researcher, he is
especially interested. The guide should attempt to avoid colouring his subject's experience although, as Houston and
Masters recognise, 'each guide ... will necessarily elicit
phenomena partially determined by himself'. (p 140)

One feature of these procedures is especially noteworthy. At one point Houston and Masters compare the guide to a shaman or priest. The relation between the investigator and his subject might also be compared to the relation between a psychotherapist and his patient. The history of both relationships is at least partly determined by the goals of the subject or patient. Both involve a peculiar blend of distance and intimacy and, perhaps most important, both result in a profound knowledge of the subject or patient which is at once 'clinical' and personal.

While Houston and Masters accepted Stace's typology of mysticism, their 'major criteria for establishing the validity of [the] most profound religious and mystical experiences' (p 267) were:

(1) An encounter with 'a Presence variously described as God, Spirit, Ground of Being ... and Ultimate or Fundamental Reality' (p 266),

(2) 'transformation of the self' (p 267), and

(3) 'in most cases' (p 267) a progression through four levels – the 'sensory' level involving altered perceptions; the 'recollective-analytic' level in which significant past experiences are vividly recalled, and personal problems and goals are examined; the 'symbolic' level in which the subject experiences symbolic images drawn from history, mythology and legend, and 'may act out myths and legends and pass through initiations and ritual observances often seemingly structured ... in terms of his own most urgent needs' (p 147); and finally the 'integral' level of 'psychological integration, "illumination", and a sense of fundamental and positive self-transformation' (p 148)

The authors recognise that these criteria cannot be mechanically applied, and point out that 'the "emotional feel" of a subject's authentic religious experience as compared to those' dismissed as inauthentic cannot be adequately conveyed 'by means of the written word'. (p 299)

It should be noted that *two* sets of criteria were employed. An experience could meet the criteria for a *mystical* experience without meeting the criteria for an 'authentic' or 'valid' *religious* experience, and vice versa.

Houston and Masters appear to have been unusually cautious in formulating their results. While 45 per cent of their subjects claimed to have had a religious experience, a 'large number of these' were rejected. (p 257f) Several subjects offered descriptions of their experience which would probably be accepted as descriptions of authentic religious experience if taken in isolation (one of these is given on p 263f), but these were discounted in view of the entire session.

'Almost one half' of Houston's and Masters' 206 subjects had extrovertive experiences. These were not regarded as authentically religious because they involved no perception of God or Being or Ultimate Reality, and were 'rarely transformative'. (p 303) Only eleven were judged to have had authentically religious experiences. (p 148) It was concluded that six had had introvertive experiences. It is significant that all six were persons who 'have in the course of their lives either actively sought the mystical experience in meditation and other spiritual disciplines or have for many years demonstrated a considerable interest in integral levels of consciousness'. and that all were 'over forty ..., of superior intelligence, and ... well-adjusted and creative personalities.' (p 307). Interestingly enough, however, these six were not included in the group whose members were judged to have had authentic religious experiences, since they failed to satisfy the second criterion. (p 321) On the other hand, this is probably less significant than it seems for, as the authors point out, these six had *already* achieved 'exceptional mental and emotional maturity and stability'. (p 311f)

II

What do these studies show? In the first place, our authors agree that 'chemical ecstasy' is a joint product of the hallucinogen, the setting in which the drug is administered, and the psychological 'set' which the subject brings to the experience. The ingestion of hallucinogens is not a causally sufficient condition of mystical experience. In the second place, the evidence that hallucinogens can trigger some kind of mystical experience is rather conclusive. Even so harsh a critic as Zæhner concedes that drugs can induce cosmic consciousness, and a sense of a 'Here' and 'Now' beyond space and time.[10] What is not clear is whether drugs can induce introvertive experiences in which the self is abstracted from empirical contents, or whether it can induce theistic mystical experiences.

A

Do drugs sometimes induce introvertive mystical experiences? The evidence is not as clear as some have supposed.

(1) Clark does not appear to have been particularly interested in showing that drugs can induce introvertive (as distinguished from extrovertive) mystical experiences. In any case, his experiment was not designed to discriminate between introvertive and extrovertive states.

His data are ambiguous. While it is difficult to deny that the experiences of K, M and W exhibited a number of the characteristics of mystical consciousness, it is *not* clear that their experiences were introvertive. All three gave high marks to 'timelessness', 'spacelessness', and 'unity and loss of self'. This fact, if considered by itself, would suggest that their experiences were introvertive. On the other hand, two of them gave relatively high marks to 'unity with objects and growing things', and all three gave high marks to 'unity with people', to colour intensity, and to the impact of music – which would suggest that their experiences were *extrovertive*.[11] Furthermore, the fact that high marks were assigned to 'timelessness', 'spacelessness', and 'unity and loss of self' is inconclusive. Extrovertive experiences also involve a kind of spatio-temporal transcendence. The space-time world is not obliterated, but time sometimes seems to stop, and the distinction between place and place is often transcended in a vision of the unity or identity of all phenomenal things. 'Loss of self' is also ambiguous. It can refer to the disappearance of the empirical ego, which is characteristic of introvertive experience, but it can also refer to the dissolution of the self in nature, which is a feature of certain types of extrovertive mystical consciousness.

It would have been helpful if the questionnaire had asked whether the subject had lost consciousness of his environment (or had ceased to be focally aware of it), but it did not. The absence of 'auto-accounts' of the subjects' experience is also unfortunate for, without them, it is very difficult to determine just what sort of timelessness or spacelessness or egolessness was experienced. (It is worth observing that in Pahnke's experiment, the subjects' descriptive reports tended to lower the overall score. ('Contribution, p 638)[12])

(2) Pahnke's results are more significant. In evaluating the follow-up questionnaire, 'internal unity' was defined by six items: loss of identity, 'pure awareness beyond any empirical content', 'fusion of the self into a larger undifferentiated whole', loss of self-identity as a positive experience, loss of self-identity as a negative experience, and 'freedom for [sic] the limitations of the self in connection with a unity or bond with what was felt to be all-encompassing and greater-than-self'. ('Dissertation', p 130) The problem is that only one of those items is peculiar to introvertive experience, viz, the second. It would be possible for a person to score highly with respect to internal unity, as defined by these characteristics, even if his experience was an instance of cosmic consciousness. The results of the second questionnaire are therefore inconclusive. In evaluating the post-drug questionnaire, 'internal unity' was defined by four items: 'loss of self', 'sense of the loss of the multiplicity of all particular sense impressions', 'pure awareness with no empirical distinctions (i.e. one is beyond the self-consciousness of sense impressions, yet one is not unconscious),' and 'sense of unity with ultimate reality at the level described by' the last two items. (*Ibid* p 130) The last three items are distinguishing features of introvertive mystical consciousness. The definition of 'internal unity' associated with the post-drug questionnaire is therefore more accurate. It is thus significant that the experimentals assigned the highest score ('strong') to one or the other of these four items twenty-four times (out of a possible forty) while the controls assigned no 'strongs' and thirty-four 'nones'. (*Ibid* p 128) It is obvious from the dissertation that the distinction between introvertive and extrovertive experiences was clearly explained to the three judges. It is therefore also significant that with respect to internal unity, six 'strongs' and three 'moderates' were assigned to the experimentals while no 'strongs' and only one 'moderate' were assigned to the controls. (*Ibid* p 128)

On the other hand, three things should make us (somewhat)

suspicious of Pahnke's results. The first is the fact that the
control group scored 8 per cent with respect to internal unity.
(This figure is presumably based upon the scores of the
member of the control group who reported a religious experience.) Given the comparative rarity of introvertive consciousness, one would have expected the score of the control group to
have been zero.[13] Of course, this consideration is not conclusive, for introvertive experiences do sometimes occur spontaneously, and members of the control group were placed in a
situation which maximised expectations of some kind of mystical experience.

The second is the quality of the subjects' written reports. In
discussing internal unity. Pahnke quotes from only three 'phenomenological accounts'. It seems reasonable to assume that
he selected the accounts which best illustrated this feature, but
the first sounds like a report of cosmic consciousness. (The
subject claims that he saw the 'orange plastic cosmos', that he
seemed to be in many places rather than in one place, that he
'floated' through the cosmos, etc.) The second is ambiguous.
(The subject speaks of life being relinquished in 'layers', of a
sense of 'oneness', of 'an eternal dimension to life', and of an
impression of 'infinite possibilities of time and space'.) Only the
third seems clearly introvertive. (The subject reported 'blank
sensation' or 'a void', and a sense of 'oneness, unity, and
harmony'. ('Dissertation', p 131) The fact that only one of
these reports is *obviously* introvertive suggests that the scores
assigned to them with respect to internal unity were inflated.

The third is the striking disparity between Pahnke's results
and the results of Houston and Masters. While internal unity
is not strictly identical with introvertive mystical consciousness, it is perhaps its principle differentiating characteristic.
The high score for 'internal unity', when taken together with
the scores for such items as 'objectivity' and 'positive mood',
suggest a high incidence of introvertive or near introvertive
mystical experience. By contrast only 3 per cent of Houston's
and Masters' subjects seemed to have had introvertive mystical experiences.

What accounts for this discrepancy? Pahnke suggests that it
is due to a difference in method. (Thus, after reporting
Houston's and Masters' results, he says 'such figures need to

be interpreted cautiously unless a careful definition with some kind of method for quantifying the experience is established.' ('LSD,' p 66)) I think that Pahnke has identified the scource of the disparity, but that he is mistaken in supposing that 'quantitative' methods are superior to the methods of Houston and Masters.

Houston's and Masters' investigation differs from Pahnke's in three important respects. First, the assessment of the subjects' experiences was made by the investigator. (In Pahnke's experiment, the subjects scored their own experiences (the questionnaires). The weighting of their written reports was done by a panel of housewives.)

Second, the investigator making the assessment had met with the subject on a number of occasions prior to the session, and was present at the session itself. He was thus personally familiar with the subject, and with his behaviour during the session. (In Pahnke's experiment, the investigator made no assessment, while the three housewives were not present at the psychedelic session. There were two brief preparatory sessions – one with the guides (who made no assessment), and one with the investigator. Two interviews were conducted after the session by the investigator. The three judges were not acquainted with the subjects, and knew nothing of their character or background. The upshot is that no overall assessment of their experiences was made by a person possessing a first hand knowledge of the subjects' character and background, and of their behaviour at the time of their experiences.)

Third, the investigator was willing to rely on his overall impressions of the authenticity or inauthenticity of his subjects experience. (While Pahnke interviewed his subjects after their experiences, primary reliance was placed upon the results of the two questionnaires and upon the numerical scores assigned to the subjects' written reports.)

Pahnke's methods may appear to be more 'objective' than the methods of Houston and Masters. If an authentic mystical experience is an experience which receives a score of at least 60 per cent in each category when Pahnke's tests are applied, it is comparatively easy to determine just who does and does not have a mystical experience. By contrast, it is not altogether clear just what counts as a positive self-transformation or as an encounter at the integral level, and it is therefore not altogether clear just what counts as an 'authentic' or 'profound' mystical or religious experience.

But this appearance of objectivity is deceptive, for the numbers assigned to Pahnke's items were themselves based on 'subjective' assessments, i.e. upon judgment rather than some sort of mechanical decision procedure. Since personal judgments are inevitable they are surely best made by learned, sensitive and balanced investigators who are familiar with the literature of mysticism, and possess a first hand knowledge of both the character and background of their subjects, and of their behaviour during their experiences.

It is not obvious that the nature and quality of a religious experience can be adequately assessed on the basis of questionnaires and brief written descriptions. We should remind ourselves of the fact that mystical literature abounds in warnings of self-deception and in admonitions to place oneself in the hands of a spiritual director who is himself adept in the contemplative life and can therefore distinguish authentic experiences from their counterfeits. The subject matter is such that the very attempt to be 'objective' or 'scientific' may cause one to be insufficiently discriminating. This is not as paradoxical as it sounds. Judging the quality and authenticity of religious experience appears to be more like judging the integrity of an acquaintance, or the style of a novel, than determining the strength of someone's eyesight or his IQ. There are 'objective' measures of the latter, i.e. standardised tests which can be mechanically applied by anyone trained to do so. The use of standardised tests to determine a friend's personal integrity or the style of a novel can yield grotesque results. I see no reason to suppose that quantitative measures of mystical consciousness will be any more successful.[14]

(3) What, then, of Houston's and Masters' study? As we have seen, Houston and Masters claim that six of their 206 subjects had introvertive mystical experiences.

The auto-accounts of three of these subjects (S_4, S_5, and S_6) are included in the text. All three experiences were, at least, in part, experiences of the 'mystic light' in which the subjects were interfused with a supernatural radiance. (S_4 says that 'all around and passing through me was the Light, a trillion atomised crystals shimmering in blinding incandescence. I was carried by this Light to an Ecstasy beyond ecstasy...' S_5 speaks of 'a pure and seething energy that was the whole of Being,' which 'was experienced as a white and radiant fire.' S_6 claims that she 'became a diffused light' that 'burst' into 'a shower of dazzling rays – each ray filled with a myriad of colours'. (pp 308 and 310)) The experiences of these subjects seem to have involved some sort of transcendence of the space-time world. We have seen (chapter 1, VC) that it is not unreasonable to regard experiences of this type as introvertive, although they could be classified as visionary.

One can also find other accounts of psychedelic experiences which might very well be accounts of introvertive mystical experiences,[15] although one seldom comes across descriptions which are unambiguously introvertive.[16]

On balance, then, the evidence does suggest that hallucinogens sometimes induce introvertive mystical states, although they appear to do so with less frequency than is often supposed.

B

Do drugs sometimes induce theistic mystical experience? Huston Smith maintains that Zæhner flies in the face of the evidence when he asserts that drugs do not induce theistic mystical states. But the only evidence to which Smith alludes is (1) James Slotkin's *Peyote Religion*,[17] which reports that members of the peyote churches 'see visions which may be of Christ Himself. Sometimes they hear the voice of the Great Spirit. Sometimes they become aware of the presence of God and of those personal shortcomings which must be corrected if they are to do His will,' and (2) the fact that G M Carstairs[18] quotes a brahmin as saying 'It gives good bhakti ... you get a very good bhakti with bhang'.[19] Houston and Masters repeat Smith's claim (*Varieties*, p 257), but provide no additional evidence.

Not only is Smith's 'evidence' slight, it provides no reason whatsoever for supposing that the experiences in question are mystical experiences. All that the first bit of evidence shows is that peyote can induce visions of Jesus and a sense of divine presence, but visions have little or nothing to do with theistic mystical consciousness, and a sense of divine presence is a feature of several states, only some of which are mystical. (Slotkin does evince some awareness of the difference between visions and mysticism. Thus, at one point, he says 'in most cases the revelation takes the form of a vision ... in some cases [it] takes the form of a mystical state, the unification of all immediate experience with God,'[20] but not enough is said about the nature and quality of the latter to be helpful.)

The second place of evidence is equally inconclusive. Bhakti is loving devotion. Some of the states associated with the higher levels of bhakti are undoubtedly mystical, but other states and attitudes associated with bhakti are not. Carstairs' article provides no indication of which states or attitudes the Brahmin had in mind. (The brahmin's remark could have meant no more than bhang intensifies feelings of devotion and love.)

Do our three studies cast any light on this question? Clark's subjects reported an intense sense of God's presence, but in the absence of information telling us what these subjects meant by 'God', or what this aspect of their experience was like, we are in no position to draw conclusions. (Many modern English speakers use 'God' as a synonym for any holy or sacred or ultimate reality.)

The studies of Pahnke and of Houston and Masters are relatively useless because they were working with Stace's typology of mystical experience, and Stace does not recognise any distinction between theistic mysticism and other forms of introvertive mystical consciousness. As a result of their commitment to this typology, no attempt was made to sort out theistic mystical experiences from non-theistic mystical experiences.

In addressing the question of drug-induced theistic mystical experiences, it is important to remember that theistic mysticism is both an introvertive mysticism and a love mysticism. One's empirical ego is temporally suspended. The soul is empty of all ordinary contents, but loves and feels itself loved by the reality which it encounters in ecstasy. This has two implications: first, unless an experience is clearly introvertive, it is not a candidate for a theistic mystical experience; second, protestations of love are relevant if and only if the love is felt to be mutual.

There are accounts of psychedelic experiences which *could* be read as descriptions of theistic mystical experience. None of the reports with which I am familiar compels a reasonable person to interpret them in this fashion.

I conclude that while it is possible that the ingestion of drugs occasionally induces theistic mystical experiences, there is little evidence that it actually does so.

III

The studies which we have examined do not pretend to show that the ingestion of hallucinogens is a causally sufficient condition of mystical experience. Nevertheless, a consideration of these and related studies inevitably suggests the possibility that science will someday discover an adequate natural explanation of religious experience. Would the discovery of an adequate scientific explanation have any tendency to show that mystical consciousness has no cognitive value?

William Alston[21] believes that it would. For consider the following argument:

(1) If an experience of x (for example, having visual impressions of pink elephants) is a perception of x, then x is a causally necessary condition of[22] the experience of x.

(2) If there are causally sufficient conditions for x which do not include y, then y is not a causally necessary condition of x. Therefore,

(3) If there are causally sufficient conditions for the experience of x which do not include x, then x is not a causally necessary condition of the experience of x. (From 2.) Therefore,

(4) If there are causally sufficient conditions for the experience of x which do not include x, then the experience of x is not a perception of x. (From 1 and 3) Therefore,

(5) If there is a set of natural conditions which is causally sufficient for the occurrence of religious experience (an

experience of God or some sort of transcendent reality),
then that experience is not a perception of God or transcendent reality. (From 4.)

I shall attempt to show that even if we were to be presented
with an adequate scientific explanation of religious experience, this argument could not be employed to establish the
proposition that religious experience is not veridical.

(1) The first premise of the argument is not clearly true. If it
is true at all it is presumably necessarily true, but its necessity
is not obvious. Suppose that we are able to produce visual
impressions of a particular table, even when that table is not
present, by stimulating certain areas of the brain, and that we
stimulate (in the right way) the brain of a person who is conscious, who possesses normal vision and whose eyes are open
and directed at the table in question which is located two feet
away from him. The presence of the table is not a causally
necessary condition of his visual impressions, for those
impressions would have occurred even if the table had been
absent. If it were clear that the first premise of our argument
was true in all possible circumstances then it would be clear
that the subject does not see the table in the circumstances
which I have described. This, however, is not clear.[23]

(2) In a general way, what is wrong with the argument is
obvious enough. It is assumed that if there is an adequate
natural explanation of religious experience, then that experience cannot be grounded in God's causal activity. (For the
argument is essentially this: if there is an adequate natural explanation of religious experience, then God is not a cause of it,
and if God is not a cause of it, then that experience cannot be a
perception of God.) But this assumption is not obvious and is
incompatible with the theist's belief that all or most phenomenal events are such that even though adequate scientific explanations can (in principle) be provided for them, they are,
nonetheless, grounded in God's causal activity.

Nevertheless, it must be admitted that Alston's argument is
plausible, and that we do not yet know exactly what is wrong
with it.

We must begin by noticing that 'causally sufficient condition' can be used in at least two senses. In the first sense, x is
a casually sufficient condition of y if and only if given x and

certain background conditions, y will occur. Thus, taking a large dose of arsenic is (in this sense) a causally sufficient condition of death, since taking a large dose of arsenic in certain familiar circumstances invariably results in death. In the second sense, x is a causally sufficient condition of y if and only if given x alone, y will invariably result. If x is a causally sufficient condition of y in this strong sense, then it must include all the necessary conditions of y. (If it does not, then it will not be true that x *alone* will invariably result in y.) Taking arsenic is not a causally sufficient condition of death in this strong sense, since given an odd physiological constitution, or the fact that an antidote has been taken in time, or something else of the sort, one can take a large dose of arsenic and not die.

If 'causally sufficient condition' is construed in the first and weak sense, then the second premise of the argument is false. As our example suggests, there are many cases in which there are causally sufficient conditions (weak sense) for an occurrence which do not include some factor y, and yet y is a causally necessary condition of the occurrence. Thus, while ingesting a large quantity of arsenic is a causally sufficient condition (weak sense) of death and does not include the failure to take an effective antidote, the latter is a causally necessary condition of death from arsenic.

If 'causally sufficient condition' is taken in the second and strong sense, the prospects for the argument look brighter. If the expression is taken in this sense, (2) is true and (assuming that (1) is acceptable) the argument is sound. Its conclusion, however, is now innocuous. If 'causally sufficient condition' is taken in the strong sense our conclusion is logically equivalent to:

(5') If there is a set of natural conditions which when taken alone will invariably result in the occurrence of religious experience, then that experience is not a perception of God or of any other transcendent reality.

(5') (and thus (5)) is innocuous because it cannot, in practice, be used to show that religious experience is not veridical. Suppose we were presented with a causal account of religious experience which was believed to be fully adequate by the scientific community. Would we be entitled to infer that religious experiences are not perceptions of God, etc.? We would be entitled to draw this conclusion on the basis of (5') only if we had good reason to believe that the causes which were specified in the scientific account could, when taken alone, i.e. in the absence of (among other things) any divine activity, produce the experiences in question. Without a disproof of the existence of God and other supra-empirical causes, it is totally unclear how we could ever know that this was the case. (We could not, for example, remove God from existence and show that the empirical causes in question still produce religious experiences.)

I therefore conclude that if 'causally sufficient condition' must be taken in one or the other of these two senses, then either the argument is unsound (since one of its premises is false) or, in spite of appearances, its conclusion is innocuous.

(3) One other possibility should be considered. In the course of his discussion, Alston suggests that:

(6) If an experience of *x* is a perception of *x*, not only must *x* be a cause of that experience, it must also occur 'somewhere (*not too far back*) in the chain of causes' which give rise to that experience.

Perhaps it is the case that if an adequate scientific explanation of religious experience can (in principle) be provided then while God's activity or the activity of some other transcendent principle may be a causal condition of that experience, it can only be a remote cause of it, in which case religious experience is not veridical.

I do not find this convincing. In the first place, I do not see why causal remoteness, or the lack of it, is relevant to a consideration of the veridical character of an experience, i.e. I do not see why we should suppose that (6) is true. In the second place, it is by no means clear that the presence of an adequate scientific explanation of religious experience (or any other phenomenon) in any way tends to show that God is a remote cause of that experience (or phenomenon). Classical theists generally distinguish between two levels of causality, arguing that God's activity is an immediate cause of all events even though the same events are members of chains of natural causes which do not include God. It is not clear that this is nonsense. If it is not, then it is entirely possible for there to be an adequate scientific account of religious experience (an account which links the occurrence of religious experience to other events on the phenomenal level and which does not, of course, mention God) even though God is an immediate cause of the experience and of each member of the chain of natural causes which leads up to it.[24]

If the argument of this section has been sound, it has not been shown that the concept of perception precludes the possibility of an adequate scientific explanation of veridical religious experience.

IV

In the previous section, I argued that the possibility of an adequate scientific explanation of veridical religious experience is not ruled out by the *nature of perception*. Nevertheless, the *object* of religious experience might be such that it precludes the possibility of an adequate scientific explanation of a veridical experience of it. If this were the case, the discovery of an adequate scientific explanation of religious experience would show that religious experience is cognitively worthless.

Different types of religious experience have different apparent objects. The apparent object of nature mysticism is either nature itself, or some energy or force or life (the world soul, prāna) which is interfused with it and sustains it. The apparent object of monistic experience is the depth of one's own soul, or some sort of impersonal unity which transcends space and time. The apparent object of numinous experience and theistic mystical consciousness is God, an all-powerful but gracious will. There appears to be no feature of nature, or of a world soul, or of one's puruṣa, or of the Ātman-Brahman, which would preclude the possibility of an adequate scientific explanation of a veridical experience of them. God is a different matter.

Robert Oakes has argued that an analysis of the concept of God shows that drugs cannot *cause* a veridical experience of God, and that it is implausible to suppose that the ingestion of a drug might *induce* God to reveal himself.[25] Oakes' arguments can be generalised to cover sensory deprivation, hypnosis, sensory overloading, and other natural causes of religious experience. They are worth examining because they articulate the uneasiness with which most theists view chemical mysticism and other forms of 'artificially' induced religious experience.

Oakes' first argument is designed to show that drugs cannot *cause* veridical theistic experiences. It can be formulated as follows:

(1) A veridical theistic experience is a revelation of God, i.e. it is a divine self-disclosure.[26]

(2) 'A revelation is an experience that is *brought about deliberately by its object*'[27] Hence,

(3) God's 'initiative and purpose' is the cause of veridical theistic experience (From 1 and 2).

(4) If the ingestion of a drug was a causally sufficient condition of veridical theistic experience, it would constitute a causal determinant of God's will. (From 3. Since God's will is the cause of all veridical theistic experience, drugs can be causally sufficient conditions of veridical theistic experiences only by being causally sufficient conditions of God's decision to reveal himself.)

(5) 'Nothing ... can constitute a causal determinant of God's will.' (p 13) Consequently,

(6) The ingestion of drugs cannot constitute a causal determinant of God's will. (From 5). Therefore,

(7) Drugs cannot be causally sufficient conditions of veridical theistic experiences. (From 4 and 6.)[28]

Oakes' conclusion can be generalised since similar considerations would show that *no* set of natural conditions can be a causally sufficient condition of a veridical theistic experience.

Oakes also argues that is is implausible to suppose that the ingestion of a drug might *induce* God to reveal Himself. Even if someone who believed in God, loved God, and burned with a desire to see God, were to ingest drugs in the hope of experiencing God, and then did so, it would be more plausible to suppose that God had been influenced by that person's faith, love and desire than to suppose that He had been influenced by his ingestion of a drug. The ingestion of a drug, unlike a person's attitudes, purposes and desires, is not the *sort* of thing which would influence God.

It may even be a mistake to suppose that God is influenced by *any* human attainment. In a number of theistic traditions, God's grace is believed to be absolutely free; it is not tied to conditions or means. God's favour is not a response to human merit or deserving; nor can anything be done to win it. If this is true, and if the 'experimental awareness of God' is a form of grace, it is a mistake to suppose that the ingestion of a drug (or anything else) might induce God to reveal Himself.

These arguments have a certain *prima facie* plausibility, but they will not survive scrutiny. The first argument is either unsound or innocuous. A natural (causal) determinant of a thing would either seem to be a natural condition upon which that thing invariably follows, or a natural condition which somehow necessitates it. Since there are invariable connections between such things as a sudden fall in temperature and water freezing, and between striking a match and its bursting into flame, there are invariable connections between a drop in temperature and God's willing that water freeze, and between striking a match and God's willing that it burst into flame. (With the possible exception of free choices, the God of classical theism is the sufficient cause of every event. Everything is brought about by His will.) If 'natural determinant' is used in the first sense, then there are many natural determinants of God's will.[29] (5) is false and there is therefore no reason to believe that (6) is true.

The world contains no natural determinants of God's will in the term's second sense. But if it follows that the ingestion of drugs does not cause veridical theistic experiences, it also follows that striking a match does not cause it to burst into flame. (A match will not burst into flame unless God wills that it do so. Hence, the only way in which striking a match could necessitate its bursting into flame would be by necessitating God's will. Since no natural condition can necessitate God's will, no natural condition can necessitate a match's bursting into flame.) Not only is this a stronger conclusion than most theists are prepared to accept, it is relatively innocuous. It is relatively innocuous because it leaves open the possibility that the ingestion of drugs or some other natural determinant may bear the same relation to veridical theistic experiences as the striking of a match bears to its ignition or a head-on collision to a person's death.

The second and third arguments also prove too much. For consider standard means of grace such as alms giving, reading the Bible, attending sermons, partaking of the sacraments, etc. One could plausibly argue that what influences God is not these *acts* but the attitudes, intentions and desires behind them. Similar considerations would show that no other human act can influence God.[30] Although some theists might be happy with this conclusion, most would not.

The third argument is exposed to a similar objection. If God's grace is *absolutely* free, *no* created condition (not even a person's attitudes, purposes and desires) can induce God to bestow grace, and this too is unacceptable to most theists.

Neither of these two arguments has the slightest tendency to show that hypnosis, the ingestion of drugs, or any other 'artificial' means of inducing religious experience cannot be a cause of veridical theistic experience in precisely the same sense in which traditional techniques of meditation and the use of God's 'ordinances' (scripture, sacraments, etc.) are causes of veridical theistic experiences.[31] To make matters worse, the very doctrines which might seem to preclude the possibility of an authentic chemical revelation in fact do the opposite. If external works have no inherent tendency to elicit God's favour, or if God's will is absolutely sovereign, then there appears to be no reason why God should not have ordained hallucinogens, or anything else whose use is not intrinsically immoral, as a means of grace.[32]

V

The principal conclusions of this chapter can be summarised as follows:

(1) There is solid evidence that given the right setting and set, hallucinogens elicit cosmic consciousness.

(2) There is good, if not absolutely conclusive evidence that hallucinogens occasionally elicit introvertive mystical experiences.

(3) The case for drug-induced theistic mystical experiences is unconvincing.

(4) No feature of perception entails that the existence of causally sufficient natural conditions of religious experience would be incompatible with its cognitive validity.

(5) No feature of the apparent object of religious experience entails that the existence of causally sufficient natural conditions of religious experience would be incompatible with its cognitive validity.

Natural explanations of religious experience have sometimes been offered with the intention of undermining its cognitive pretensions. If the argument of this chapter has been sound, the discovery of an adequate scientific explanation of religious experience would have little bearing upon its cognitive status.

Notes

[1] Aldous Huxley, *The Doors of Perception and Heaven and Hell*, New York, 1963 p 18.

[2] *Drugs, Mysticism and Make-Believe, op cit*, p 79.

[3] Raymond Prince and Charles Savage, 'Mystical States and the Concept of Regression', *The Highest State of Consciousness*, ed by John White, Garden City, N Y, 1972. (Originally published in the *Psychedelic Review* 8 (1966), pp 59–75.)

[4] Pahnke's work is described in his thesis ('Drugs and Mysticism: An Analysis of the Relationship between Psychedelic Drugs and Mystical Consciousness', Doctoral Dissertation: Harvard University, 1964). He discusses his results in 'Drugs and Mysticism', (*International Journal of Parapsychology* VIII (1966), pp 295–320), and 'The Contribution of the Psychology of Religion to the Therapeutic Use of the Psychedelic Substances', (*The Uses of LSD in Psychotherapy and Alcoholism*, ed by Harold Abramson, Indianapolis, 1967). These two papers are substantially identical. See also his 'LSD and Religious Experience', (*LSD, Man and Society*, ed by R C Leaf, Middletown, Conn, 1967), and a paper which he co-authored with William A Richards entitled 'Implications of LSD and Experimental Mysticism', (*Journal of Religion and Health* 5 (1966), pp 175–208). Clark's study is described in chapter 6 of his *Chemical Ecstasy, Psychedelic Drugs and Religion*, New York, 1969.

For the work of Houston and Masters, see their *The Varieties of Psychedelic Experience*, New York, 1967, especially chapter 9. References to this material will be incorporated in the text. The experimental study of chemical mysticism was aborted. Most interested investigators happened to be Americans. When legal restrictions were placed upon the experimental use of hallucinogens in the mid-sixties, research came to an effective halt. Street users could, of course, be examined as in some of Clark's later work, but the type of study described in this section is no longer possible.

5 Pahnke says that the interview was 'intensive'. In view of the fact that the interview was only two hours long and included a physical examination, one wonders just how intensive it could have been

6 The rankings of the three judges turned out to be highly correlated. ('Dissertation', p 109)

7 The score for 'internal unity' was thus higher than the score for 'external unity'. Pahnke suggests that the setting (a darkened chapel) encouraged introvertive rather than extrovertive experiences. ('Dissertation', p 229)

8 All page references in this section are to *The Varieties of Psychedelic Experience (op cit)*.

9 Although the first two conditions are formulated as recommendations for future investigators, it seems fairly safe to assume that these conditions were met by the Houston-Masters study.

10 *Drugs, Mysticism and Make-Believe, op cit.*, p 109.

11 It is possible that these features were not experienced simultaneously; that an experience which displayed many of the marks of extrovertive vision was succeeded by an experience which displayed the marks of introvertive consciousness or vice versa. But Clark says nothing which would indicate that this was the case.

12 Although Pahnke suggests that this may have been due to the fact that these reports were relatively incomplete. ('Dissertation', p 230)

13 Another thing which suggests that the subjects inflated their scores is the fact that on the pre-drug questionnaire, five out of twenty subjects scored four (out of a possible five) with respect to whether their previous religious experience had been characterised by a 'sense of presence, mystical union, or experience of the numinous'. ('Dissertation', p 116) This is a surprisingly high score.

14 The reason why personal judgment is necessary is not the presence of some occult quality, but the number and complexity of the relevant factors, and the difficulty in quantifying qualitative considerations. I do not wish to be misunderstood as implying any criticism of Pahnke's experimental set-up, or his use of questionnaires. Control groups should be used. The results of the questionnaires can be highly suggestive and should not be disregarded. My point is only that one's final assessment of a subject's experiences should not be entirely, or even primarily, based on quantitative data.

15 For example, the report of John Robertson entitled 'Uncontainable Joy', (*The Ecstatic Adventure*, ed by Ralph Metzner, New York, 1968, pp 86–91).

16 It is difficult, for example, to find accounts which explicitly state that the mind was emptied of all percepts, images and clear concepts.

17 James Slotkin, *Peyote Religion, A Study in Indian-White Relations*, Glencoe, Illinois, 1956.

¹⁸ G M Carstairs, 'Daru and Bhang', *Quarterly Journal of Studies on Alcohol*, 15 (1954), pp 220–37. Bhang is a preparation made from a hemp plant of the same name.

¹⁹ Huston Smith, 'Do Drugs have Religious Import?', *The Journal of Philosophy* LXI (1964), p 523.

²⁰ *Peyote Religion, op cit*, p 75.

²¹ William Alston, 'Psychological Explanations of Religious Belief', *Faith and the Philosophers*, ed by John Hick, New York, 1964, pp 88–90.

²² I think this is what Alston means: one might suppose that all that is necessary is that *x* be a causal condition of the experience of x, not that it be a *necessary* casual condition of the experience of *x*. However, if the premise is construed in this way, the argument loses much of its force. Other premises must be modified accordingly and while it is plausible to suppose that if there is a set of causes which does not include *y* and which is sufficient for the occurrence of an event, *x*, then *y* is not a necessary condition of that event (our second premise), it is considerably less plausible to suppose that if there is a set of causes which does not include *y* and which is sufficient for the occurrence of *x*, then *y* is not *a* cause of *x*, for the effect might be overdetermined. (That there cannot be two sets of conditions for *x*, both of which are present and operating, and one or both of which are sufficient to produce *x* is, I think, a mere dogma.)

²³ There is another proposition which is similar to (1), which may be necessarily true, and with which it is (barely) possible that (1) is being confused, viz, that *x* must be present to a person who experiences *x* if his experience of *x* is to count as a perception of *x*. This proposition does not clearly entail (1). (For one thing, though the notion of presence is imprecise and undoubtedly varies with the type of experience which is in question, it seems reasonably clear that 'x is present to y' does not entail 'x is a causally necessary condition of y's experience of x'.)

²⁴ One might suggest that the kind of causality which is involved here is not the kind which must be present if experiences of God are to count as perceptions of God. But why say this?

²⁵ Robert A Oakes, 'Biochemistry and Theistic Mysticism', *Sophia* XV (1976), pp 10–16.

²⁶ One could argue for this in several ways. (1) As Oakes points out, God cannot be experienced *against* his will. (For nothing can happen except by God's permission.) *If* a person who knowingly permits another to perceive him can be said to disclose or reveal himself to that person, then every veridical experience of God is a revelation or self-disclosure. (2) Some theists believe that everything is deliberately brought about by God. If they are correct, experiences of God are deliberately brought about by God and are therefore self-disclosures. (3) Or one might simply argue that God is a hidden God who can be known only if He chooses to reveal himself. (There is a sound Biblical basis for this claim.)

²⁷ Oakes is quoting George Mavrodes (*Belief in God, A Study in the Epistemology of Religion*, New York, 1970, p 53).

²⁸ One might object that the argument is invalid: (4) does not follow from (3) since it is logically possible for God to reveal Himself *by means of* an hal-

lucinogen, i.e. it is logically possible that a divine decision is the causally sufficient condition of someone's ingesting an hallucinogen, and that this in turn is a causally sufficient condition of a veridical experience of God. Under these conditions, the ingestion of a drug is a causally sufficient condition of a veridical theistic experience. Nevertheless, it does not determine God's will but is determined by it. While there is truth in this objection, it does not get to the heart of the matter. A veridical theistic experience is a deliberate act of God (a self-disclosure). It is *constituted* by God's revealing Himself to a subject. Therefore, if any empirical event is a causally sufficient condition of a veridical theistic experience, it is a causally sufficient condition of a divine act, and this does appear to be incompatible with the doctrine underlying Oakes' fifth premise, viz the doctrine of God's absolute freedom.

[29] Does God's willing that the match ignite *follow* its being struck? Classical theism maintains that God's continued activity is necessary for the continued existence of contingent being. There are three ways of interpreting this doctrine: (1) A new divine volition is the cause of each new event. (This *need* not imply that God changes in any significant sense. *If* one can decide at t_m to decide to do x at t_{m+n} without actually deciding at t_m to do x at t_{m+n} then God could have eternally decided to decide to bring about the ignition of a match at t_{m+n} without having actually made that decision prior to t_{m+n}. God's decision to bring it about that a match bursts into flame would thus be new, even though the event had been decreed from eternity.) (2) God everlastingly wills that (e.g.) this match burst into flame at this time and place. (3) God's decrees are timeless. In the first case, God's willing that the match burst into flame clearly *follows* the striking of the match. In the second case, it both precedes and follows it. In the third case, it neither precedes nor follows it. In all three cases, however, God's *act*, viz, His intentionally bringing about the match's ignition *follows* its being struck. It follows it because God's bringing it about that the match bursts into flame involves at least two things – His volition (which may or may not be eternal or everlasting) and its effect, viz, the match's bursting into flame.

[30] Certain acts (e.g. worshipping God, forgiving one's enemies) logically include attitudes which are highly prized in theism. Others (e.g., reading the Bible and alms giving) do not. The argument may have no tendency to show that acts of the first sort cannot induce God to reveal Himself. Nevertheless it still proves too much. The ingestion of a drug is an act of the second sort, but then so are a number of the traditional means of grace.

[31] The use of hallucinogens might not be 'fitting'. Thus Zæhner, noting that Houston and Masters compare the use of drugs to traditional ascetic practices, points out that the Buddha, the *Bhagavad-Gītā*, etc. condemn such 'ascetic excesses'. (*Drugs, Mysticism and Make-Believe, op cit*, p 81f) (Zæhner fails to explain just why the use of hallucinogens *is* an 'ascetic excess'.) Arguments of this type may have their value but they do not show that there is some kind of conceptual tension in the notion of a drug-induced theistic revelation.

[32] The arguments we have considered fail to establish the existence of a con-

ceptual tension in the notion of a drug-induced theistic revelation. Furthermore, if it is conceptually possible for drugs to be a cause of veridical theistic experiences, I see no reason why it should be conceptually impossible for any other natural condition to be a cause of veridical theistic experiences. Does it follow that the discovery of an adequate scientific explanation of theistic experience would have no bearing on the authenticity of theistic experiences? I believe it does not. The God of the Bible or of the *Qurān*, and perhaps also of the *Bhagavad-Gītā*, is a hidden God who reveals Himself if and when He pleases. His ways are mysterious and incalculable. Unpredictability does not appear to be a logically essential feature of God. (It is not a feature of the God of liberal theology, for example. God's personality may entail that His self-disclosures are free acts, but this does not imply that they are unpredictable. On a traditional view, *all* contingent occurrences are freely caused by God. It does not follow that the course of contingent events is unpredictable.) Nevertheless, unpredictability is believed to be a property of God by many theists. But if unpredictability really is one of God's attributes, then no natural condition is either a causally sufficient condition of veridical theistic experience, or a condition which makes its occurrence highly probable. Hence, if a significant correlation was discovered between some natural condition and theistic experiences, theists who believe in God's unpredictability would be forced to conclude either that these experiences are inauthentic or that God's ways are not as mysterious as they had previously supposed.

CHAPTER 3

The Cognitive Status of Mystical Experience

In part I of this chapter, I shall argue that mystical experience is sufficiently similar to sense experience to create a presumption in favour of its cognitive validity. Part II will examine attempts to defeat this presumption. The conclusion of the chapter is that there are good reasons for believing that mystical consciousness is a mode of cognitive experience.

I

Mystical experience is often said to involve a kind of 'seeing' or 'tasting' or 'touching'. We are told that mystical experience is an 'experimental knowledge' of the divine. Mystical experiences are believed to involve a direct or immediate awareness of reality or some aspect of reality which is normally hidden from us. It is clear that an analogy with sense experience is intended and that part of what is implied in ascribing cognitive value to mystical experience is that these experiences are, in some important respects, like ordinary perceptual experience. In the opposite camp we find critics like C B Martin[1] who assume that ordinary perceptual experiences provide us with the paradigm of a cognitive or perceptual experience and go on to argue that religious experiences cannot be cognitive or perceptual because they deviate in certain important ways from that paradigm.

The analogy (or lack of it) between mystical experience and sense experience appears, then, to be critically important both to those who ascribe cognitive value to mystical experiences and to those who refuse to do so.

A

Mystical experiences and sense experiences are alike in two important respects. (1) Both types of experience are noetic. (2) On the basis of both types of experience claims are made about something other than the experience itself. These claims are corrigible and independently checkable. In each case there are tests for determining whether or not the object of the experience is real and tests for determining whether or not an apparent perception of that object is a genuine one.

(1) Sense experiences (whether veridical or not) have a noetic quality. This involves two things. (a) The experiences have an object, i.e. they are experiences of something (real or imagined). In this respect sense experiences are unlike pains, feelings of depression and so on. The latter may have causes. They may be aroused or occasioned by certain kinds of events or objects but (in spite of certain continental philosophers) they are not experiences *of* those events or objects. (To the question 'What is the object of a visual [auditory] experience?' we can reply 'Colours and shapes [sounds]'. The question 'What is the object of a dull pain [a feeling of depression]?' cannot be answered so easily.) (b) Sense experience typically involves the conviction that the object on which the experience is focused is 'really there', that it exists and that one 'experimentally' apprehends it. To use Berkeley's language, the experience has 'outness'. This conviction is not an interpretation which is placed upon the experience, but part of the experience itself.

In spite of the fact that some mystics speak as if their experiences transcended the subject-object structure of ordinary perceptual experience, many mystical experiences (and perhaps all of them) are noetic in this sense. (For example, monistic mystics by and large agree that they experience something which transcends space and time, is devoid of distinctions and is supremely valuable. Theistic mystics believe that they experimentally perceive God.)

(2) No type of experience can be called cognitive if it induces those who have it to make false claims. Thus, the experience of a mirage or the experiences one obtains by pressing one's eyeball and seeing double are called delusive because they are inherently misleading – the very nature of these

experiences is such that (until one learns better) one is likely to
base false claims upon them, (that water is really present or
that there are two candles rather than one). There is no conclusive reason to suppose that mystical experiences are delusive in this sense. The mystic does not make false empirical
statements on the basis of his experiences because he does not
make empirical statements. Rather he claims to know, on the
basis of his experience, that God is real and present to him or
that there is an 'uncreated, imperishable Beyond', or something of the sort. It would therefore seem that we are entitled to
assert that these experiences are delusive only if we have good
independent reasons for believing that claims of this kind are
false. It is by no means clear that we do.

But the fact that experiences are not delusive does not imply
that they are cognitive. Pains are not delusive, but they are not
cognitive either. One of the reasons for calling sense
experiences cognitive is that not only do they not induce *false*
claims, they also provide a basis for making *true* claims about
something other than the experience itself. This involves two
things. First, sense experiences are means of apprehending
(some aspect of) reality. Those who have them are more likely
to discern certain truths than those who do not, or can at least
discern them more easily. Second, sense experiences can be appealed to, to justify the truths which have been made out by
their means. For example, people with normal vision are
more likely to discern truths about colours and shapes, and
can do so more easily, than those who are blind, and they are
entitled to appeal to their visual experiences to justify their
claims.

Are mystical experiences like sense experiences in this
respect? We can at least say this: on the basis of their
experiences, mystics make claims about something other than
their own experiences. They believe that they have directly
apprehended a reality which others accept on faith, or on the
basis of certain arguments, and they appeal to their
experiences to justify their claims.[2] Furthermore (assuming
that there is no disproof of God's existence, or of the reality of
the One, etc.) these claims are not known to be false. We seem
therefore to have found a respect in which sense experiences
and mystical experiences are like each other and unlike pains.

The analogy extends further. When a person claims to see, hear or touch something, his claim is not self-certifying. Things other than his own experience are relevant to a determination of the truth or falsity of his claim. C B Martin and others have asserted that sense experiences are radically unlike mystical experiences in this respect, for (they say) when the mystic claims to experience God or the Brahman, his claims are not corrigible – there are (to use Martin's phrase) no independent tests and check-up procedures which he and others would regard as relevant to a determination of the truth or falsity of the claims he makes. His claims are therefore private (like first person psychological reports), not public (like ordinary perceptual claims).

This is simply false. Misled by the fact that certain familiar tests (for example, the appeal to the agreement of others) play at most a minor role in the evaluation of mystical experiences, critics like Martin have illicitly concluded that mystics, therefore, dismiss all tests and check-up procedures as irrelevant and regard their claims as incorrigible.

Suppose someone claims to have seen an elephant in his backyard. There are at least two ways in which his claim might be attacked. One might try to show that no elephant was there at all, or one might try to show that he could not have seen it because, for example, he was not in a position to observe it, or his sensory equipment was defective. When we turn to mystical experience we find both sorts of test and check-up procedure (at least in a rough and ready way), that is, we find independent procedures for determining whether its object is real and we find independent procedures for determining whether the experience is a genuine perception of its object.

Even when claims about such things as God or Nibbāna are grounded in mystical consciousness, they are not self-certifying. Things other than the experience itself are relevant to an evaluation of their truth. For example, considerations of logic are relevant. *Pace* Stace, these claims cannot be true if the concepts of God or Nibbāna are self-contradictory. Again, considerations adduced in arguments for and against the existence of God have some bearing on the truth of the claims made by theistic mystics. Even the statement that there is a One beyond distinctions does not appear to be self-certifying though, since what is claimed is relatively minimal, it would be harder to disprove. (Considerations of logic, and considerations adduced by positivists and naturalists, might count against it.) When the mystic asserts that he has experienced God (or Nibbāna, or Brahman) he implies that what he has experienced is real. He should therefore recognise that things besides his own experience are relevant to an evaluation of his claim. It is true that mystics are usually certain of the truth of the claims that they make, but this is no more incompatible with their corrigibility than the fact that I am certain that there is a red pen in front of me is incompatible with the fact that that claim is corrigible. In short, claims about God, or Nibbāna and other things of that kind are not self-certifying, and we have some idea of the sorts of things which count for and against them.

There are, then, independent tests for determining whether the object of mystical experience is real. There are also independent tests for determining whether an experience of this object is a genuine perception of it. Consider theistic mystical experiences, for example. Even if God exists and a direct experience of Him is possible, it does not follow that every claim to be immediately aware of God is justified. How, though, do we distinguish experiences of God which are veridical from those which are not? If we turn our attention to the communities in which theistic mysticism has flourished we find that various tests have been used to distinguish the experiences which genuinely involve a perception of God from those which do not. Each of the following six criteria is employed in the Christian (particularly the Catholic) community. Similar criteria are used in other communities.

(1) The consequences of the experience must be good for the mystic. The experience must lead to, produce, or reinforce, a new life marked by such virtues as wisdom, humility and charity. (Sanity should be subsumed under this criterion. A genuine experience of God is believed to have a tendency to produce a life of rather extraordinary goodness. It seems reasonable to suppose that sanity is a necessary condition of such a life.) This criterion helps to explain why people are bothered by the presence of certain kinds of causes. Many

people find it impossible to believe that the use of drugs, nervous and physical disorders and so on, can play a part in the best sort of life. Consequently, if they find that these things play a major role in the life of a mystic, they will tend to discount his experience.

(2) One must consider the effect which the experience has on others. For instance, one should ask whether the mystic's words, actions and example tend to build up the community or weaken it.

(3) The depth, the profundity and the 'sweetness' (Jonathan Edwards) of what the mystic says on the basis of his experience counts in favour of the genuineness of that experience. On the other hand, the insignificance, or the silliness, of what he says counts against it. (On the basis of this criterion many would reject the claims of Margery Kempe.[3])

(4) We must examine what the mystic says on the basis of his experience and see whether it agrees or disagrees with orthodox talk. (It should be noted that this test is not circular. The statement being tested is a statement like 'Teresa saw God', or 'John received heavenly consolations'. Statements of this kind are not Christian dogmas.)

(5) It will be helpful to determine whether the experience in question resembles other mystical experiences regarded as paradigmatic by the religious community. (In the Roman Catholic church, experiences are often compared with the experiences of Teresa of Avila or of John of the Cross.)

(6) We must also consider the pronouncements of authority. In some communities (for example, Zen) the word of the spiritual director, guru or master is final. In other religious communities, the voice of the spiritual director is important though not conclusive. In some cases the relevant authority may be the community as a whole, or some special organ of it. (For example, the standing enjoyed by the experiences of John of the Cross and Teresa in the Roman Catholic community is largely a consequence of their acceptance by that community and its official representatives.) In some cases all of these authorities may be relevant.

If I am correct, these criteria are similar to the tests which we employ in ordinary perceptual cases to determine whether an apparent perception of an object is a genuine perception of it, that is, they are similar to the tests which take things into account like the position of the observer and the condition of his sensory equipment. Of course, the *nature* of the tests is not much alike. Nevertheless, the point of them is, viz, to show not that the object of the experience is real or unreal but that there is or is not a genuine perception of it. (One would not expect the nature of the tests to be much alike. For example, in the case of introvertive mystical experience there is no sensory equipment which can go awry because sense organs are not involved. Nor does there appear to be anything which clearly corresponds to the position of the observer in sense experience.)

B

Among the more important tests and check-up procedures which are used to evaluate ordinary perceptual claims are (1) the agreement and disagreement of others occupying similar positions, and (2) the success or failure of predictions which have been based upon the experience whose claims are in question. Are similar tests used to assess the cognitive status of mystical experience?

(1) The claim that mystical experience is cognitive is frequently supported by appealing to the rather surprising amount of agreement that exists. Extrovertive mystics, monistic mystics and theistic mystics can be found in radically different cultures, in places which have had little or no contact with each other, and in all periods of history. Not only are their experiences alike, they base remarkably similar claims upon them. But some kinds of agreement are irrelevant. The visual and auditory experiences of persons from different cultures, with diverse social backgrounds and different psychological makeups, are often quite similar. Analogously mystics from different cultures, with diverse social backgrounds and different psychological makeups often have similar experiences. It is also the case that people suffering from migraines or indigestion undergo similar experiences in spite of differences in culture, social background, psychological makeup and many other factors. Sense experiences are widespread and so are mystical experiences, but so also are migraines and stomach-

aches. Since migraines and stomachaches are paradigm cases of non-cognitive experience, the presence of this sort of agreement has little tendency to show that a mode of experience is cognitive.

There are other sorts of agreement. People who make visual (or auditory or tactual) observations are normally able to describe conditions under which others can make similar observations. ('If you go into the room on the left, you will see the body.' 'If the telescope is trained on such and such a place at such and such a time, you will obtain a sighting of the moons of Jupiter.') Now mystics are able to do something like this. For example, they can prescribe procedures which are likely to lead to introvertive experiences. (These include special postures, breathing techniques, a deliberate withdrawal of the attention from sense objects, mental concentration and so on. Sometimes these procedures are specified in detail. Furthermore, in spite of some variation – particularly in the emphasis placed upon physical techniques – there is a great deal of agreement as to just what these procedures involve.)

Now the only agreement or disagreement which is directly relevant to the cognitive value of a sense experience, is agreement or disagreement among those who use the procedures associated with that type of experience, and try to make the relevant observation under the prescribed conditions. Agreement among people who fail to follow these procedures is not expected, and its absence is therefore regarded as beside the point. If sense experience provides the model for all cognitive modes of experience, then the fact that most of us have never had a mystical experience is irrelevant, for most of us have made no attempt to use the mystic's techniques.

Nevertheless, agreement among those who employ a set of prescribed techniques is not decisive. This kind of agreement is characteristic of sense experience, but it is also characteristic of subjective experiences. (For example, it can be safely asserted that people eating ten *bratwurst* sandwiches within twenty minutes will undergo strikingly similar and equally unpleasant digestive experiences.)[4] What sort of agreement, then, is relevant? People who see, hear and touch, base claims about the world upon their experiences, and a lack of agreement among those following the appropriate procedures is believed to have an important bearing on the truth of their claims. People suffering from headaches or indigestion, on the other hand, do not base claims about the world upon their experiences and hence do not consider the agreement or disagreement of others to be relevant to the *truth* of such claims.

Mystics base claims about 'objective' reality upon their experiences. They differ in this respect from people suffering from headaches and indigestion. But do they believe that the agreement or disagreement of others is relevant to the truth of their claims? Do they take the fact that some people have similar experiences when following the appropriate procedures as counting *for* their claims? And do they take the fact that there are others who do not have similar experiences when following these procedures as counting *against* their claims? If they do, then we have discovered what may be an important analogy between mystical experience and sense experience. If they do not, we have uncovered what many would regard as a significant disanalogy. Unfortunately, the situation is ambiguous.

I am inclined to think that at least some mystics believe that the fact that others have had similar experiences, and have made similar claims, supports the claims which they base upon their own experiences, and that because of this agreement these mystics are more confident of the cognitive value of their experiences than they would otherwise be. However, no distinction appears to be made between those experiences which are obtained by employing techniques of prayer and meditation and those which occur spontaneously. *All* similar experiences are thought to confirm (equally) the claims which are made or (which comes to more or less the same thing) the cognitive value of the experiences upon which those claims are based.

It is not clear whether mystics believe that disagreement has any bearing upon the cognitive value of their experiences.[5] Mystics are clearly not disturbed by the fact that most people never enjoy mystical experiences. Nor do they seem to be bothered by the fact that some people earnestly employ the appropriate techniques but never achieve illumination or union. These points are not decisive, however, for it might nonetheless be true that if there *was* more disagreement than in fact obtains, the mystic would withdraw or qualify his claim. The mystic regards disagreement as relevant if there is *any* degree of disagreement which *would* be taken as counting against his claim if it *were* to occur. Suppose, for example, that the mystic were to discover that those whom he thought had achieved a unitive experience by employing the standard techniques had not really done so. Would he regard this discovery as counting against the cognitive value of his own experiences? Of course he might (particularly if he had used these techniques himself) but he might only conclude that the techniques were not as effective as he had believed them to be. Suppose, however, the mystic stood alone. While it is by no means clear that the mystic would (or should) repudiate his experience under these conditions (it is, perhaps, too impressive for that) he might nevertheless be bothered by the absence of supporting claims. (There is some evidence that those who believe that their religious experiences are comparatively unique are more suspicious of them than those who are aware of the fact that others have had similar experiences.[6]) If he would, then perhaps the mystic does regard disagreement as having at least *some* relevance to the evaluation of his experiences.

What emerges from these considerations is this. The mystic bases ontological statements upon his experiences and seems to believe that the fact that others have similar experiences confirms those claims (or the veridical character of his own experience). It is *possible* that if others were to fail altogether to have similar experiences, he would take this fact as counting against the veridical character of his own experience. In these respects mystical experience appears to be more like sense experience than like feelings of nausea or depression.

On the other hand there are significant disanalogies. (i) *All* similar experiences are believed to confirm the mystic's claim. The fact that some of these experiences were not obtained by employing the appropriate procedures but occurred spontaneously is ignored. (ii) Furthermore, it is not clear that a breakdown of the procedures for obtaining these experiences would induce the mystic to hedge his claims. In both respects mystical experience differs from sense experience. In the case of the latter, the only *relevant* agreement is that which is found among those who satisfy certain appropriate conditions, and a failure to obtain similar experiences after meeting those conditions casts serious doubts upon the experience's validity.

What is perhaps most significant is the fact that the presence of agreement or disagreement is not regarded as a crucial consideration by those who have had mystical experiences. It is not even clear that it is considered to be important. In the case of sense experience, on the other hand, the presence or absence of agreement (among those who employ the appropriate procedures) is always important, and often crucial.

(2) In evaluating a particular instance of sense experience, we consider predictions which have been based upon that experience. Successful predictions count for its verdicality and unsuccessful predictions count against it. Furthermore, if anyone were to attempt to justify the claim that sense experience in general is a cognitive mode of experience, he would undoubtedly appeal to the fact that a very large number of successful predictions about the course of external events have been based upon experiences of that type.

A few predictions do appear to be based upon mystical experience. On the basis of their experience mystics frequently assert that the soul is immortal and, of course, this involves a prediction.[7] Furthermore, mystics occasionally claim that their experiences confirm theological systems which include certain predictions as an integral part. Thus, Christian mystics have sometimes regarded their experiences as confirmations of the truth of Christian dogma, and Christian dogma includes a belief in the general resurrection and the transfiguration of heaven and earth.[8] A mystic may also, on the basis of his experience, predict that if one subjects oneself to the appropriate discipline (for example, practises the Jesus prayer or follows the noble eight-fold path) he will obtain a vision of God or pass into Nibbāna or something of the sort.[9]

Now many, perhaps most, of the predictions made by those who can see or hear (etc.) can be checked *both* by others who can see or hear *and* by those who cannot. Suppose, for example, that I see thunderclouds approaching and predict it will rain. A blind man cannot do this (though he might predict rain on the basis of other factors). He can, however, *check* this prediction. If it rains he will not see it, but he will (if suitably situated) feel, hear, and perhaps even taste the rain. If he does not, he is entitled to conclude that my prediction was a failure.

The claim that we are immortal and the claim that human beings will be resurrected are, I think, verifiable (though not falsifiable). However, the experiences which would justify them are (in the first case) post-mortem experiences, and (in the second case) post-Advent experiences. Neither mystics nor non-mystics can verify these claims in this life, or before the second Advent. If one verified the third prediction one would be a mystic. The conclusion then is that none of these predictions can be checked in this life by the non-mystic, and the first two predictions cannot be checked in this life by anyone.

Since these predictions cannot be checked, they cannot be appealed to in order to establish the cognitive value of mystical experience as such, or to establish the cognitive value of a particular instance of mystical experience. It would thus appear that a blind man may have a reason for ascribing cognitive value to visual experience (*qua* mode of experience) or to a particular visual experience, which the non-mystic does not have for ascribing cognitive value to mystical experience (*qua* mode of experience) or to a particular mystical experience, viz, that the blind man knows that visual experiences in general, or a particular visual experience, have led to successful predictions, whereas the non-mystic does not know that mystical experiences in general, or a particular mystical experience, have led to successful predictions. This difference is striking and perhaps significant.

(3) A consideration of the presence of agreement or disagreement, and of the success or failure of predictions which have been based upon the experience play an important role in the evaluation of the cognitive status of sense consciousness but not in the evaluation of the cognitive status of mystical consciousness. These differences are intelligible if sense experiences are cognitive and mystical experiences are not. However, there is another way to account for them. The differences can be explained by the fact that the *objects* of these two kinds of experience are radically different.

Suppose[10] that God is the object of a mystical experience (rather than Nibbāna or the Ātman, etc.). If God is what He is supposed to be (omnipotent, omniscient, mysterious, other, transcendent and so on), then whether or not one has an experience of Him will, in the last analysis, depend upon His will; there will be not set of procedures the correct use of which invariably results in illumination or union. Hence, while these experiences may be repeatable in the weak sense that given *exactly* the same conditions (including God's gracious activity), the same experience will occur, there is no reason to suppose that they will be repeatable in the strong sense, viz, that certain procedures or methods can be described which are such that (almost) all who correctly employ them will obtain the experience in question.

God is radically unlike physical objects in this respect. Physical objects exhibit spatio-temporal continuity, are relatively accessible and behave in law-like and regular ways. Given the nature of physical objects, one reasonably supposes that if one's experience of the object is veridical, others will enjoy similar experiences under similar conditions.[11] One expects experiences of these objects to cohere and mutually support one another in certain familiar ways. If the nature of physical objects were different, however, these expectations would not be reasonable; experiences of these objects would not be repeatable in the strong sense, *even though the objects were real and experiences of them were veridical*. Suppose, for example, that mountains jumped about in a discontinuous fashion, randomly appeared and disappeared, and behaved in other lawless and unpredictable ways. If these conditions obtained, observation under similar conditions would not normally yield similar results even if mountains were real and experiences of them were veridical. There would be no reason to expect experiences in this area to cohere and support one another in the way they do.

The general point is this. The nature of an object should (at least partly) determine the tests for its presence.[12] Given the nature of *physical* objects it is reasonable to suppose that genuine experiences of those objects can be confirmed by employing appropriate procedures and obtaining similar experiences, and that non-genuine experiences can be disconfirmed by employing the same procedures and obtaining different experiences. God's nature, on the other hand, is radically different from the nature of physical objects. It is therefore not clearly reasonable to suppose that (apparent) experiences of God can be confirmed or disconfirmed in the same fashion.

The difference in the nature of their respective objects thus explains why the presence or absence of agreement is an important test in the one case, but not in the other. This difference also explains other disanalogies. (1) God bestows His grace upon whom he pleases and is therefore not bound by our techniques. One person may employ mental prayer and fail to obtain the desired experience, while another who does not practise contemplation may experience (some degree) of illumination. It is therefore only to be expected that little distinction is made between similar experiences which are obtained by these techniques and similar experiences which occur spontaneously. In so far as agreement is considered to be relevant, *both* are regarded as confirmatory. (2) Since God freely bestows the experience upon whom He will, we have no idea of how many of these experiences to expect. Hence it is not clear at just what point (if any) a mystic should begin to be bothered by the absence of agreement. We should, therefore, not be surprised if we find it difficult to specify a degree of disagreement which is so great that in the face of it a mystic would or should withdraw his claim.

Similar considerations show that, in the case of theistic mystical experiences, the demand for successful predictions may be inappropriate. It is reasonable to insist on successful predictions when the type of experience which is involved is supposed to provide access to ordinary empirical objects – objects which exhibit spatial-temporal continuity, which are accessible, and which behave in law-like and regular ways – for the nature of these objects is such that testable predictions can be made about them.[13] However, it is not clear that the demand for successful predictions is reasonable when the object in question is (like God) a-spatial, a-temporal (?), and neither accessible in the way in which ordinary objects are accessible nor law-like and regular in its behaviour.

In short, there is no reason to believe that genuine experiences of God will be supported by the experience of others in the way in which veridical sense experiences are supported by the experience of others, or that veridical experiences of God will provide data which can be used to predict the future. The fact that mystical experiences are not supported by the agreement of others in the way in which veridical sense experiences are supported by the agreement of others, and that they afford no glimpse of the future, is therefore not decisive.

But suppose that the object of a mystical experience is Nibbāna, the nirguṇa Brahman, or one's own puruṣa rather than God. These realities do not dispense favours, but are impersonal and inactive. Since they do not act, their 'behaviour' cannot be irregular and unpredictable. Nor do they appear to have any other features which would make it unreasonable to include agreement and disagreement among the tests and check-up procedures that are used to assess experiences of them.[14] However, there is a reason for disregarding the lack of successful predictions. By definition, predictions are concerned with the temporal order; their content is the future. Nibbāna, the nirguṇa Brahman, and one's puruṣa are nontemporal realities. They are neither in time nor do they intervene in the temporal order. There is thus no reason to suppose that veridical experiences of these things will lead to successful predictions.

C

For a mode of experience to be accepted as cognitive, it is not sufficient that there be tests for evaluating the cognitive character of instances of that type of experience. It is necessary that these tests be relevant to the cognitive status of these experiences, and that they can be satisfied by many (most?) instances of that type of experience. We would dismiss a test which specified that valid experiences occur only in months the English name of which contains the letter r, on the ground that whether or not an experience occurs in those months has nothing to do with its cognitive status. Furthermore, if in most instances the relevant tests yielded negative results, we would not regard experiences of that type as cognitive. (For example, we would not regard visual experiences as cognitive if they normally conflicted with one another and were an unreliable guide to future experience.)

Two significant sorts of disagreement are thus possible.

People may disagree as to the relevance of the tests which are used to evaluate instances of an experience whose cognitive status is in question, or they may disagree as to whether the appropriate tests are met in a significant number of instances.

Whether the appropriate tests are met depends, of course, upon just what the appropriate tests are. The six tests considered earlier are met in many instances.[15] On the other hand, while mystical experiences do not lead to patently false predictions, the few predictions which are based upon them are not *known* to be true. Nor is it clear that mystical experiences agree and cohere in the way in which sense experiences agree and cohere. We have seen however that neither of the last two tests is especially relevant to the evaluation of certain types of mystical experience. Therefore, the fact that they fail to satisfy them, or satisfy them very imperfectly, is of no particular importance. Or at least it is not crucial.

But are the tests relevant? As we have seen, there are two kinds of tests for evaluating mystical experiences – tests which are used to determine the reality of the *object* of mystical experience, and tests which are used to determine the genuineness of an *experience* of that object.

In determining the truth of the claim that God is real, one would address oneself to considerations of logic, review the more telling points made by theists and atheists, and so on. (One would do similar, though not identical things, in order to determine the reality of the Brahman or Nibbāna.) It would be generally agreed that this procedure is legitimate and that these considerations do bear upon the reality of the object of mystical experience. It is the other set of tests – the procedures which are used to determine the genuineness of an experience of the object – which create suspicion. Nevertheless, there are good reasons to believe that, at least under certain conditions, these tests too are relevant.

(1 and 2) The first two tests are moral tests. A veridical experience is one which is fruitful and edifying both for the mystic himself and for others. If the (apparent) object of a mystical experience is God, then these tests are relevant. For, if God is good and cares for His creatures (things analytically connected with the notion of God), then one would expect a direct experience of Him to be fruitful and edifying, to result in

spiritual beauty and goodness, in holiness and in wisdom.

(3) The third test is also relevant when God is the (apparent) object of an experience; for if God is perfect goodness, omniscient, omnipotent, necessary, the 'mysterium tremendum,' holy, numinous, etc. (attributes which are once again analytically connected with the notion of God), then one would not expect a vision of Him to lead to twaddle. Quite the contrary.

(4) The fourth test is relevant to an evaluation of experiences which seem to involve a direct awareness of God provided that (a) God is not a deceiver, and that (b) orthodox beliefs are true. If God is a God of truth and orthodox beliefs are true, one would not expect a genuine experience of God to lead to (very much) non-orthodox talk.

(5 and 6) The relevance of the fifth and sixth tests depends upon the truth of doctrines concerning the holiness and authoritative character of the individual or community in question. For example, the claims of the Christian community and its representatives would be supported by an appeal to the notion that the Church is the body of Christ and the temple of the Holy Spirit, to the claim that its bishops possess teaching authority, and so on.

The relevance of the first three tests depends upon the truth of certain *conditional* propositions (viz, that *if* God is good and cares for His creatures, then genuine experiences of Him will be fruitful and edifying for the mystic and for others, etc.). One may be uncertain that God exists and yet admit that if an experience really *is* an experience of God, it will be fruitful and significant, and that there is therefore good reason to examine a mystic's verbal and non-verbal behaviour and its consequences. One need not be a theist to admit the relevance of these tests.[16] The last three tests, on the other hand, are relevant only if the specific tenets of some particular religious community are true. One would have no reason to compare the talk of a mystic with orthodox Christian talk, or to stress the ways in which his experience is like and unlike the experience of John of the Cross (rather than some Sufi or Theravādin mystic), or to appeal to the concensus of the Church, if one were not a Christian.[17]

These tests are therefore relevant to an evaluation of

experiences that purport to be experiences of God. Are they relevant to the evaluation of extrovertive and monistic experiences? They are relevant to their evaluation when the person who has them claims they are perceptions of God (as they sometimes do. Although Eckhart's experiences appear to have been monistic, he thought they were experiences of God.) Suppose, though, that the object of an extrovertive experience is alleged to be nature's unity, or its inner life or soul. Or that the 'object' of a monistic experience is alleged to be an undifferentiated One, or one's own 'naked essence'.

Because nature embraces both good and evil and because an undifferentiated unity (or the essence of one's own soul?) transcends good and evil, there is no reason to suppose that the first two tests are relevant. One would not expect a vision of these things to promote righteousness and active charity. On the other hand, *other* behavioural tests may be relevant. One might, for example, expect that a vision of an undifferentiated unity transcending time and space would produce detachment and inner peace, or that a vision of nature's unity would lead to empathy with other creatures.

The other four tests may still be relevant. A vision of nature's unity or of an undifferentiated One should not lead to twaddle. If some kind of orthodox talks is true, then, since veridical experiences do not lead to (many) false claims, no veridical experience of *any* kind will lead to (very much) unorthodox talk. If some community or its representatives are authoritative, then the fifth and sixth tests are also relevant.[18]

A minor problem remains. If I am correct, agreement is a test, although an unimportant one. Now we have seen that, because of the peculiar nature of its object, there is no reason to expect that veridical, theistic experiences will be confirmed by the experiences of others in the way in which veridical sense experiences are confirmed by the experiences of others, and having seen this, we may wonder whether there is any logical connection between the presence of agreement and a genuine perception of God. True, agreement seems to be implicitly appealed to, and the mystic might feel uncomfortable in the absence of any agreement, but this does not imply that agreement and disagreement have any *logical* significance. (Most of us take comfort in numbers and are uneasy when we find ourselves alone.)

Two considerations suggest that agreement and disagreement have some logical bearing upon the cognitive status of these experiences. If God's behaviour were completely erratic and unpredictable, then agreement and disagreement would not count at all. But it is not. Although God's behaviour does not possess the regularity and law-like character which belongs to the behaviour of physical objects, it is not thought to be completely erratic and lawless either.

The second consideration is this. Other things being equal, it *may* be reasonable to expect instances of a genuinely cognitive mode of experience to occur under radically different social and psychological conditions. (Similar visual experiences are of course, enjoyed by people with radically different natures and radically different backgrounds.) The presence of widespread agreement shows that this expectation is satisfied.[19]

D

Are there, then, reasons for supposing that mystical experiences are cognitive? I believe that there are. Consider the following argument:

(1) If the analogy between mystical experience and sense experience is very close,[20] then we are entitled to regard mystical experience as a mode of cognitive experience.[21]

(2) The analogy is very close. (Both experiences are noetic. Both are the basis of corrigible and independently checkable claims about something other than the experience itself. In both cases there are tests for determining the reality of the object of experience as well as tests for determining the genuineness of an apparent perception of that object. (The tests are different in the two cases, but the differences can be explained by differences in the nature of the objects of the two experiences. (The tests are relevant in both cases, and their application yields positive results in a large number of instances.[22])

(3) Therefore, we are entitled to regard mystical experience as a mode of cognitive experience.

A variant of this argument may be more persuasive:

(4) The analogy between mystical experience and sense experience is close enough to warrant the conclusion that mystical experiences are cognitive *provided that* we have independent reasons for believing mystics when they assert that they have directly experienced some transcendent aspect of reality.

(5) We have independent reasons for believing mystics when they assert that they have experienced a transcendent aspect of reality. (For example, arguments for God's existence, and for the sanity, sanctity and intelligence of the great mystics.[23])

(6) We are therefore warranted in concluding that mystical experiences are cognitive.

Sense experience is the paradigm case of cognitive experience. (1) therefore seems plausible. The plausibility of (5) largely depends upon the success or failure of natural theology, and here opinions can and do differ. (2) and (4) involve the same problem. One's opinion of these premises will be determined not only by one's estimate of the number of respects in which sense experience and mystical experience are like and unlike each other, but also by one's judgment as to the relative importance of these resemblances and differences. (Thus, when evaluating sense experiences the presence or absence of agreement is regarded as vitally important; when evaluating mystical experiences, as relatively unimportant. One's assessment of the significance of this fact will depend upon whether or not one believes that the appeal to the presence or absence of agreement is an appropriate test for the evaluation of mystical experience, upon whether or not one thinks that this test *must* be among the tests used to determine the cognitive value of an experience, and so on.) No mechanical decision procedures are available which can be used to determine the truth value of these premises, just as there are no mechanical decision procedures which can be appealed to, to determine what one should do when moral obligations conflict, or how one should appraise a new style of art, or the general plausibility of a world view. These cases call for judgment and reasonable people may differ. (There are criteria, but it is sometimes difficult to see whether or not they have been applied correctly. For example, in choosing a world view, we should attempt to determine which view has the most explanatory power. But this itself calls for judgment.) In spite of these considerations, I submit that, if the argument of the preceding sections has been correct, the analogy between mystical experience and sense experience is sufficiently striking to justify (4) and, somewhat less clearly, (2).

Although I believe that the two arguments being considered in this section are good arguments, their failure would not show that mystical experiences are non-cognitive. It is often assumed that no experience can be cognitive which is unlike sense experience in very many important respects. This is, of course, quite vague. (What deviations are *important* and how many deviations are *very many*?) More significantly, it is not clear that the assumption is true. As far as I can see, all that we *mean* when we say that an experience is cognitive or perceptual is that through this experience we come to know something which we could not know, or could not know as easily, in other ways, and (probably) that the knowledge in question is non-inferential. If this is even roughly correct, then 'x is a cognitive experience' does not entail 'x is very much like sense experiences'. Of course sense experiences clearly are cognitive experiences. Therefore, if we can show that mystical experience is very much like sense experience, we have provided a good (if not conclusive) reason for supposing that mystical experience is cognitive. On the other hand, if the analysis I have provided is correct, then, even if mystical experience and sense experience were radically dissimilar, this dissimilarity, would not be decisive. (Even if mystical experiences were radically unlike such objective experiences as seeing or hearing, it would not follow that they were like paradigmatic subjective experiences. They might – as Stace suggests – be like neither.[24])

II

But the conclusion that mystical experiences are cognitive, may be premature. There are several substantial objections to mysticism's cognitive pretensions. These must be shown to be inconclusive before we are entitled to assert that mystical consciousness is a means of knowledge.

A

Antony Flew, Paul Schmidt and Ronald Hepburn maintain that the cognitive claims which are made for praeternatural experiences must be certified by independent checks.[25] Schmidt's argument is typical. He asks us to look at a case in which we judge that we have a cavity because we have a toothache. He suggests that this judgment is warranted only because we have independent criteria (criteria other than the toothache) by which we can establish the existence of a cavity and because we know (on the basis of past experience) that toothaches and cavities are correlated. Schmidt concludes that, in general, we can move from a first person psychological report about feelings (or some other kind of private experience) to a claim about a non-psychological entity or event only if we have independent criteria for determining the truth or falsity of the claim and have discovered by experience that a correlation exists between the occurrence of that sort of feeling and the existence of that type of entity or event.[26]

The implication, of course, is that the mystic is only entitled to base religious and metaphysical claims upon his experience if he has independent criteria for establishing the existence (or presence) of the alleged object of his experience, and if he can show that experiences of that type and objects of that type are correlated.

What exactly is being demanded? We must distinguish (1) the demand that independent checks be provided for claims based on an instance of mystical experience from (2), the demand that one be given an independent certification of the claim that mystical experience as such provides an adequate basis for cognitive claims of a certain kind. In the latter case one is asking for a justification of the cognitive validity of an entire mode of experience.

The first demand is rather easily met. Just as there are tests other than the visual experiences of a person who bases a cognitive claim upon one of those experiences (for example, his own auditory and tactual experience, the sense experiences of others, etc.) so there are tests other than the mystical experiences of a person who bases cognitive claims on *those* particular experiences (for example, his sanity, the similarity of his experiences to those of other mystics, etc.). But this is clearly not what is at issue. What is at issue is the cognitive status of mystical experience in general. It is the second demand which is being made rather than the first, and Schmidt's argument is designed to show that this demand cannot be met.

Is Schmidt's argument convincing? There are reasons for thinking that it is not. (1) It is wrong to suppose that 'having certain feelings and sensations' is an adequate description of the subjective side of mystical experience. No description of these experiences is adequate which neglects their intentional character. As we have seen, these experiences are noetic. They have an object and incorporate the conviction that one is in the presence of that object. Having a mystical experience is not like feeling pain or being depressed.

(2) In the second place there may be independent reasons for thinking that (for example) God exists and that there is a correlation between the presence of God and the occurrence of certain kinds of religious experience. (These reasons might be provided by natural theology, tradition or authority.) Critics like Schmidt would not accept these reasons but it is not clear that this is significant. Again (though this is obviously not what Schmidt is looking for) one might suppose that a kind of independent certification of the cognitive character of mystical experience is provided by the arguments of the last section.

(3) Perhaps some other kind of experience can be used to confirm the claims made for mystical experience (by showing that judgments based on mystical experience cohere with judgments based on this other sort of experience). For example, it might be suggested that numinous experience corroborates theistic mystical experience in the way in which auditory and tactual experience corroborates visual experience, or (and this is essentially the same point) that theistic mystical experiences and numinous experiences support and reinforce one another in the way in which the various kinds of sense experience support and reinforce one another. Of course Schmidt would not accept this. In his view numinous and mystical experiences are equally suspect. What Schmidt is demanding is that we justify the claim that religious experience of any kind involves an awareness of the presence of God (or some transcendent being or state) in precisely the same

way in which we would justify the claim that toothaches are a sign of cavities.

(4) It is not clear that this demand is reasonable. Suppose we were asked to justify the claim that sense experiences involve an awareness of something distinct from those experiences, viz, physical objects. It is not clear that we would know how to satisfy this request. In particular, it should be noticed that we cannot independently (of those experiences) establish the existence of physical objects and the occurrence of sense experiences, and observe that the two are correlated. (To suppose that we could, would be to suppose that there are tests for ascertaining the presence of physical objects which neither directly nor indirectly appeal to our own sense experiences, or the sense experiences of other people, and there are no tests of this kind.) In short, while the connection between mystical experiences and a transcendental object cannot be justified in the manner which Schmidt demands, the connection between sense experiences and physical objects cannot be justified in that manner either. Since the latter hardly entitles us to conclude that sense experiences do not provide cognitive access to physical objects, it is unclear why the former should entitle us to conclude that mystical experiences do not provide cognitive access to a transcendent object. Schmidt's demand *might* be in order when we are dealing with experiences which are not 'perception-like', for example, toothaches, twinges, depression, etc. It is not clear that it is in order when the experiences in question are 'perception-like', for example, visual experiences and mystical experiences.[27]

One might object, however, that the two cases differ in the following important respect. When we learn the meaning of a physical object word like 'tree' we learn what trees look like, what they feel like, what they sound like when the wind blows through their branches, etc. That is, in learning the meaning of the word 'tree' we learn the connection between the presence of trees and experiences of this type. On the other hand numinous and mystical experiences are not connected in this way with the meaning of 'God' or 'Brahman'.[28] A person who has never had numinous or mystical experiences and has no idea of what they are like can learn the meaning of 'God' or

'Brahman'. On the basis of these considerations it might seem reasonable to conclude that tree experiences and trees are analytically connected, whereas mystical or numinous experiences and God (or Brahman) are not, and that therefore while some kind of independent justification must be provided to connect mystical or numinous experiences and God (or Brahman), no such justification is needed to connect tree experiences and trees.

This move would be plausible if statements about trees and other physical objects could be translated into statements about sense experiences (i.e. if phenomenalism were true) and if statements about God (or Brahman) could not be translated into statements about mystical and numinous experiences. It is reasonably clear that statements about God (or Brahman) cannot be translated into statements about religious experience.[29] A number of good philosophers have thought that statements about physical objects could be translated into statements about sense experiences but it is by no means clear that they are correct.

Consider the following: (1) There is a gap between the phenomenological object of mystical experience and its apparent object. For example, although the phenomenological object of theistic mystical experience is a loving will, theistic mystics typically experience or interpret this object as God. But there is also a gap between the phenomenological object of sense experience and its apparent object. When I look at my desk, the phenomenological object of my experience is a desk-like surface seen from a particular point of view. However, its apparent object is the desk itself. There is another gap between the claim that one appears to be confronted with a loving will and the claim that this loving will is real but, similarly, there is a gap between the claim that one is appeared to in a desk-like way and the claim that there really is something which appears to one in that fashion.

(2) It is logically possible for physical objects to exist and for no one to have sense experiences, just as it is logically possible for God (or Brahman) to exist and for there to be no mystical or numinous experiences. As far as I can see, it is also logically possible for there to be sense experiences even though independent physical objects do not exist just as it is logically

possible for there to be religious experiences even though God (or Brahman) does not exist.[30]

(3) Nevertheless, while there is no necessary connection between the existence of physical objects and the occurrence of sense experiences, there may be a necessary connection between the existence of physical objects and the *possibility* of sense experiences, e.g. it may be necessarily true that if a tree exists, then, if a normal observer is present under standard conditions, he will enjoy sense experiences of a certain type. But it should be noticed that a similar claim can be made about God and mystical experiences, viz, that it is necessarily true that, if God exists, then if there is an adequately prepared mystic whom God chooses to visit, he will enjoy mystical experiences.

The point is this. It is by no means clear that the logical relations between sense experiences and physical objects are significantly different from the logical relations between mystical or numinous experiences and an object like God.[31] It is thus not clear that some sort of special justification is needed in the one case which is not needed in the other. If a special justification is not needed in the case of sense experience, and it does not seem to be, then it is not needed in the case of mystical experience. I conclude therefore that the first objection is unsuccessful.

B

It is sometimes argued that religious experiences cannot be cognitively valid because they support conflicting claims (about Allah, Jesus, Nibbāna, etc.).[32] As it stands, this argument is unconvincing. 'Religious experience' is an umbrella term covering many different types of experience – charismatic phenomena, numinous feeling, possession, conversion, experiences, mystical consciousness, visions, voices, and so on. Religious experience in general may indeed support conflicting claims, but the most that follows is that not all of these experiences or types of experience can be cognitive. In particular, it does not follow that mystical consciousness (or numinous feeling) is delusive.

But even if we were to restrict our attention to types of experience which are not known to be delusive,[33] and thus have some legitimate cognitive pretensions, the argument would still be unsound. Visual experiences support conflicting claims, for people hallucinate and misperceive in other ways, but it is surely wrong to conclude that visual experience is not cognitive. Our attention should be confined not only to types of experience with legitimate cognitive pretensions, but to instances of those types that pass the tests which are used to distinguish veridical experiences of that type from those which are not veridical. No cognitive claims are being made for the latter.

Finally, the only relevant conflicts are conflicts between propositions which are *immediately* based upon the experiences in question. Claims which are indirectly based upon veridical experiences can be infected with error from other sources. Thus, if I claim that the hat I see in front of me is Jack's, I may be mistaken, not because my visual experience is in error, but because I am wrong in thinking it belongs to Jack. If someone standing nearby says that he sees Tom's hat, then his claim conflicts with mine, but this conflict has no tendency to show that either of us our visual experiences are delusive.[34]

Nevertheless, the argument can be reformulated to take account of these objections:

(1) If the criteria which are used to sort out veridical experiences from those which are not veridical are adequate, then all the experiences which meet those criteria are veridical.

(2) If an experience is veridical, then the claims which are immediately based upon it are true. Therefore,

(3) If the criteria which are used to sort out veridical experiences from those which are not veridical are adequate, then the claims which are immediately based upon an experience which meets those criteria are true. (From 1 and 2.) Therefore,

(4) If the criteria which are used to sort out veridical, mystical or numinous experiences[35] from those which are not veridical are adequate, then the claims which are immediately based upon an experience which meets those criteria are true. (From 3.)

(5) Conflicting claims are immediately based upon mystical and numinous experiences which meet the criteria

that are used to sort out veridical experiences of that type from those which are not veridical. (Among these claims are the claim that God exists and is the supreme reality, the claim that Nibbāna is the supreme reality, and so on.) Therefore,

(6) If the criteria which are used to sort out veridical mystical and numinous experiences from those which are not veridical are adequate, then conflicting claims are true. (From 4 and 5.)

(7) Conflicting claims cannot be true. Therefore,

(8) The criteria which are used to sort out veridical mystical and numinous experiences from those which are not veridical cannot be adequate. (From 6 and 7.)

(8) has significant implications for the cognitive status of mystical consciousness and numinous feeling, for if the criteria of validity which are actually used *cannot* be adequate, one suspects that

(9) Adequate criteria cannot be provided.

But it is plausible to suppose that

(10) For any cognitive mode of experience, there are (adequate) criteria for distinguishing veridical instances of that mode of experience from those which are not veridical. Hence,

(11) Mystical consciousness and numinous feeling are not cognitive modes of experience. (From 9 and 10.)

Although one might question (10), this line of response is not particularly promising, since the only type of cognitive experience for which there seem to be no criteria of this sort is the immediate awareness of some of our own mental states.[36] For example, while there are criteria for determining whether others are in pain, our awareness of our own pain is self-certifying; there are no criteria by which we distinguish those cases in which we really feel pain from those in which we only think we do. As we have seen, the mystic's claims are not private and they are not self-certifying. There is therefore no reason to suppose that they constitute an exception to the general rule.

However, it is by no means clear that (5) is true. We must remember that the only relevant conflicts are conflicts between claims which are *immediately* supported by religious experience.

Many of the conflicting claims which people try to support by
appealing to mystical or numinous experience are not *immediately* supported by it. For example, that God (as defined by
Anselm) exists, or that the Ātman-Brahman is the ground of
being, or that Nibbāna is real. None of these propositions
would appear to be immediately warranted by the religious
experiences upon which they are (partly) based.[37] If all the
conflicting claims which people attempt to support by appealing to mystical experience or numinous feeling fall into this
category, then premise (5) is false.

It is true that nature mysticism, monistic mysticism, theistic
mysticism and numinous experience (immediately?) support
different claims – that nature is one and sacred, that there is an
undifferentiated unity transcending space and time, that an
overwhelming loving consciousness exists, that there is a holy
Other. But it is not clear that these claims *conflict*. (Monistic
and theistic experiences might be experiences of different
objects, for example.) In order to establish (5), one must show
that claims immediately supported by mystical experience or
numinous feeling are not only different but incompatible, and
it is by no means clear that this can be done.[38]

I therefore conclude that the objection from conflicting religious experiences or intuitions is inconclusive.

C

The similarity between mystical experiences and certain psychotic experiences have led some to dismiss mystical experience as delusive.[39] There are, of course, differences between
mystics and psychotics. Thus, as Kenneth Wapnick points
out,[40] although both mystical experience and schizophrenia
involve a withdrawal from social reality, the mystic is able to
maintain a certain amount of control over this process while
the schizophrenic is not. Furthermore, the mystic is able to
integrate his special experiences with his normal experiences,
and to function successfully in society. The schizophrenic is
not able to do this, but lives in his own private universe.
Wapnick believes that these differences can be partly attributed to the tradition and training of the mystic which
enables him to handle his experiences when they occur.

While there is truth in Wapnick's observations, they are not

entirely satisfactory. Nature mysticism is usually spontaneous, not consciously induced, and many nature mystics
belong to no tradition. Nevertheless, cosmic consciousness
does not normally interfere with the mystic's ability to function socially, and the nature mystic is frequently able to integrate his mystical experience and his other experiences.
(Bucke is a case in point.) Control and training are not sufficient to explain the difference between mysticism and schizophrenia.

But there is a more important point. Wapnick speaks as if
the essential difference between mystics and schizophrenics
was not a difference in their states, but a difference in the
effects of their states, and the ways in which they handle them.
This is misleading. Wapnick, for example, focuses on the case
of Lara Jefferson, but the experience in which she abandoned
control and allowed what she called 'Madness' to rage through
her, did not, as Wapnick admits, involve an experience of
unity. It was thus significantly unlike mystical experience.
William James speaks in a similarly misleading fashion.
According to James, 'diabolical mysticism' or 'mysticism
turned upside down' involves 'the same sense of ineffable importance in the smallest events, the same texts and words
coming with new meaning, the same voices and visions and
leadings and missions, the same controlling by extraneous
powers; only this time the emotion is pessimistic: instead of
consolations we have desolations; the meanings are dreadful;
and the powers are enemies to life.'[41] These remarks are misleading because the experiences which James has described
are not the obverse of mystical experience, but the obverse of
visionary and occult experiences.[42]

Nevertheless, psychotic mysticism is a genuine phenomenon. In his manic periods, John Custance appears to have
enjoyed extrovertive mystical consciousness. He experienced a
sense of well-being that was 'sometimes ecstatic'. His 'sense of
reality' was 'heightened'. For example, lights seemed 'deeper,
more intense,' and the taste of strawberries or raspberries gave
'ecstatic sensations'. The experience included a 'sense of com-
munion' extending 'to all fellow-creatures', and a feeling of
expansion. Thus, in describing these states, Custance says 'in
a sense I am God . . . I am utterly and completely immortal; I

am even male and female. The whole universe ... is within me
... I reconcile Good and Evil and create light, darkness,
worlds, universes.' His consciousness was infused with 'a sense
of ineffable revelation'.[43]

In his depressive periods, Custance suffered from extrovertive states which parodied states of cosmic consciousness. In
these experiences everything appeared as phantasmagoric and
potentially evil, and, instead of expanding, his soul contrac-
ted; it 'turned into nothingness – except unending pain', 'an
almost infinitesimal point of abject misery, disgust, pain and
fear'.[44]

Psychotic 'mysticism' is thus a genuine phenomenon: it
appears to be of two sorts. Some psychotic states seem to be
phenomenologically identical with normal mystical states.
Custance's manic experiences are an example. One of E W
Anderson's cases reported merging 'into everything ... [and]
an intense consciousness of power and absolute ecstasy,' and
went on to say 'things appear more real ... The whole being
expands ... I notice everything I haven't seen before, lights
and sounds ... Everything is absolutely new ... I seemed
above time and yet it was intensified in some way ... It
seemed like something which served a purpose, which was
used to divide, to limit something, but not real.'[45] Other psychotic experiences bear a family resemblance to mystical
experiences but contain components which are in some sense
the opposite of components contained in normal mystical experience. For example, they may involve a sense of unreality
instead of a sense of heightened reality.

The world now looks remote, strange, sinister, uncanny. Its colour is gone,
its breath is cold, there is no speculation in the eyes it glares with. 'It is as if I
lived in another century,' says one asylum patient. 'I see everything through
a cloud,' says another. 'I see,' says a third, 'I touch, but the things do not
come near me, a thick veil alters the hue and look of everything'. 'Persons
move like shadows, and sounds seem to come from a distant world.' – 'There
is no longer any past for me .... it is as if I could not see any reality, as if I
were in a theatre; as if people were actors, and everything were scenery ...
Everything floats before my eyes, but leaves no impression.' – 'I weep false
tears, I have unreal hands: the things I see are not real things.'[46]

Rather than a living presence, nature seems dead. 'The immo-
bility became more immobile, the silence more silent, things

and people, their gestures and their noises, more artificial, detached one from the other, unreal, without life.'[47] Instead of expansion, a psychotic 'mystic' like Custance experiences contraction. Instead of joy, the dominant emotion is fear and horror.

What implications do these facts have for the cognitive status of mystical experience? As we have seen, some psychotic 'mysticism' is aberrant, but some is not. Custance's manic experiences appear to have been genuine cases of extrovertive mystical consciousness. These cases should not trouble us. The fact that psychotics sometimes have extrovertive mystical experiences is no more disturbing than the fact that psychotics sometimes see physical objects in a perfectly normal way, or hear and understand correctly. If most of the people who had mystical experiences were psychotic, it would perhaps be reasonable to dismiss their experiences as delusive, but they are not.

The aberrant experiences present a different problem. These experiences bear a family resemblance to normal mystical experiences, but are essentially restricted to psychotics. It would be generally agreed that these experiences are delusive. 'Horrorific' visions fail to meet at least five of the six tests described in the first part of this chapter. (They *might* meet the third test; the content of these experiences is not silly or insignificant, though it is hardly 'sweet.')[48] Even people who are suspicious of the tests would dismiss horrorific visions as delusive. (There seem to be essentially two reasons for this. First, our assumption that, in the long run, men and women who see things as they really are will lead happier and better lives than those who do not. Second, our assumption that truth is coherent – that, in the long run, valid insights will be seen to cohere, or at least not conflict. The lives of those afflicted by the horrorific vision are morally and spiritually wretched, and their 'insights' conflict with the insights of others, and the insights of their own lucid and manic moments.[49])

Does the occurrence of these delusive parodies of mysticism cast doubt upon the cognitive validity of mystical experience? I believe that it does not. Hallucinations bear a family resemblance to normal sense experience, and some philosophers have suggested that the occurrence of experiences of this type

casts doubt on the cognitive validity of sense experience. Their
argument is essentially this:

    (1) The existence of sensory illusions and hallucinations
          shows that it is possible for an apparently veridical
          sense experience to be delusive. But if
    (2) Delusion is possible in any given case, then
    (3) It is possible in all cases. Therefore,
    (4) The cognitive pretensions of sense experience are
          suspect.

Each step in this argument is questionable. (2) does not
entail (3). (The inference from a proposition of the form 'for
every x, it is possible that x is Ø' to a proposition of the form 'It
is possible that every x is Ø' is invalid. For example, while for
any logically contingent proposition, it is possible that it is
true, it is not possible that every contingent proposition is
true.) (1) implies (2) if only if there are no relevant differences
between the illusions and hallucinations referred to in (1) and
other instances of sense experience. But of course there are,
viz, the presence of precisely those features which led us to
classify them as illusions or hallucinations (viz, their failure to
cohere with the rest of the subject's experience and with the experience of others). Neither (2) nor (3) implies (4). Even if (2)
or (3) are true, their truth should not bother us unless we have
reason to suspect that the possibilities to which they allude are
actually realised. The bare possibility of error is not disconcerting; what is disconcerting are special reasons (for example,
the lack of agreement) for thinking that the experiences in
question are cognitively defective.

    The point is clear. The existence of aberrant parodies of
mystical experience should bother us only if the reasons which
led us to dismiss them as delusive are present in normal cases.
The principal reason, viz, their correlation with psychosis or
insanity, is not.

D

There may be special reasons for thinking that cosmic consciousness is delusive.

    In the third chapter of *The Comparison of Religions*,[50] Zæhner
argues that because the mystic is not identical with nature, he
cannot perceive that he is identical with it. Why, then does he

believe that he is identical with nature? Zæhner finds a clue in Aristotle who argues that, in ordinary cognition, the mind is in a sense identical with what it cognises. But only in a sense. When the mind cognises a stone it is clearly not identical with the stone itself. It is instead identical with something 'like' the stone, viz, its form, or concept, or image. Analogously, Zæhner argues, the nature mystic is not identical with nature and so does not experience identity with it. He instead experiences a temporary identity with the *form* of nature, or 'imago mundi', which is part of every person's unconscious. (This image can be identified with Jung's collective unconscious, and/or with man as a microcosm (p 88).)

Aside from its imprecision, Zæhner's theory suffers from two substantive weaknesses. First, Zæhner *seems* to think that the 'imago mundi', and not nature, is the real object of the nature mystic's experience; but this is doubtful. In at least some cases (that of Richard Jefferies, for example, or of Thomas Traherne) nature mysticism is clearly an experience *of nature*, i.e. it is an experience in which the *external world* appears to the mystic in a certain (perhaps illusory) way. In these cases, at least, the object of the mystic's experience is not an image.

But perhaps this is not really Zæhner's position, for he sometimes speaks as if the nature mystic was aware of nature, and not merely its image. Thus, he says that the nature mystic establishes 'a physico-psychic *rapport* with the macrocosm [and not merely its image. Thus, he says that the nature mystic establishes 'a physico-psychic *rapport* with the macrocosm [and nature mystic makes contact with 'the spirit animating all Nature [and not just an image] ... a terrible, a ruthless, and a mindless spirit ... a *material* absolute ... the animating principle of the non-rational universe ... [which] is totally indifferent to man' (the prāna of the *Upanishads*, the world soul of Neoplatonism). (p 86–7)[51] In *Concordant Discord*, Zæhner speculates that the experience may involve a union with matter, where matter is thought of as something pregnant with movement, or inherently vital (the 'food' of the *Upanishads*, prakṛti). Zæhner is not always consistent, but it is possible that his position is that (1) *through* the 'imago mundi' the nature mystic genuinely experiences *union* with nature (prāna, prakṛti), but

that (2) his sense of *identity* is a reflection of his temporary identity with the 'imago mundi'.

In any case, Zæhner's position is internally incoherent. His
objection to the claim that the nature mystic experiences identity with nature is that man and nature are not (literally) identical. A similar objection can be made to the claim that the
nature mystic experiences identity with the 'imago mundi'.
Man and the 'imago mundi' are not (literally) identical either.
The 'imago mundi' does not smoke a pipe or cross the street.
Nor is Jefferies, or any other nature mystic, the collective
unconscious, or some kind of form or image. Hence, if
Zæhner's argument for the delusive character of cosmic consciousness is sound, his own theory of cosmic consciousness is
defective.

Nevertheless, these considerations fail to get to the heart of
the matter. Delusive experiences are inherently misleading.
Their very nature is such that, (until one learns better), they
tend to induce false judgments. Zæhner believes that there are
three reasons for regarding cosmic consciousness as delusive.
(1) Nature mystics tend to believe that they are, at least for a
moment, identical with nature; and yet no one is ever identical
with nature. (pp 75–6) (2) To the nature mystic, the world
appears transfigured, resplendent and wonderful whereas it is
actually 'cruel' and 'senseless'. As Jefferies said, it is 'anti-
human ... outre-human ... almost grotesque in its attitude
towards' what is human. (Quoted p 85)[52] (3) These
experiences tempt one mistakenly to conclude that the distinction between good and evil is invalid.[53]

Although Zæhner's case cannot be dismissed out of hand, it
is far from conclusive.

(1) Identity talk may be nothing more than an exaggerated
expression of an experience of unity. In another connection, al-
Ghāzālī pointed out that lovers in ecstasy say things which in
the sober light of reason they know to be (literally) false. Exaggeration and hyperbole are natural effects of intense emotion
and heightened sensibility.

(2) In positive moods and moments of exaltation, we temporarily forget nature's dark side. It seems unduly harsh to
conclude that these experiences are therefore delusive. If
cosmic consciousness led people to deny that things like cancer

are real or harmful, it would be delusive, but it does not. It instead leads people to believe that these things weigh little on the cosmic scales and that, on the whole, nature is overwhelmingly good. This opinion, which is shared by many non-mystics, may be erroneous but it is not *known* to be false.

(3) Whether cosmic consciousness has a tendency to blind people to the importance of moral distinctions will be discussed in chapter 5. We shall see that the evidence is ambiguous. In any case, it is not *certain* that moral mistakes are cognitive mistakes. If non-cognitivist theories are correct, moral judgments are neither true nor false and, in that case, the notion of inducing a *false* moral judgment is incoherent.[54]

Although the judgments which are incorporated in cosmic consciousness may seem fantastic, they are not easily shown to be false. For example, consider the claim that time stands still. This does not imply that things do not change, or that it is not now a quarter past four. It may imply that our ordinary experience of time is 'relative' (one of only several ways of doing so), but this is not clearly false. Similar remarks can be made about the other judgments which are incorporated in the experience. Because it is not clear that these judgments are false, it is not clear that the experience which includes them is delusive.

E

Special problems are created by the (alleged) fact that introvertive mystical consciousness is entirely devoid of conceptual content, and by the fact that one mode of introvertive mystical consciousness even seems to lack an object. It is difficult to see how a non-conceptual or objectless experience could be cognitive.

(1) I have assumed that mystical experience incorporates judgments. But is this assumption compatible with the claim that even theistic mystics bury concepts, images, and other familiar contents of consciousness beneath a 'cloud of forgetting'? It might seem that it is not, and that one could argue that, because introvertive mystical experience is non-conceptual, it cannot incorporate judgment and is, therefore, not even a *candidate* for a cognitive experience.

There are three ways of responding to this objection. The

first is by denying that cognitive experiences always incorporate judgments. The second is by denying that judgments always incorporate concepts. The third is by denying that introversion involves the exclusion of all conceptual content.

The first two responses are unacceptable. Non-controversial cases of cognitive experience, such as perception and memory, incorporate judgment (thinking that something is the case). A bare 'intuition', totally devoid of judgment, would be similar to the reception of raw sense data by newly born children. The reception of sense data will eventually become incorporated in genuinely cognitive experiences (for example, seeing a table) but is itself no more cognitive than pains or itches.[55]

Jacques Maritain adopts the second response. He believes that because theistic mystical consciousness is a form of knowledge, it incorporates judgment,[56] but that it incorporates judgment without incorporating concepts. Although all knowledge involves judgment, not all knowledge is conceptual. The beatific vision is cognitive but non-conceptual,[57] and while animals do not possess concepts, they do know certain things. For example, my dog knows that I am its master.[58]

This is not persuasive. In order for a theistic mystic to be convinced that he is in the presence of a person-like reality, he must possess the concept of a person. The notion of a judgment without concepts is as incoherent as the notion of a sentence without words. To judge or affirm just is to use concepts in a certain way. If mystical experience involves judgment it cannot be totally non-conceptual.[59]

But can this be reconciled with the way in which introvertive mystics describe their experience? Allowing for some occasional exaggeration, I believe that it can.

First, the fact that an experience is non-discursive (does not involve comparing, analysing, inferring, etc.) does not entail that it is non-conceptual. For example, the contemplation of a seascape is sometimes non-discursive. Nevertheless, the experience is not a chaotic confusion of unrelated impressions, but is conceptually structured. One sees the sea and sky as sea and sky, though one is not thinking about them 'conceptually'. The fact that mystical consciousness is non-discursive is therefore not decisive.

Second, the fact that introvertive mystical consciousness is devoid of imagery does not entail that it is devoid of conceptual content. Many Christian students of mysticism are heirs of a scholastic tradition which asserts that conceptual thought is never free from accompanying imagery. Joseph Maréchal, for example, assumes that ideas or concepts must always be accompanied by 'subtle traces of representation ... very attenuated semi-sensorial, semi-emotive symbolism ... a vague image of a word such as God, Infinite, Goodness ... and so on.'[60] If this is true, and if introvertive mystical consciousness is devoid of imagery as introvertive mystics maintain, then introvertive mystical consciousness *must* be non-conceptual.[61] It is not really clear, however, that conceptual thought *is* always accompanied by imagery. The fact that introvertive mystical consciousness is devoid of imagery is therefore inconclusive.[62]

Third, it may be true that introvertive mystics bury all *clear* and relatively *specific* concepts beneath a cloud of forgetting. It might also be the case that any general and obscure concepts (for example, 'being', 'consciousness', 'bliss', 'love') which may happen to be involved in the mystic's experience, are not explicitly attended to. It does not follow that introvertive mystical consciousness is entirely non-conceptual.[63]

Fourth, that all thoughts *of creatures* are buried beneath a cloud of forgetting, does not imply that all *thoughts* are buried beneath a cloud of forgetting, and in fact, fifth, the consciousness of the theistic mystic, at least, has a determinant content, viz, union with God.

If these points are kept in mind when one turns to the texts, one will find that mystical autobiographies and impersonal accounts of mystical experience provide little evidence that introvertive mystical consciousness is devoid of *all* conceptual content.[64]

(2) Monistic mystical consciousness presents another problem. Contemplatives in different cultures, and at different periods of history have had experiences which they describe as experiences of undifferentiated unity – ecstatic experiences in which consciousness, without destroying itself, empties itself of its contents, and all distinctions disappear. Whether or not these mystics are accurately describing their experience, two things are clear. First, people really do have experiences which

they feel compelled to describe in this fashion. Second, these experiences of blissful, empty consciousness provide an experential basis or model for such concepts as 'nirguṇa Brahman', 'puruṣa', 'Ātman,' and 'citta mātra'.

But at least two things about these experiences are problematic – the claim that consciousness *can* occur without an object, and the application of terms like 'true', 'valid', 'knowledge', and 'sight' to experiences of this type.

Westerners have usually assumed that consciousness is necessarily intentional, i.e. that the notion of empty consciousness or a consciousness without contents is self-contradictory. Thus, earlier students of mysticism, such as Leuba, assumed that introvertive states either had some ordinary but very attenuated object (for example, a faint image) or were states of complete unconsciousness.[65] There is little empirical support for this position, but they were forced to adopt it because of their *a priori* conviction that consciousness is always intentional. It would seem, however, that the cross-cultural occurrence of this type of introvertive experience, together with the fact that an entire culture (viz, that of India) has supposed that consciousness can exist without an object, casts doubt on both the necessity and truth of this assumption.

But if the experience has no object, can it have any cognitive value? Paradigm cases of cognitive experience, such as sense perception and memory, have objects. Paradigm cases of non-cognitive experience, such as pains, headaches and feelings of depression, do not. It would appear to follow that if monistic states have no object, they are more like paradigm cases of non-cognitive experience than like paradigm cases of cognitive experience. Furthermore, an objectless experience cannot be noetic, i.e. an experience *of* something which is believed to be real, and yet it is difficult to see how it could possibly be cognitive if it is not noetic. It would seem, then, that if monistic experiences have no object *of any kind*, they are not cognitive experiences.

It might, nonetheless, be appropriate to speak of them as 'true' or 'valid', for 'true' and 'false' can be used in non-cognitive senses. Thus consider the following sentences: 'I am the truth', 'God is truth', 'she revealed her true self'. In these sentences, 'true' means 'real', 'authentic', 'genuine', 'valuable' or 'important'. An experience can be true in these senses but lack cognitive value. It would seem, however, that the mystics who have these experiences believe that they are cognitive, and not merely authentic, valuable, or important. Unless they are simply confused, their experience must therefore have some sort of content.

There are at least two reasons why monistic mystics might describe their experiences as empty even if they had an object. (1) These experiences clearly have no ordinary object. The mind of the monistic mystic is empty of percepts, images and clear concepts. (2) In these experiences, the sense of mutual distance or 'overagainstness' which characterises 'ordinary perceptual experience, especially seeing and hearing, is either minimal or non-existent. Monistic experiences are even more unlike ordinary experience in this respect than theistic or extrovertive experiences.

Certain things suggest that these experiences actually do have some sort of identifiable object or content. The most important is the fact that monistic mystics themselves often speak as if their experiences were experiences *of* something. (For example, the Ātman-Brahman, one's puruṣa, Reality, Being, or an undifferentiated One.)

The non-reflective self-awareness involved in ordinary consciousness or awareness might provide an appropriate model for these experiences. In thinking of (perceiving, doing) this or that, I am aware of myself without being an *object* for myself, i.e. without standing over against myself, or reflecting upon myself, or making myself an *object* of explicit cognition. Monistic experiences are often understood as experiences of the 'real I'. It is not entirely unreasonable to suppose that monistic mystical consciousness involves something like this non-reflective self-awareness, and thus has a kind of 'object' or 'content'.

(3) The critic has made an important point. Paradigmatic instances of cognitive experience incorporate judgments (and thus concepts), and they have objects. Since 'cognitive experience' is defined in relation to experiences of this kind, it is at best misleading to apply the term 'cognitive' to experiences which are either non-conceptual or lack an object. I have argued, however, that there are reasons for supposing that

introvertive mystical experiences are not totally devoid of conceptual content, and that even monistic experiences have a kind of 'object'. The objection is therefore inconclusive.

F

According to Robert Gimello, 'Buddhists do not ontologise the contents of their mystical experiences.'[66] A number of things can be said in favour of this view. (1) Buddhists value trance states less highly than discernment and insight (the inward appropriation of the Buddha's teachings about dependent origination, impermanence, etc.). Wisdom 'is the proximate cause of enlightenment'; without it mystical states have no soteriological significance.[67]

(2) Buddhists freely admit that Hindu yogins have mystical experiences, but reject the conclusions which they draw from their experiences (especially the conclusion that there is some kind of permanent self or substance). In spite of their mystical attainments, it is believed that these yogins fail to perceive the nature of reality. (3) Buddhist analysis is applied to introvertive trance states as well as to more familiar experiences. For example, since these states are also impermanent they too are duhkha ('unsatisfactory').

David Kalupahana makes a similar point. Kalupahana argues that the Buddha rejected any sort of transcendental reality, that Nirvāna is essentially desirelessness or non-attachment, and that while mystical states, like 'cessation', have an instrumental value and provide a temporary relief from attachment, they have no cognitive significance.[68]

That 'Nirvāna,' merely refers to non-attachment or the cessation of becoming is, of course, contentious. (Although it appears to have been the view of the Sautrāntikas.[69]) Nevertheless, Kalupahana's remarks call our attention to the fact that the Buddhist attitude towards mystical states of consciousness is strikingly different from the attitude of other traditions.

The contention, then, is that: 'Buddhists do not ontologise the contents of their mystical experiences.' These experiences are helpful devices which can be used to calm the mind and break up harmful patterns of thought and behaviour, but they have no cognitive value. If true, this contention is interesting for it suggests that mystical experiences might not be *inherently* noetic; that claims about the nature of reality are not built into their very structure, but are adventitious interpretations which have been *added* to these experiences. How else, one might ask, can one explain Buddhism's attitude towards mystical experience?

The contention must, however, be treated with caution. There are reasons for believing that (1) Buddhism's strictures are primarily directed towards introvertive experiences rather than towards mystical experience in general, and that (2) its reluctance to ontologise the contents of introvertive experience is not due to the nature of the experience but to extra-mystical considerations. We will consider the last point first.

The trance states associated with the eighth and ninth dhyāna (the state of 'neither perception nor non-perception', and the state of 'cessation') appear to be monistic – experiences of pure, empty consciousness. It is significant that Buddhists themselves sometimes succumb to the temptation to erect a transcendental metaphysics upon the basis of these experiences. Perhaps the clearest example is Yogācāra which identified the suchness of things with Mind Only.[70] But it is not implausible to suppose that the Hīnayāna concept of Nirvāna has connections with monistic states of consciousness, and the concept of Nirvāna has metaphysical implications.[71] Some Mahāyāna speculations about the Buddha nature or Dharmakāya may also be rooted in these experiences.

These considerations suggest that the experiences in question *are* noetic or inherently 'metaphysical', but that Buddhists for some reason wish to repudiate their cognitive implications. Why would they want to do so?

Some Buddhist schools (for example, Mādhyamika) reject *all* views concerning the nature of reality. Although this is an extreme position, Buddhism in general is very suspicious of 'metaphysics'. (Although why the Hīnayāna analysis of the nature of space-time world or Mahāyāna accounts of the suchness of things should not be regarded as metaphysics is at best unclear.) Metaphysical speculation is a distraction from the task at hand, viz, to extinguish thirst and enter Nirvāna. It is therefore not surprising that Buddhism would reject the metaphysical implications of monistic experiences.

Most important, however, is the anātman doctrine. The repudiation of any kind of permanent self or substance is at the very heart of Buddhism. Belief in self (ātman) is both a cause and effect of self-assertion and the will to live. It is thus inextricably bound up with the attachment to self which binds us to this world. Since monistic experiences almost invariably lead to talk of a 'true self' or 'real I' (an Ātman or puruṣa, etc.), it is not surprising that Buddhists are suspicious of them.

There therefore seems to be no reason to suppose that Buddhists have noticed something which has escaped other observers, viz, that mystical experiences are not really noetic. Furthermore, the Buddhists' rejection of the ontological claims that appear to be built into these experiences is inextricably bound up with the anātman doctrine, the attack on 'views', and other teachings peculiar to Buddhism. No reason for repudiating the cognitive implications of mystical experiences has been provided which is independent of the idiosyncrasies of Buddhist doctrine.

But there is another point. In chapter 1, I suggested that a certain type of extrovertive experience is highly prized by at least some Buddhists, viz, an experience in which the world is viewed without conceptualisation and without attachment. I argued that this experience is properly called 'mystical', and that it plays an important role in both Mādhyamika and Zen. It is difficult to believe that this experience has nothing to do with what Gimello calls their 'view about views', viz, that all views of reality distort it. It is at least possible that a more accurate description of the attitude of these Buddhists towards mystical experience would be that the noetic content of more familiar mystical experiences (for example, introvertive experiences) is discounted partly upon the basis of a certain type of extrovertive mystical experience. If this is correct, then the objection of these Buddhists is not to the cognitive claims of mysticism as such, but to the cognitive claims of certain types of mysticism.

If this is their position, it is problematic. A non-conceptual and non-attached vision of the space-time world either incorporates a 'view' (a judgment), or it does not. If it does not, then it can no more conflict with views than a feeling of nausea conflicts with views. But if it does not conflict with views, it provides no reason for discounting them, and therefore provides no reason for discounting the claims (about a 'real I' or an undifferentiated One) which are built into monistic experiences. If it does incorporate a 'view' (a judgment), it is presumably that things really are as they appear in the experience, and that conceptual views of the space-time world, which distinguish one thing from another and are inherently abstract and static, are incoherent or invalid. But this alternative would expose these Buddhists to three objections. First, that all conceptualisations of the space-time world break down does not entail that all conceptualisations (for example, the belief in a transcendent self) break down. Since the experience in question is an experience of the *space-time world*, it is difficult to see how its content could conflict with the content of monistic experiences. Second, if this experience (with its incorporated 'view') is privileged, then one is after all committed to a view. (And to deny that this view is metaphysical, or to assert that it is merely a meta-view about views, is obfuscating.) Third, if this experience really does incorporate the conviction that every view about the world is equally inadequate, there is reason to believe it is inherently delusive. For not only does it conflict with our ordinary experience, it also conflicts with other equally compelling forms of mystical experience (for example, experiences in which one seems to perceive a holy power permeating nature). I would suggest, however, that perhaps the most that is actually built into these experiences is the belief that all ordinary conceptualisations (of the space-time world) are inadequate (which does not entail that all views are *equally* inadequate). This is undoubtedly true, but has no implication for the validity of other types of mystical experience.

I conclude therefore that a consideration of Buddhism's attitude towards mystical experience provides no compelling reason for distrusting its cognitive pretensions.

III

A pramāṇa is a 'source or means of acquiring new knowledge'.[72] For example, sense perception, yogic intuition, inference and testimony are pramāṇas. According to Advaita Vedānta, all pramāṇas are 'intrinsically valid'. Ideas, judgments and experiences are to be accepted as valid except where they are called into question by other ideas, judgments or experiences. (As our (apparent) experience of a snake is called into question by the experience which is obtained when we examine the object more closely and discover that it is only a rope.) To suppose that an apparent cognition must be justified before it is accepted commits one to the necessity of an infinite regress. An apparent cognition, C_1, can only be justified by another apparent cognition, C_2. Given our supposition, C_2 must itself be justified, and this requires yet another apparent cognition, C_3, and so on. Only Brahman-knowledge (jnāna) is self-certifying in the sense that there are no conceivable circumstances in which the presumption of its validity could be overriden, but all apparent cognitions are 'self-luminous' in the sense that they are presumptively valid.[73]

Advaitins believe that Brahman-knowledge is self-certifying because it is an experience of undifferentiated unity. Since the experience has no content or object, it is impossible to show that its content or object is defective. Hence, the experience cannot be shown to be in error. This is not altogether convincing. As we have seen, it is not clear that monistic mystical experiences have no 'object' or 'content'. Nor is it clear that the only way in which an apparent cognition can be shown to be in error is by cancelling or 'sublating' its content. (As the content of the snake experience is cancelled when we look at the object more closely and see that it is only a rope.) For example, regardless of their content, we reject experiences on the basis of their causes when we have reason to believe that apparent cognitions with those causes are invalid.

Nevertheless, I would suggest that the Advaitin doctrine contains an important truth. If there is no type of apparent cognition which is presumptively valid, then it is impossible to avoid an infinite regress. Furthermore, to suppose that one type of apparent cognition is presumptively valid while another is not is arbitrary. It follows that any type of apparent cognition is presumptively valid, and should be accepted in the absence of adequate reasons for doubting its validity.

The argument of this chapter should be placed within the

framework of these considerations. Part I attempted to show that various types of mystical experience are presumptively valid apparent cognitions. Part II examined the most important attempts to defeat the presumption of their validity. Since there appears to be a presumption in favour of the cognitive validity of mystical experience, and since attempts to defeat that presumption are unsuccessful, mystical experience should be accepted as a valid means of knowledge.[74]

Notes

[1] C B Martin, *Religious Belief*, Ithaca, New York, 1959, chapter 5.

[2] I do not wish to be understood as implying that mystics appeal to their experiences to demonstrate (e.g.) God's reality or the reality of Brahman, or that they are uncertain of God's reality or the reality of Brahman before they have their experiences. Nevertheless, mystics do appeal to their experiences to support the claim that they taste God or experience Brahman, and these claims entail that God exists or Brahman is real. Furthermore, mystics do seem to believe that their experiences confirm the latter although they usually think that there are other grounds (e.g. scripture) on the basis of which one can be justifiably certain of their truth.

[3] David Knowles, *The English Mystical Tradition*, London, 1960, chapter VIII.

[4] R M Gale makes a similar point in the last section of 'Mysticism and Philosophy', (*The Journal of Philosophy* LVII (1960), pp 471–81); Walter Stace makes a similar point in *Mysticism and Philosophy*, *op cit*, pp 135–9.

[5] The fact that the mystic believes that agreement is relevant does not entail that he believes (or should believe) that disagreement is relevant. True, if he thinks that the presence of agreement strengthens his claim, he must acknowledge that in its absence his claim would not be as strong as it is. It does not follow that he should concede that its absence counts *against* his claim. In general, that A recognises that e counts from p and that in the absence of e the case for p is not as strong as it would otherwise be, does not imply that A should take the absence of e as counting against p. For example, the fact that Smith helps Jones, with whom he is barely acquainted and to whom he has no obligation, supports the claim that Smith is a good man, and if this fact did not obtain, the evidence for that claim. In general, that A recognises that e counts for p and that in the man who has no claim on him and whom he hardly knows would not count against his goodness.

[6] J A Symonds and Richard Jefferies *may* be cases in point.

[7] Stace, (*Mysticism and Philosophy*, pp 308–10) suggests that perhaps these

claims ought not to be taken at face value: (1) He points out that the conviction is not universal. Bucke refers to a case of cosmic consciousness in which the subject remained convinced that the self does not survive death. (Or consider the case of Richard Jefferies.) (2) As he says, not all mystics express the conviction that the soul is immortal. (Though of course, it does not follow that they do not possess that conviction.) (3) He suggests that it is possible that those who express this conviction are only speaking of an aspect of their experience (e.g. the feeling that time drops away) and not of survival after death. (However, there is no compelling reason to believe that this is the case.)

[8] Though, again, one should probably be careful. I am not aware of any instance in which a Christian mystic claimed that his experiences confirmed the doctrine of a general resurrection. Any confirmation of this doctrine which is provided by mystical experience is at best indirect. (These experiences allegedly confirm problematic elements of a 'theory' which includes certain predictions as an integral part. By providing new 'evidence' for these elements, the mystic's experiences confirm the theory as a whole, and thereby confirm its consequences. Whether the experiences of Christian mystics actually do confirm such peculiarly Christian doctrines as the doctrine of the Trinity is, of course, debatable.)

[9] This should be regarded as a kind of prediction of the course of 'external' events. The vision of God or passing into Nibbāna are not just inner experiences. Neither can occur if God or Nibbāna are unreal, and the vision of God depends upon God's causal activity. The events referred to by 'a vision of God' or 'passing into Nibbāna' have a non-psychological dimension.

[10] I am indebted to William Alston for the main point of the next three paragraphs. (See his *Religious Belief and Philosophical Thought*, New York, 1963, pp 124–5.)

[11] Or similar experiences under certain conditions. (If the object is moving, we can sometimes predict its future locations.) Or dissimilar but connected experiences under certain conditions. (If the object is rapidly changing, similar experiences cannot be obtained but we can often specify conditions under which related experiences can be obtained.) I shall continue to ignore these complications.

[12] As H P Owen asserts in various places in *The Christian Knowledge of God*, (London, 1960).

[13] Thus, since psychic experiences, like clairvoyance, purport to provide extraordinary knowledge about perfectly ordinary events and objects, the demand for a large number of successful predictions is entirely appropriate.

[14] One might therefore expect to find more emphasis placed upon agreement (and disagreement) by monists and pantheists than by theists. But as far as I can determine, there is no evidence that this is the case. (One might argue that because these objects are 'incomprehensible', agreement and disagreement is an unreliable test. If Brahman, for example, is neti, neti (not this, not that), there is no reason to suppose that veridical experiences of Brahman will be repeatable. However, this argument

suffers from two defects. In the first place, the object is usually described with some precision. Thus, though Brahman is said to be neti, neti, it is characterised as pure, blissful, empty consciousness. In the second place, if the argument were sound, it would prove that *all* tests are unreliable; it would not show that there was any *special* problem with the test of (dis) agreement.)

[15] One should point out that not only Christian experiences satisfy the fourth and fifth tests. Theistic experiences from other traditions may also satisfy them. Furthermore, if we can distinguish claims that are directly based upon an experience from claims which are part of its interpretation, then the experiences of some non-theistic mystics might also satisfy these tests. Thus, if Saṁkara's monistic claims are part of an interpretation of an experience of the naked essence of his own soul, then the fact that his claims conflict with orthodox talk is not conclusive. According to the sixth test, certification by authority counts for the genuineness of an experience (and rejection by authority counts against it). However, because the appropriate Christian authorities have said little about most non-Christian experiences, the latter are not explicitly excluded by the sixth test. The point is that, even though the last three tests are the tests of a particular religious community, it does not follow that the only experiences which will pass those tests are experiences which occur *within* that community.

[16] One cannot deny that God exists and assert that it is nevertheless appropriate to employ these tests. But the reason is obvious. If God does not exist, the experience cannot be valid and the issue is closed. There is therefore no point in using the tests.

[17] The relevance of the tests is grounded in conditionals linking the presence of God to the states of affairs specified in those tests (the production of good fruits, etc.). In the last three cases, the conditional itself depends upon a condition. (For example, *if* orthodoxy is true then, if God is a God of truth, genuine experiences of Him will not lead to very much unorthodox talk.) One is required to accept the conditional which justifies the test only if one also accepts the condition upon which the conditional depends.

[18] The God of classical Christian theism is the apparent object of some theistic mystical experiences. (Viṣṇu of Śiva are the apparent objects of others.) Their phenomenological object appears to be an overwhelming loving consciousness with which one unites in ecstasy. The claim to have perceived the experience's phenomenological object might be true even if the claim to have perceived its apparent object is false. Are there tests for the former which are distinct from tests for the latter? It is clear that not all tests for the latter are tests for former. For example, a demonstration of the incompatibility of immutability and omniscience would count decisively against the latter (since it would entail that the God of classical Christian theism cannot exist), but not against the former. But neither are the tests altogether different. Since the phenomenological object of an experience is typically a part, aspect, mode or property of its apparent object (or more accurately, the sort of thing which would be a part,

aspect, mode or property of its apparent object if the latter were real), tests for the former will usually be included among the tests for the latter. The tests for perceptions of desk-like surfaces are part of the tests for perceptions of desks. Similarly, tests for perceptions of God include tests for perceptions of an overwhelming loving presence. For example, one would expect experiences of an overwhelming loving consciousness to be edifying, significant, and not inherently misleading. The evidence for naturalism would count against them; and so on. Similar remarks can be made about monistic experiences and cosmic consciousness.

[19] If testable predictions were based upon mystical experience, then a consideration of their accuracy would be relevant. But they are not. (Locutions and visions, however, sometimes *do* incorporate testable predictions.)

[20] At this point we might add 'with respect to those features which lead us to speak of the latter as cognitive'. I have not done so because it is not entirely clear just what those features are. Of course we are not entirely in the dark. In my opinion, they would include the presence of tests and check-up procedures, but not the fact that sense experiences are bound up with certain bodily organs. (The latter has recently been denied by Peter Donovan. (*Interpreting Religious Experience*, London, 1979, pp 51–3.) As far as I can determine, Donovan has only two reasons for his denial: (1) the importance of the fact that we have several senses which can be used to check one another, and (2) our scientific understanding of the 'processes involved in the production of our sense experiences'. Neither is convincing. While it is true that our confidence in our senses is partly based upon the fact that they corroborate one another, I fail to see how the possibility of mutual corroboration depends upon the existence of different *physical organs* (as distinguished from the existence of different modes of experience). (Notice, too, that an appeal to such things as agreement or successful predictions would seem to be relevant to the evaluation of visual or auditory experiences even if no physical organs were involved.) Donovan is undoubtedly correct in asserting that our scientific knowledge of sense experience is largely made possible by the fact that it is intimately bound up with physical organs. But how relevant is this knowledge to an appreciation of sense perception's cognitive validity? It is certainly not necessary, for, it it were, it would follow that sense experiences and the criteria used to evaluate them were not known to be reliable until quite recently.)

It is unclear whether the special *character* of the tests (the emphasis upon agreement and successful predictions) is among the features which lead us to speak of sense experiences as cognitive. Though I cannot prove it, I believe that, with one exception, I have considered all of the features one might reasonably suppose to be logically bound up with the cognitive status of sense experience. The exception is causality. Some would argue that in order for a sense experience to be veridical, its object must be among its causes. It is not certain that this is correct. In any case, if theism is true, this condition is met by theistic mystical experiences, since God is a cause of everything that exists. Similarly, although the Ātman-

Brahman is not strictly a cause, it is believed to be the ground of all experience. (It is the awareness or consciousness in any act of awareness or consciousness.) It follows that if Advaita Vedānta is true, this condition is met by experiences of the Brahman. Again, nature (or some part of it) is a partial cause of extrovertive mystical experiences, and so on. Whether crucial or not, the condition in question may be met (in a rough and ready way) by mystical experiences. It is true, however, that (with the possible exception of extrovertive mystical experience) one cannot determine *whether* the condition is met independently of metaphysical and theological considerations. The practical value of an appeal to this consideration is therefore limited.

²¹ Or perhaps more accurately (since there are different types of mystical experience), as a *cluster* of modes of cognitive experience. Sense experience, too, is a cluster of modes of cognitive experience, although there is a difference since different modes of sense experience ultimately have the same object, viz, physical reality, whereas the different modes of mystical experience *may* have different objects (God, nature, one's own soul, etc.).

²² In addition, there are less significant similarities. For example, in both cases agreement is sometimes appealed to, to support the claim that the experience is authentic.

²³ The first consideration provides us with a reason for believing the *claims* which the (theistic) mystic makes. The second consideration provides us with a reason for believing *the mystic* when he makes those claims.

²⁴ But not for the reason Stace gives. According to Stace, ordinary visual or auditory experiences cohere with our other experiences and are hence objective. Hallucinatory experiences conflict with the rest of our experience and are therefore subjective. Since mystical experience excludes multiplicity, it neither coheres nor conflicts with experience as a whole. It is therefore neither objective nor subjective. Stace's argument will be criticised in chapter 4, but even if it were sound, it would not show that mystical experience is not subjective in the sense in which headaches and feelings of depression are subjective. Stace fails to distinguish 'noncognitive', i.e. 'providing *no* information' from 'delusive', i.e. 'providing *false* information'. Both can be meant by 'subjective'. That mystical experience does not conflict with the rest of our experiences shows that it is not delusive and is therefore not subjective in that sense. It does not show that it is not non-cognitive. For all Stace has shown to the contrary, mystical experience may be subjective in the same sense in which pains are subjective. (Cf Ninian Smart, 'Mystical Experience', *op cit.*)

²⁵ Antony Flew, *God and Philosophy*, London, New York, 1966, chapter 6; Paul Schmidt, *Religious Knowledge*, Glencoe, Illinois, 1961, chapter 8; Ronald Hepburn, *Christianity and Paradox*, London, 1958, p 37.

²⁶ I am slightly modifying Schmidt's argument, but not weakening it. Schmidt's argument is rather more lucid than the arguments of Flew and Hepburn, but all three make essentially the same point. For example, Hepburn argues that even if we (and no one else?) saw a red circle in the air whenever John was angry, we would be entitled to claim that John was angry on the basis of this experience only if we had learned by ordi-

nary procedures that the 'code' was reliable (i.e. to justify these claims we would have to show that a correlation obtained between seeing a red circle and John's anger, the latter being established by normal criteria).

27 H P Owen has made a similar point (*The Christian Knowledge of God, op cit*, pp 276–80). The demand for pragmatic justification leads to similar difficulties. People sometimes attempt to justify the cognitive validity of sense experience by appealing to the fact that it enables us successfully to deal with the external world. Whether religious experiences assist successful adaptation depends upon the nature of the external world. If supernaturalism is true, it is reasonable to suppose that they do. If it is objected that supernaturalism is only reasonable upon the assumption that religious experiences are veridical, one may reply that (1) this is not obviously true (since there are other reasons for believing in supernaturalism), and that (2), in any case, the pragmatic justification of sense experience involves a similar circularity. That sense experience leads to successful adaptation can only be justified by appealing to statements about human beings and their environment which are ultimately supported by sense experience.

28 Though mystical experience *might* be connected with the meanings of 'Ātman' and 'Nibbāna'.

29 *Pace* Schleiermacher as sometimes interpreted. (See *The Christian Faith*, Edinburgh, 1928.) John Wilson also attempted a reduction of this kind. (*Language and Christian Belief*, London, New York, 1958; *Philosophy of Religion*, London and New York, 1961.)

30 This might be doubted but it seems to me to be logically possible for God to annihilate the physical world without annihilating particular minds, and for Him to produce impressions in those minds which are similar to those which they would have had if the physical world had continued to exist. And if this is possible, it would seem to be possible for God to have created particular minds without having created a physical world at all, but instead to have produced impressions in those minds which are similar to those which they would have enjoyed if He had chosen to create a physical world. An idealism of this sort *may* be incoherent, but that it *is* incoherent is at least controversial.

31 Though I would admit that the fact that phenomenalism is more attractive in the one case than in the other, *might* indicate some underlying logical difference.

32 John Hospers offers an argument of this kind in *An Introduction to Philosophical Anlysis*, 2nd ed, Englewood Cliffs, New Jersey, 1967, pp 444–8.

33 Or which are such that there is no compelling reason to believe that they are delusive. It should be pointed out in this connection that experiences of God or Nibbāna cannot be as easily discounted as visions of Thor, since there are better reasons for doubting the existence of Thor than for doubting the existence of God or the reality of Nibbāna. Again, mystical experience is less suspect than visionary experience for the contents of the latter do seem to conflict, and are more obviously culturally conditioned. (Though one must be careful. While the content of Teresa's visionary experiences of Christ seems to conflict with the content of a Norseman's vision of Odin, the existence of Christ and the existence of Odin are not

logically incompatible. The conflict appears to be between the value and importance, the existential meaning and significance, of the visionary objects (which is itself part of the visionary content) rather than between the visionary objects as such.)

[34] Strictly speaking, what is immediately warranted by a veridical noetic experience is the claim to have perceived its phenomenological object. When a experience's phenomenological object (e.g. a desk-like surface) is distinct from its apparent object (e.g. a desk), two types of perceptual error are possible; one's claim to have perceived the experience's apparent object may be mistaken, or one's claim to have perceived its phenomenological object may be mistaken. Although both mistakes are perceptual mistakes, they have very different implications. A claim to have perceived an experience's apparent object not only reflects the subject's experience and his linguistic competence (e.g. his understanding of the concept of a desk), but also reflects (true or false) beliefs which he brings to his experience (e.g. that desk-like surfaces normally belong to desks). Perceptual error may be due to these beliefs and not to any defect in the experience upon which his perceptual claim was based. By contrast, when a claim to have perceived an experience's phenomenological object is mistaken, the experience itself is delusive. Suppose, for example, that I claim to see a desk-like surface because I am having the sort of visual experiences which I would have had if a desk-like surface had been present, but that in fact there is no desk-like surface in front of me. In this instance, my *experience* has misled me, not my beliefs about how things are.

[35] It seems to me that numinous experience is the other type of religious experience with legitimate cognitive pretensions. If other modes of religious experience have legitimate cognitive pretensions, then they too should be included. (Remember that the point of the original argument is that apparently valid religious 'intuitions' conflict.)

[36] Or at least this is the only type of experience which is (*pace* Wittgenstein) non-controversially cognitive and of which this is true. Self-evident intuitions of moral truths and rules of logic might also be experiences of this type, but their cognitive value is controversial.

[37] To be in a position to make these claims one must not only have mystical or numinous experiences, and be linguistically or conceptually competent, one must also know or believe certain things about God, or the Brahman or Nibbāna. One must know, for example, that an invisible loving presence is probably God, or that empty consciousness is an aspect of Brahman, or that Nibbāna is cessation ('stopping').

[38] There is another objection to (5). One of the criteria which in practice is used to distinguish veridical religious experiences from those which are not is the compatibility of the claims that are immediately based upon a religious experience with orthodox talk. Because this is the case, the adherent of a religious tradition can argue that the only mystical or numinous experiences which meet *all* of the appropriate criteria are experiences which are such that the claims which are immediately based upon them are compatible with orthodoxy. Since the only experiences

which will pass the tests are those which are compatible with orthodoxy, it is unlikely that there will be many serious conflicts between the claims which are immediately based on mystical or numinous experiences meeting the appropriate criteria. The only possible conflicts will be between claims neither of which are unorthodox, and it is difficult to find clear examples of conflicts of this type.

39 See, for example, James H Leuba, *The Psychology of Religious Mysticism*, London, New York, 1925.

40 Kenneth Wapnick, 'Mysticism and Schizophrenia', *The Highest State of Consciousness*, ed by John White, Garden City, New York, 1972. (The article originally appeared in the *Journal of Transpersonal Psychology*, 1 (1969), pp 49–67.)

41 William James, *Varieties of Religious Experience*, New York, 1936, p 417.

42 Again, a number of the examples cited by Ben-Ami Scharfstein (*Mystical Experience*, Oxford, New York, 1973) are also misleading. 'Self-loss' experiences which consist in observing oneself from outside or in a sense of breaking apart (p 137) are not especially reminiscent of mystical ex-perience.

43 John Custance, *Wisdom, Madness and Folly: The Philosophy of a Lunatic*, New York, c 1952. The quoted passages occur between pp 30 and 52. Sexual inhibitions were also relaxed. This is of some interest in view of the contention that nature mysticism is amoral. (See chapter 5.)

44 *Ibid* pp 73 and 79.

45 Quoted in Carney Landis, *Varieties of Psychopathological Experience*, New York (etc.), 1964, p 290. I am not aware of any instances in which a psychopath experienced states that were phenomenologically *identical* with those of (normal) monistic or theistic mystics.

46 William James, *op cit*, p 149.

47 Quoted in Landis, *op cit*, p 252.

48 It might be argued that the first test is irrelevant since, if the world really is as it appears in the horrific vision, insane reactions (and not wisdom, humility or charity) are appropriate. On the other hand, the *thrust* of the first test is that the effects upon the mystic should be what one would expect them to be if he had actually encountered what he allegedly encountered. Now the horrific vision purports to be an experience of the real character of the space-time world. Most of us believe that the space-time world is not as the psychotic apprehends it, and therefore conclude that his reactions are inappropriate.

49 The content of mystical experience does not conflict with the content of ordinary experience in this manner. One indication of this is the fact that there are many philosophical and theological systems which are subscribed to by large numbers of non-mystics that can accommodate the content of mystical experience. (The major religions, Platonism, Absolute Idealism, etc.) The only theological or philosophical system which *might* accommodate the content of the horrific vision is the system which Jean-Paul Sartre articulated in *Being and Nothingness*. The experience of *things* (as distinguished from consciousness) that he describes in *Nausea* is somewhat similar to the horrific vision.

50 R C Zaehner, *The Comparison of Religions*, Boston, 1962. (Published in Great Britain as *At Sundry Times*, London, 1958.) Page references in this section will be to this work unless otherwise noted.

51 Cf *Mysticism, Sacred and Profane, op cit,* pp 48 and 99.

52 Cf *Concordant Discord, op cit,* p 277, and *Drugs Mysticism and Make Believe, op cit,* pp 57–8.

53 See especially *Our Savage God*, London, 1974, chapter 1. There are passages in which Zæhner seems to ascribe a certain validity to nature mysticism. He suggests, for example, that nature mysticism 'is a revelation of the unity of man with the spirit that sustains all nature' (prakṛti? prāna?) (*Mysticism Sacred and Profane*, p 104). In *The Comparison of Religions*, he considers the possibility that this spirit 'is the Spirit of God in its relationship to the subrational order for which the moral law does not apply,' and asserts ' that such a spirit exists seems to be attested by the experience of all nature mystics.' (p 183; cf *Mysticism, Sacred and Profane*, p 201) Nevertheless, Zæhner's last word on the subject appears to be that the experience is 'purely subjective' and 'bears no relationship to Nature as seen objectively'. (*Drugs, Mysticism and Make Believe*, p 50; cf p 60)

54 I happen to think that non-cognitivism is false, but my point is that the claim that moral mistakes are cognitive mistakes is controversial.

55 Cognitive experiences are ways of knowing. A veridical visual experience, for example, involves knowing that certain things are the case. ('I see a table' entails 'I know that a table is there.' If I do not know that a table is there, then I am at most entitled to say that I think I see a table, or that I seem to see one.) A mere experience, whether the experience of pain or the experience of being appeared to redly, is not knowledge. Pains, being appeared to redly, and other experiences of this kind are neither veridical nor non-veridical; they just occur.

56 Maritain thinks that all knowledge incorporates judgment. (*Distinguish to Unite, or the Degrees of Knowledge*, transl by Gerald B Phelan, London, New York, 1959, p 89.)

57 *Ibid* p 310

58 That Maritain wishes to say this is suggested by his remarks on pp 95–6.

59 But what about animals? According to Aquinas, animals apprehend that a particular man is friendly, or that a particular object is harmful, but their apprehension of these things does not involve concepts, since concepts are universals and the power to grasp the universal belongs to the rational intellect. Animals thus judge, but do not use concepts. (See Frederick Copleston, *Aquinas*, Harmondsworth, 1955, pp 174–8.) I am inclined to respond that if animals judge, then they *must* use concepts. If, on the other hand, they only do something *analogous* to what we do when we judge, they need only employ something *analogous* to concepts, for example, images or habitual associations. Now Maritain might concede this, for he could be construed as arguing that, because contemplation is a form of knowledge, it must involve some analogue of the concept. If Maritain's account of mysticism is correct, this analogue is the consciously experienced effects of infused charity. If this is indeed Maritain's view, then he and I agree that mystical knowledge must involve something like

a concept, but disagree as to its nature. I am convinced that 'obscure' and 'general' concepts are involved in the theistic mystic's apprehension of God, and perhaps in other introvertive experiences as well. Maritain believes that the 'passion' of infused charity functions *like* a concept. (Maritain's hypothesis will be examined in detail in chapter 4.)

[60] Joseph Maréchal, *Studies in the Psychology of the Mystics*, transl by Algar Thorold, Albany, New York, 1964, p 187.

[61] A move of this sort appears to be made by Maréchal on p 194.

[62] Notice that the (alleged) fact that conceptual thought is ultimately grounded in sensation and imagination, and that concepts are abstracted from 'sensible species', does not entail that imagery *accompanies* all conceptual thought.

[63] For example, John of the Cross says that 'in order for the understanding to be prepared for this Divine union, it must be pure and void of all that *pertains to sense*, and detached and freed from all that can *clearly* be apprehended by the understanding.' (*Ascent of Mt Carmel*, transl and ed by E Allison Peers, Garden City, New York, 1958, p 200. My italics.) He speaks of the absence of '*distinct* knowledge', and contrasts this with a knowledge which is '*general* and dark'. (*Living Flame of Love, op cit*, p 113. My italics.) Notice that while John insists on the absence of *all* sensible content, he only insists on the absence of all *clear, distinct*, and *specific* intellectual content.

[64] Or at least they provide little evidence that introvertive mystical consciousness is always, or normally, devoid of conceptual content. It is interesting to find Maritain asserting that although 'distinct concepts are all silent', 'confused' or 'indistinct' concepts may 'intervene' and, while remaining 'quite unperceived, play a ... material role' in the experience even though they do not function as 'formal means of knowing'. (*Distinguish to Unite*, p 264; cf p 109 fn2, and pp 339–40) According to Maritain, then, concepts may *accompany* theistic mystical experience although the object of the experience is not in any way grasped *through* these concepts. However, once it is conceded that the theistic mystic is not abstracted from all concepts, there no longer seems to be any reason to deny that those concepts structure his intuition. Theistic mystical experience would resemble sense experience in this respect. Although the sense object is immediately apprehended, it is apprehended through concepts. The tree is seen *as a tree*.

[65] According to Leuba, the introvertive mystic progressively reduces the contents of his consciousness until he lapses into complete unconsciousness.

[66] Robert Gimello, 'Mysticism and Meditation', *Mysticism and Philosophical Analysis, op cit*, p 193.

[67] *Ibid* p 185.

[68] David Kalupahana, *Buddhist Philosophy: An Historical Analysis*, Honolulu 1976.

[69] See Edward Conze, *Buddhist Thought in India*, Ann Arbor, Michigan, 1967, pp 161–3.

[70] Yogācāra placed particular emphasis upon the cultivation of the trance

states; it is difficult to believe that there was no connection between their mystical experiences and their metaphysics.

[71] Theravāda at least *seems* to speak of Nibbāna as some sort of transcendent state. Furthermore, some of the best known characterisations of Nibbāna (e.g. *Udāna* 80–1, or *Milindapañha* 268–71) are reminiscent of descriptions which monistic mystics have given of the 'object' of their experiences. These facts are not conclusive, but they are suggestive.

[72] Ninian Smart, *Doctrine and Argument in Indian Philosophy*, London, 1964, p 220.

[73] For an excellent discussion of the Advaitin view, see Eliot Deutsch, *Advaita Vedanta, a Philosophical Reconstruction*, Honolulu, 1973, pp 86–8.

[74] Of course this is oversimplified. In establishing a presumption in favour of the cognitive validity of mystical experience, I was necessarily forced to consider objections, particularly the objection that mystical experience is not cognitive since it is radically unllke paradigmatic cognitive experiences. Nevertheless, the thrust of part I was that, because mystical experiences are more like sense experiences than like paradigmatic instances of subjective experience, they are apparent cognitions with claims upon our belief.

CHAPTER 4

Some Theories of Mysticism

This chapter will examine two theories of mysticism. The first was formulated by Walter Stace in *Mysticism and Philosophy*. The second was developed over a number of years by Roman Catholic neo-scholastics. We will consider two of its versions – the version of Étienne Gilson, and that of Jacques Maritain. Stace's theory is familiar to most students of mysticism. Although the neo-scholastic theory is less widely known, it is equally sophisticated. Both purport to be theories of mysticism in general, but because Stace equates a fully developed mysticism with an absolutely unitary consciousness, and because the neo-scholastics tended to dismiss non-theistic mysticism as spurious or inferior, their theories are in fact theories of monistic mysticism and theistic mysticism respectively.

I shall argue that these theories are inadequate. Nevertheless, both theories are impressive attempts to make sense of (certain kinds of) mystical experience, and their mistakes will prove instructive.

The argument of this chapter will provide support for the following contentions:

(1) There is no reason to believe that mystical experience transcends the distinction between subjectivity and objectivity.

(2) There is no reason to believe that mysticism transcends logic.

(3) There is no reason to believe that (monistic) mysticism supports the position that a person's true self is identical with the Ground of Being and with the true selves of other persons.

(4) There is no reason to believe that 'dualism' is false, i.e. that the 'One', selves and nature are not ontologically independent realities.

(5) There is no reason to believe that the apprehension of
the object of introvertive mystical experiences is mediated through other contents in the way in which our
apprehension of physical objects is mediated through
sense impressions.

These contentions are important since the beliefs in
question have a number of influential adherents, and in some
cases are part of the popular lore about mysticism.[1]

I

Stace contends that (1) mystical experience is neither subjective nor objective, that (2) the laws of logic do not apply to
statements about the mystical experience or its object, that (3)
the Pure Self of any one person is the same as the Pure Self of
any other person, and the same as the World Self, and that (4)
the mystical One both is and is not identical with souls and
with nature.[2] These theses are not novel. Similar theses are frequently found in the literature of mysticism. What *is* novel is
that Stace's attempt to explain and defend them is both clearer
and more careful than usual. As such, any serious consideration of mysticism must sooner or later come to terms with
Stace. What follows is an examination of his account of these
claims.

A

According to Stace, an objective experience is an experience
which is orderly, in the sense that its object (not the experience
itself, although Stace does not always make this clear) displays
'internal' and 'external' order. By this he means that the items
which are experienced, their connection with one another, and
their connection with other items in the world, must be such
that they can be subsumed under, and (with the help of certain
antecedent conditions) explained by, true empirical laws. An
experience is subjective if the items which are experienced are
empirically impossible, or if they fail to cohere with each other
or with other items in the world in empirically law-like and
orderly ways, i.e. if the existence or occurrence of the
experienced items is ruled out by true empirical laws (and
antecedent conditions).[3]

Having provided a characterisation of what it means for an experience to be objective or subjective, Stace then argues in the following way:

(1) The (object of) introvertive mystical experience contains no distinguishable items at all. Therefore,

(2) The (object of) introvertive mystical experience contains no items which conform to law or which are connected with other items in empirically law-like and orderly ways, and it contains no items which conflict with empirical laws or with other items. (From 1.) Therefore,

(3) The experience is neither objective nor subjective. (From 2 and the characterisations of objectivity and subjectivity.)[4]

Stace often appears to use 'the experience of the One' ('the mystical experience', 'the unitary consciousness') and 'the One' (the object of mystical experience) interchangeably. He would undoubtedly wish to defend this practise on the grounds that the mystic experiences 'no duality of subject and object'. Nevertheless, I think that the distinction can be made, and that the failure to make it is confusing. This is true in the case at hand. It sometimes appears that what is crucial is that the *experience* is undifferentiated. (pp 144–5) At other times the crucial consideration appears to be that the *object* of mystical experience is free from distinctions. It follows that Stace's argument can be interpreted in two ways, depending on whether we understand him to be speaking of the experience as a whole or of its object.

If we suppose that Stace is speaking of the experience as a whole, then the argument is a valid one. If the experience contains no distinguishable items, it presumably has no object. But if it has no object, then it has no object which could be lawful, or unlawful, either in itself or in its relations. Therefore, such an experience is neither objective nor subjective. The point of the argument, when construed this way, is that nothing is a candidate for an objective or subjective experience unless it has an object (as dreams, hallucinations, and veridical sense perceptions have objects). If the mystical experience has no object, it is not a candidate and so is neither objective nor subjective.[5]

If we interpret Stace's argument in this way, then, while the argument is valid, its first premise is not clearly true. Theistic mystical consciousness is introvertive and has an object. Of course Stace believes that all introvertive experience is essentially monistic but, if I am correct (chapter 3, II*E*), monistic experience, too, has a kind of object. If it does not, it is not a candidate for a cognitive experience. To say that the experience has no object (not even the Pure Self) makes nonsense of the analogy with sense experience, and of the mystic's claim to an immediate knowledge or awareness of something which transcends ordinary experience.

As we have seen, one must handle the texts carefully. It is clear that the world sometimes vanishes from the view of the introvertive mystic, and that his experience has no ordinary or empirical object. It does not follow that the mystic's experience has no object at all. Therefore, any text which can plausibly be interpreted as merely denying the absence of sensuous content, ordinary discursive thought, etc. fails to support the claim that the experience is *completely* devoid of content and multiplicity. Again, it is one thing to say that the mystical object is an undifferentiated unity, and quite a different thing to say that mystical experience is an undifferentiated unity. Even if the One is free from multiplicity, it does not follow that an experience of the One is a bare unity devoid of content. If one approaches the texts with these points in mind, he will find that the evidence which is offered for the first premise (as presently interpreted) fails to establish it. (See, for example, the texts Stace cites on p 88ff.)

If we suppose that Stace is speaking of the *object* of mystical experience, then not only is his first premise dubious, his argument is invalid. (1) His first premise is dubious. Although monistic mystics do sometimes speak as if the object of their experience was an undifferentiated unity, they also, upon occasion, distinguish various moments or aspects or properties of that object.[6] For example, Advaita Vedānta speaks of the nirguna Brahman as 'being-consciousness-bliss'. Plotinus sometimes refers to his highest principle as the One, but sometimes as the Good. (2) On the second interpretation, Stace's conclusion does not follow from his premises and the characterisations of objectivity and subjectivity. To establish (3) we would have to show not only that the object does not *contain* items which are lawful or lawless and which cohere or conflict with other items, but also that the object of the experience *as a whole* is neither lawful nor lawless, and neither coheres nor conflicts with other items. It seems clear that the latter does not follow from (1) and (2) and the characterisations of objectivity and subjectivity, and that therefore (3) does not follow from (1) and (2) and the characterisations of objectivity and subjectivity.

In practice, mystics frequently claim that the object of their experience is related to other things in a number of real and important ways. For example, the One is often said to be the ground of the world and the Self, thus giving it a kind of semi-causal status. The relations in question are not empirical relations however, i.e. they are not the sorts of relations which could be discovered by science.

A moment's consideration of this point is worth while for it suggests that, given Stace's characterisations of subjectivity and objectivity, (3) is true, even if it is not established by his argument.

An experience is objective if its object is lawful and coheres with other objects in law-like ways. An experience is subjective if the existence of its object would falsify laws which do in fact hold. The laws in question are empirical laws, i.e. the sort of laws or connections which can be discovered by science or common sense. It follows that an experience is objective or subjective only if its object is the sort of thing whose existence or occurrence *can* conform to or conflict with empirical laws. The object of mystical experience does not seem to be the sort of thing whose existence could conform to or conflict with empirical laws. (It is often said to be spaceless, timeless, causeless, unchanging, etc.) It follows that the mystical experience is not objective and not subjective in Stace's sense.

But the *most* that Stace has established is that mystical experience is neither objective nor subjective in this sense. His conclusion is thus much weaker than it appears to be.

A person who calls an experience 'objective' or 'subjective' may have a number of different things in mind. For example, in calling an experience subjective, someone may be calling our attention to any one of the following facts:

(1) That the object of the experience is empirically lawless (Stace).

(2) That the experience is more like pains, feelings of depression and headaches than like sense perception.

(3) That the experience is delusive – the kind of experience which leads to error. (Though one may learn that this kind of experience does so and not be misled.) A mirage experience would be subjective in this sense.

(4) That the experience is causally connected with making certain kinds of subjective statements (but not with making objective statements), and that the experience in question is typically appealed to in order to justify statements of that kind.

Similarly, in calling an experience objective, someone may be calling our attention to any one of the following facts:

(1') That the object of the experience is empirically lawful (Stace).

(2') That the experience is more like sense perception than like pains, feelings of depression and headaches.

(3') That the experience leads to new truths, or to a confirmation of old truths.

(4') That the experience is causally connected with the making of a kind of objective claim which can be legitimately backed by an appeal to that sort of experience.

By a subjective claim, one may mean:

(a) A first-person psychological report.

(b) A claim which cannot satisfactorily be justified by the person who makes it. (For example, suppose I say, 'There are purple lemons on some planet.')

(c) A claim which is in principle untestable, or such that one does not know what a reason for or against it would be like.

(d) A claim whose truth or falsity cannot, in principle, be decisively determined by every normal person with the necessary intelligence. (Philosophers have occasionally suggested that there are certain truths which cannot be made out by just any intelligent and trained individual, but only by those who possess some special qualification. For example, a 'well constituted soul', 'openness to the transcendent', etc. One might want to call these truths subjective.)

(e) A claim which is unreasonable, absurd or wildly wrong.

In a similar way an objective claim may be thought of as:

(a') A claim about something other than the psychological states of the person who makes it.

(b') A claim which can satisfactorily be justified by the person making it.

(c') A testable claim and/or a claim such that one has an idea of the kind of thing that counts for or against it.

(d') A claim whose truth or falsity can, in principle, be determined by any normal person with the necessary intelligence, training and equipment. (Scientific claims are objective in this sense.)

(e') A claim which is true and such that good reasons can be provided for it.

I do not contend that this is an exhaustive list of the possible meanings of 'objective experience', 'subjective experience', 'objective claim', and 'subjective claim'. Some of the characterisations I have offered are somewhat vague and imprecise. Furthermore, when someone speaks of an experience or a claim as objective or subjective, he is more likely to have some of these things in mind than others. All of this must be admitted. Nevertheless, enough has been said to show that one may prove that mystical experiences are neither subjective nor objective in one sense, but leave open the possibility that they are objective or subjective in some other, important sense. More strongly, to show that mystical experience is neither objective nor subjective in one sense (and this is, at most, what Stace does) is *not* to show that the experience is neither objective nor subjective. To show that mystical experience is neither objective nor subjective, one would have to show *either* that the experience was neither objective nor subjective in any of the senses which can be given to the expressions 'objective experience' and 'subjective experience', *or* that the senses in which it is objective or subjective are not interesting or important or what anyone has in mind when he speaks of experiences as 'objective' or 'subjective'. Stace has performed neither of these tasks.[7]

B

Theories of mysticism must take account of the fact that mystics sometimes employ language which is, if taken literally, logically incoherent. Those who are sympathetic to mysticism often try to explain these apparent contradictions away. Stace, however, adopts the position that (1) the mystics' paradoxical remarks are to be taken literally, and that (2) what is said is true or correct.[8]

Stace argues that because (1) mystics who have had a number of mystical experiences continue to use paradoxical language, because (2) mystics from different cultures and different historical periods use paradoxical language, and because (3) these mystics are, for the most part, unfamiliar with each other's traditions, it is reasonable to assume that their language correctly describes mystical experience and/or its object. Stace's argument is, of course, a non-sequitur. His premises support the conclusion that paradoxical language often *seems* appropriate, but not that it *is* appropriate.[9]

But let us suppose that the mystic's paradoxical language is in some sense true, apt, correct or appropriate. Why should we take it at face value? Because, according to Stace, attempts to eliminate the mystic's contradictions are subject to decisive objections. These attempts are of essentially three kinds. The mystic's paradoxes may be explained as instances of rhetorical exaggeration, as metaphors, or as instances of verbal ambiguity.[10]

(1) Mystical paradoxes are sometimes explained as rhetorical devices. For example, when a mystic says that he both is and is not identical with God, he may be using exaggerated language to express an experience of intimate union. This theory is not implausible since we often use exaggerated language to express ecstatic or deeply moving experiences and intense emotional excitement. Stace dismisses the theory on the grounds that it ignores the fact that it is the mystic's *thought*, and not merely his language, which is paradoxical. Although this begs the question, it may be conceded that the theory of rhetorical exaggeration works better in some cases than in others. (While 'I am and yet am not identical with God' can be plausibly explained as an instance of rhetorical exaggeration, 'reality is neither void nor non-void, nor both,

nor neither' cannot.)

(2) But perhaps the mystic's paradoxes can be interpreted as metaphors. If Stace is correct, one cannot coherently suppose that *all* mystical language is metaphorical. In the first place, one is only entitled to say that x is metaphorically y when x and y resemble one another. But if x and y resemble one another, they have some property, P, in common and, in that case, x is literally P. For example, if it is appropriate to speak of mystical love as a flame, then mystical love must have some property in common with flames which it literally possesses.[11]

In the second place, although one can initially explain one metaphor by another, one must ultimately provide a non-metaphorical explanation if one's metaphor is to be intelligible. For example, the Brahman's relation to the world may be expressed by the image of the sun which emits light and heat, and the point of this image may be explained by other images. (Water welling from a spring, for example, or a plant growing from a seed.) Nevertheless, in the absence of a literal account of the Brahman's relation to the world, these images will ultimately prove unintelligible.

Neither of these arguments is convincing. In the first place, it is not clear that 'x is like y' entails 'There is some P such that x is like y in that both are P.' The scholastics, for example, argued that the being, goodness or unity of such diverse things as stones, oaks, lions, men and angels were analogous or similar even though it is impossible to abstract a set of common characteristics in which that similarity consists. Nor is it clear that every instance of colour similarity can be explained by the possession of a common property.[12] In the second place, it is not true that literal paraphrases are always necessary. As Stace admits, a person may understand a metaphor because he is directly acquainted with its terms. For example, even though I am unable to provide a literal paraphrase, I understand 'the sound of a trumpet is like scarlet' because I know what scarlet looks like and what trumpets sound like. This possibility is especially relevant in the case at hand, since mystics claim to be immediately acquainted with the objects which they describe.

But even though Stace's arguments are unsound, his conclusion is undoubtedly correct. Some mystical language is not metaphorical.[13] (For example, 'the experience is bliss'.) Nevertheless, unless all mystical language is paradoxical, this is irrelevant.[14] From the fact that some mystical language is literal, it does not follow that all mystical language is literal: some of it may not be. Hence, with respect to any paradox, it is possible that what is said is intended metaphorically, and that the contradiction is only apparent.

(3) Even if there are some mystical paradoxes which can neither be explained as metaphors, nor as instances of rhetorical exaggeration, it does not follow that they are self-contradictions, for terms are sometimes used ambiguously. Thus, Stace considers the possiblity that 'mystical consciousness is something (i.e., not nothing) and nothing' is consistent because 'nothing' in its first occurrence means 'non-existent', while in its second occurrence it means 'is nothing to the intellect, i.e. is something which cannot be conceptually understood'. He argues, however, that even if ambiguation can resolve this particular paradox, it cannot resolve such central paradoxes as 'The world is the same as God and yet different from Him', and 'In the unitary experience, I both do and do not continue to exist.'[15]

It is significant that mystics have sometimes attempted to resolve their own paradoxes by ascribing contradictory predicates to different subjects. For example, Saṁkara and Eckhart attribute emptiness, rest and unity to the nirguṇa Brahman (the Brahman without attributes) or the Godhead, and fullness, movement and multiplicity to the saguṇa Brahman (the Brahman with attributes) or God. Stace believes that these theories of 'double location'[16] are inadequate. In the first place, both Śaṁkara and Eckhart speak as if the higher Brahman or Godhead *produced* the lower Brahman or God. But in speaking in this way, they have introduced motion and activity into something which is essentially motionless and inactive. Therefore, they have not eliminated the contradiction. (p 172f) In the second place, the double location theory is unable to resolve the two paradoxes to which I have already alluded – that God (i.e. the One) is and is not the same as the world, and that, in the unitary experience, the I ceases to exist and yet somehow continues to exist. We cannot assign sameness to

God (and not to the world) and difference to the world (and not to God) because sameness and difference are relations between the two terms and not properties which might be possessed by one but not the other. Again, while it may be possible to distinguish two divine principles, it makes no sense to suppose there that there are two selves.

This is unconvincing. That a motionless and inactive Godhead produces God may be self-contradictory. But that the lower Brahman depends upon the higher Brahman for its reality, or that the lower Brahman just *is* the way in which the higher Brahman appears to the spiritually immature, is not obviously self-contradictory. Furthermore, it is much closer to what Śaṃkara had in mind. It is thus not clear that the relation between a higher and lower divine principle cannot be expressed without self-contradiction.

The double location theory is able to resolve the paradox that the One both is and is not the same as the world, not by assigning sameness to the One and difference to the world, but (for example) by assigning difference to the relation between the higher principle and the world, and sameness to the relation between the lower principle and the world. There is a basis for this in Advaita Vedānta. The Brahman without attributes transcends the world, but the Brahman with attributes has three forms or aspects – Īśvara, which is roughly Brahman thought of as a kind of seed or germ from which the world develops; the hiranyagarbha, or Brahman thought of as a kind of world soul; and the virāt or Brahman as the manifest universe. These three are in some sense identical with different aspects of nature.[17]

The second paradox can be easily resolved by the double location theory. Mystics typically distinguish between a person's true self (nous, Ātman, puruṣa, etc.) and his empirical self (soul, jīva, manas, etc.). This distinction can be used to explicate 'I cease to exist and yet continue to exist.' In its first occurrence 'I' refers to the empirical ego. In its second occurrence it refers to the pure ego. There is thus no contradiction.

My point is not that all mystical paradoxes can either be explained as metaphors, or instances of rhetorical exaggeration, or resolved by ambiguation. Some of them cannot. (For example, the claim that reality is neither void, nor not void, nor both, nor neither.[18]) My point is that Stace has not shown that any of these strategies is unable to resolve *some* paradoxes, and he has not shown that there is *any* paradox which cannot be resolved by some strategy of this type. He has thus not shown that mystical paradoxes must be taken at face value.[19]

But let us suppose that there are mystical paradoxes which should be taken at face value, i.e. that mystics sometimes make statements which express genuine contradictions, and that they do so deliberately. If Stace is correct, these statements are true. And yet how can a statement be true if it is logically incoherent?[20] Stace tells us that it cannot be if the statement is about a multiplicity of items, but that it can be if the statement is about an undifferentiated unity. Principles of logic hold only in those 'experiences, realms, or worlds' which contain two or more items. Therefore, while statements about the world or the items in it can be logically evaluated, statements about the One cannot be, and thus, if a statement about the One is self-contradictory, we cannot draw the conclusion that that statement is false. (pp 270–4)

Stace's remarks are not transparent, but it is fairly clear that he is maintaining that principles of logic only hold in worlds which contain two or more members, and/or that logic applies to experiences that involve multiplicity, but not to unitary experiences, and/or that statements which are not about two or more items cannot be logically evaluated. No matter which alternative we choose, Stace's argument is unsound.

(1) Let us suppose that what Stace is suggesting is that a statement of, for example, the form $(p \rightarrow q. \& p) \rightarrow q$ (and the corresponding inference rule) holds in any possible world which contains two or more items, but not in a possible world which contains no more than one item. Just what this suggestion amounts to is not entirely clear, but one might conjecture that one of the following three propositions is intended. (a) Statements of, for example, the form $(p \rightarrow q. \& p) \rightarrow q$ are true (and the corresponding inference rule may be applied), if and only if the statements which are substituted for p and q are about, or describe, or apply to items in a universe with two or more members. (Thus, if one of a pair of propositions, A and B, is not about, and does not describe, and does not apply to items in a world with two or more members, then $(A \rightarrow B. \&$

A) → B is either false or neither true nor false [and the corresponding inference rule is either inapplicable, or neither applicable nor inapplicable, to the statements A → B and A].)
(b) Statements of, for example, the form (p → q. & p) → q are necessary (and the corresponding inference rule is binding), if and only if the statements which are substituted for p and q are about, or describe, or apply to, items in a universe with two or more members. (Thus, if one of a pair of propositions A and B, is not about, and does not describe, and does not apply to, items in a world with two or more members, then it is logically possible that (A → B & A & not-B) or (A → B. & A) → B is neither necessary nor possibly false [and the corresponding inference rule does not bind, or neither binds nor does not bind, a person who makes the statements A and A → B].)[21] (c) If one were to make a statement of, for example, the form (p → q. & p) → q (or use the corresponding inference rule) one would make a true statement (a legitimate inference) if and only if one were a member of a world with two or more members.

Even if one of these claims were true it would not yield the conclusion Stace wants. For example, if a proposition of the form (p → q. & p) → q is not true, or not necessary, or cannot be truly stated, in a world which is free from multiplicity, it does not follow that (A → B. & A) → B is not true, or not necessary, or cannot be truly stated, when A and B are statements about the One. This *would* follow *if* statements about the One did not describe, were not about, and did not apply to items in a world with two or more members, or if the person who makes these statements were not a member of a world with two or more members, but neither of these is the case.

The mystic does not (except metaphorically) gain access to a possible world which is different from our own, but to the underlying reality in that possible world of which we are all members. Unless monism is true (where monism is the view that, in spite of appearances, nothing is real except the undifferentiated One), statements about the One are statements about an item or items in a possible world (namely, our own) which contains two or more members. Stace does not think that monism is true. (pp 211 and 237ff) It follows that we have been given no reason to suppose that, for example, (A → B. &

A) → B is not true, or not necessary, or cannot be truly asserted, when A and B are statements about the One. Since similar points can be made if we replace (p → q. & p) → q with any other tautologous statement form or truth of logic, we may conclude that no reason has been given to suppose that principles of logic do not apply to the One.

(2) Stace asserts that logic applies to experiences and to objects of experience which involve multiplicity, but not to experiences or to objects of experience which are free from multiplicity. However, logic does not apply to experiences or objects, but to statements. (Experiences and objects do not entail one another, are not necessarily true, or self-contradictory, or logically contingent, etc.) Therefore, to say that logic only applies to experiences and to objects of experience which involve multiplicity, must be to say that statements which are about unitary experiences or their objects are not subject to logical evaluation, while statements about non-unitary experiences or the multiple realities which are their objects are subject to logical evaluation.

It follows that if the mystic's statements are about a unitary experience or its object, they are not subject to logical evaluation. The difficulty is that several important and *apparently contradictory* statements made by mystics appear to be about experiences, or objects, which involve multiplicity. For example, 'God and the world are distinct and identical', and 'each distinct item in the world (each stone, each blade of grass, etc.) is one'. Both of these statements appear to be about two or more items – items, moreover, which (at least in the second case) are clearly given in the mystical experience itself. The laws of logic should therefore apply to these statements. Yet if the laws of logic do apply to them, and they are taken at face value, both statements are necessarily false.

Stace sees this difficulty, but I do not think he avoids it. Consider the following argument:

(1) If logic applies to a statement *s* (if *s* is subject to logical evaluation) then, if *s* is contradictory, *s* is (necessarily) false.

(2) Logic applies to statements which are about non-unitary experiences (or the complex object of these experiences).

(3) Our two statements are about (the complex object of) experiences which involve multiplicity.

(4) The statements in question are contradictory. Therefore,

(5) The statements in question are false.

The argument is valid and Stace finds the conclusion unacceptable. Therefore, if it is to have any point, his reply must show that one or more of the premises is false or dubious. It appears to be directed against the truth of (3).

Stace points out that some mystics think that realisation is incomplete until one no longer sees any distinction between Nirvāna and Samsāra (or the One and the Many), and adds that when we say that the Many is the sphere of logic and that the One is the sphere of paradox, we are standing in the Many, speaking from the point of view of everyday consciousness. The thrust of these remarks is not clear. Stace appears to be saying one or more of the following three things: (a) When one entertains one or more of premises (1) through (4), one is in an ordinary frame of mind. (b) Propositions (1) through (4) appear to be true to (a properly informed and reasonable) ordinary consciousness, but (c) one or more of these propositions appear false or neither true nor false to a fully developed mystical consciousness. If this is what Stace is saying, his reply is a failure. While (a) and (b) may be true it does not follow (from (a) and (b)) that (1), (2), (3), or (4) is false. But (c) is false, for Stace thinks that a fully developed mystical consciousness is a unitary consciousness, and *no* proposition appears to be true or false, or neither true nor false to unitary mystical consciousness. In order for a proposition to be considered true or false, etc. it must be considered, but if it is considered, we do not have a unitary mystical consciousness.[22]

In any case, to dispose of (3) would not dispose of the difficulty. Stace asserts that logic does not apply to statements which are about a unitary experience (or its object) but only to statements about experiences which involve multiplicity. But it is clear, I think, that it is not that the statements are about an *experienced* unity or multiplicity (or a unitary or multiple *experience*) which is crucial, but that they are about a unity or multiplicity. That is, Stace thinks that logic is restricted to statements about an experienced multiplicity (or about an experience in which there is multiplicity), only because he thinks that logic applies to statements about any multiplicity, but not to statements which are not about two or more items. This brings us to the last alternative.

(3) Stace believes that logic only applies to statements which are about a multiplicity of items. To meet this claim, we can reformulate our argument in the following way:

(1) If logic applies to a statement s (if s is subject to logical evaluation) then if s is contradictory, s is (necessarily) false.

(2) Logic applies to statements which are about two or more items.

(3) 'God is distinct from and identical with the world' and 'each distinct thing is one' are statements about two or more items.

(4) The statements in question are contradictory. Therefore,

(5) The statements in question are false.

It is again the case that the argument is valid and that its conclusion is unacceptable to Stace.

There is no indication that Stace wishes to take exception to (1) (and indeed (1) appears to be necessarily true). While it is hardly clear that logic fails to apply to statements which are *not* about two or more items, (2) would appear to be true. In any case, Stace, accepts it. (4) is dubious. The first statement may be infected by ambiguity, and the second statement may be an instance of rhetorical exaggeration. Nevertheless, Stace not only believes that (4) is true, but has argued for it at some length. This leaves him with only one option. Though Stace realises that the two statements appear to be about a multiplicity of items, he must deny (3). Nevertheless it is difficult to see what possible ground he could have for doing so.[23]

Stace, then, is in the following position. He must either deny (3) or accept (3). If he denies (3), he is denying something which is patently true. If he accepts (3) then (since (1) is necessary, and (2) and (4) and not (5) are part of his theory) he is inconsistent. In either case his position is untenable.

In summary, even if Stace were correct in contending that logic only applies where multiplicity is involved, he has not succeeded in showing how statements made by mystics can be both true and contradictory. He has not shown that the mystical paradoxes are not about items in a multiple world, or that they are not in many cases about two or more items, or that they are not made within a multiple world, and so on. Since he has not shown this, he has not shown that logic does not apply to the statements in question, and since he has not shown that logic does not apply to them, we must continue to suppose that they are false if they are logically impossible.

C

Stace offers the following argument to show that each individual's Pure Self is identical with every other individual's Pure Self, and with the World Self.

(1) There are Pure Selves. (Each individual *has* a Pure Self; the introvertive mystic becomes *aware of*, or *identical* with, his Pure Self.)
(2) Each Pure Self is contentless. Therefore,
(3) There is nothing to differentiate one Pure Self from another. (From 2 and the principle that, if *x* and *y* are contentless, there is nothing to differentiate *x* from *y*.)
(4) If there is nothing to differentiate *x* from *y*, then *x* = *y*. Therefore,
(5) Each Pure Self is identical with every other Pure Self. (From 3 and 4.) Therefore,
(6) There is one and only one Pure Self. (From 1 and 5.) Let us call this Pure Self, which is the same in all individuals and which the introvertive mystic finds by turning inward, 'the Introvertive One'.
(7) One and only one Unity or One lies 'behind' the world and its multiplicity. (This One is apprehended by the extrovertive mystic who turns outward to find the Unity 'within' things or 'behind' things.) We will call this Unity 'the Extrovertive One'.
(8) The Extrovertive One is contentless. Therefore,
(9) There is nothing to differentiate a Pure Self from the Extrovertive One. (From 2, 8, and the principle that if *x* and *y* are contentless, then there is nothing to differentiate *x* from *y*.) Therefore,
(10) Any Pure Self is identical with the Extrovertive One.

(From 4 and 9.) Therefore,

(11) There is something which is both a Pure Self and an Extrovertive One, and which is such that any Pure Self or Extrovertive One is the same as that thing, i.e. the Introvertive One and Extrovertive One exist and are identical. (From 6, 7, and 10.) (pp 149–52)

Stace admits that the claim that there are Pure Selves and a World Self is controversial. Indeed, he recognises that the very notion of a Pure Self is problematic. What I will show is that *even if* there are Pure Selves and a World Self, Stace's argument does not establish their identity.

The difficulty arises from the claim that the Pure Self is contentless. This claim could mean any one of four things:

(2a) A Pure Self has no properties.

(2b) A Pure Self has no empirical properties.

(2c) A Pure Self (at least during the period in which the mystic has temporarily freed it from its entanglement in nature) is aware of nothing.

(2d) A Pure Self (at least during the period in which the mystic has temporarily freed it from its entanglement in nature) is not aware of any empirical or ordinary object.[24]

Any one of these four propositions might be what is *meant* by the claim that Pure Selves are contentless. They should be distinguished from four other propositions which could be offered as reasons for them. These are:

(2i)   A Pure Self exhibits no property (to the introvertive mystic).

(2ii) A Pure Self exhibits no empirical property (to the introvertive mystic).

(2iii) During his experience the introvertive mystic is aware of nothing.

(2iv) During his experience the introvertive mystic is aware of no empirical or ordinary object.

While (2ii) and (2iv) appear to be true, (2i) and especially (2iii) are dubious.[25] Be this as it may, we are now in a position to see why Stace's argument is unsatisfactory.

If (2a) is true, then we can argue that, since there is *no* property which distinguishes one Self from another Self, each Self is identical with every other Self. Only (2a) is strong enough to yield this conclusion. If no properties differentiate x and y, we can conclude that they are identical. But we cannot draw this conclusion from the proposition that no *empirical* properties differentiate x and y, or from the proposition that x and y are aware of nothing empirical or from the proposition that they are aware of nothing at all. (It is almost certain that Stace thinks that (2d) implies (2c)[26] and he may think that (2c) and (2d) imply (2a) and (2b), respectively, and that (2b) implies (2a).[27])

(2a) is not clearly true. For one thing, 'the Self of any individual, A, has the property of being the Self of A' is a proposition which is plausible and which is incompatible with (2a). But there is a more serious difficulty. (2a) is incompatible with (1) (there are Pure Selves). Assuming that it is necessarily true that something exists only if it has some property or other, (2a) entails that there are no Pure Selves. If that is the case, (2a) and (1) cannot both be true. Since Stace accepts (1), he ought to reject (2a), but if he does his argument collapses.

In any case, none of the propositions (2i) through (2iv) entails (2a) (or (2b)).[28] Furthermore, the most plausible of these propositions (viz, (2ii) and (2iv)) have no tendency to show that (2a) is true. If Stace had some other ground for (2a) (i.e. some ground other than one or more of the propositions (2i) through (2iv)) these points would not be particularly damaging, but as far as I can see, he does not.[29]

In short, because Stace needs (2a) in order to establish his conclusion, and because there are good reasons for believing that (2a) is false and none for believing that (2a) is true, his argument is unsuccessful.

D

'Dualism' may be defined as the belief that God (or the 'One'),[30] the world and individual selves are three distinct things. Stace believes that dualism is incompatible with the implications of mystical consciousness, but he also thinks that it is a mistake simply to identify these things, or to suppose that there is nothing *but* the One ('monism'). The only viable position, according to Stace, is that God, the world and individual selves are *both* the same *and* different ('pantheism').[31]

Why are dualism and monism inadequate?

Dualism is inadequate for four reasons. First, dualists are unable to account for the fact that the mystic actually *experiences* identity with the One. Second, dualists cannot account for extrovertive mysticism. Third, mystics maintain that the One transcends relations. If the One is not related to anything else then there is nothing else, and dualism is false. (If there were something else, then the One would stand in *some* relation to it, if only the relation of difference.)[32] Finally, even dualists admit that God is infinite. But to be infinite is either to be mathematically infinite or to be unlimited by anything else, i.e. to be all there is, 'one without a second'. Since dualists deny that God is mathematically infinite, they cannot coherently maintain that the world and individual selves are different from God.

Stace's case against dualism is unconvincing. In the first place, Stace believes that even monistic mystics experience differentiation and not merely identity. Stace concludes that the (monistic) mystic is different from the One as well as identical with it, but unless the experiences of differentiation and (apparent) identity are successive, it would be equally plausible to conclude that what monistic mystics experience is not identity but union.[33]

Be this as it may, dualists can account for monistic experiences in which the mystic seems to experience identity and not merely union. For example, they can be explained as experiences of the mystic's 'naked essence' or true self.

Dualists can also account for extrovertive mysticism. For example, Zæhner has interpreted cosmic consciousness as an experience of the world viewed through the eyes of innocence, as an experience of the spirit of God in its relation to the subrational order, as an experience of a 'mindless' spirit diffused through the whole, and as an experience of 'matter'. Given theistic ('dualistic') presuppositions, none of these theories is *clearly* inadequate.[34]

That mystics sometimes fail to *experience* relations between the One and other things, hardly implies that there *are* no relations between the One and other things.

Finally, there are other relevant senses of 'infinite'. For example, 'God's infinity' may refer to the fact that God's power, knowledge and goodness are boundless, or it may refer to the fact that God's existence is underived and necessary and, in that sense, unlimited. Dualists are not forced to choose between mathematical infinity and 'being one without a second'.

Stace's arguments against monism are equally inconclusive. According to Stace, monism can take two forms – that God and the world are identical, and that God alone is real. The first is dismissed as silly. 'God' and 'the world' do not mean the same thing. If one wishes, one can use 'God' for what other people call the 'the world', but to do so is pointless and misleading. The second form of monism regards the world as an illusion, and this is incoherent. Illusion is explained by ignorance. But there is no such thing as ignorance *simpliciter*. Ignorance is always the ignorance of someone or something. Ignorance therefore must either be ascribed to the One or to something else, and yet neither alternative is acceptable. To say that the One is ignorant introduces the multiplicity of illusion into an undifferentiated unity. To locate ignorance in something else presupposes that that in which it is located is real[35] when, by hypothesis, nothing is real but the One.

Stace's first argument is seriously flawed. He appears to assume that in identifying God and the world, one is committed to the assertion that 'God' and 'the world' mean the same thing. In general, this sort of claim is false. Scott is identical with the author of *Waverley*, but 'Scott' does not mean the same thing as 'the author of *Waverley*,' and the criteria for their application may be quite different. (A person may know how to apply 'Scott' correctly and do so without knowing that Scott is the author of *Waverley*, and a person may know how to apply 'the author of *Waverley*' correctly and do so without ever having heard of Scott.) Suppose then, that someone says that while he uses 'God' (or the 'One', or 'the Divine') and 'the world' to refer to the same thing, he does not mean the same thing by these expressions. When he applies 'God' to the spatio-temporal manifold he has in mind one set of features (viz, those disclosed to the extrovertive mystic), but when he applied 'the world' to it, he has in mind a quite different set of features (viz, those disclosed to ordinary consciousness). This view may be mistaken but it is not *clearly* wrong, and it is not silly. (Although the use of 'God' is misleading since God is typically defined as omnipotent, omniscient, etc., and the thing to which 'the world' refers does not seem to exhibit these features. The use of 'the Divine' or the 'One' however would not be subject to the same strictures. Of course, one might argue that it is idolatrous to identify the divine and the world, but this is controversial.)

Stace's objection to the second form of monism is essentially sound, but he is not in a position to make it! As we have seen, Stace believes that logic does not apply to mystical consciousness or to the One, and that the mystic can therefore say incompatible things about them which are both true. If this is the case, then it is difficult to see how Stace can object to a theory of the One on the grounds that it is logically incoherent. Stace is aware of this problem, and responds by arguing that his objection is to the point since 'the monistic philosophy ... professes to be self-consistent'. (p 239) But even if this is true, it is irrelevant. The question is not whether monists are correct in thinking that their theory is consistent. The question is whether what they say about the One is true. Since Stace believes that the truth about the One need not be logically coherent, the fact that what monists say about the One is inconsistent is beside the point.

In summary, Stace's arguments against dualism and his first argument against monism are unsound. His second argument against monism is sound, but he is not in a position to use it. Stace's case for 'pantheism' is dependent entirely upon his case against dualism and monism. He has therefore failed to establish that the world, individual selves and the One both are and are not the same.

E

We have examined Stace's arguments for four contentions which are frequently encountered in the literature of mysticism. These arguments are unsuccessful. Let me conclude by suggesting that Stace's failure to establish his contentions is due neither to a lack of acumen nor to the fact that arguments are inappropriate in this realm. He fails because the contentions are false.

II

Towards the end of the last century, Roman Catholicism experienced a renewed interest in the Christian contemplative tradition. Although the philosophical and theological literature which grew out of this revival was sophisticated and interesting, it is not as widely known as it should be. In the second part of this chapter we will examine one strand of this material, viz, the accounts given by several of those philosophers and theologians of the cognitive component of theistic experience. At one extreme it was argued that the presence of God is merely inferred from the effects which God creates in the soul. At the other extreme it was contended that the mystic perceives God directly, without any kind of intervening medium.[36]

The first theory was generally, and I think correctly, dismissed on the grounds that it does not account for the perception-like character of mystical experience. Albert Farges speaks for most mystics and for most mystical theologians when he asserts that the experience involves ‘“an experimental knowledge of divine things or realities” – that is to say, not an abstract knowledge, but one that is concrete, intuitive, and without reasoning, analogous to that of the senses’.[37] Nevertheless, the first theory is by no means devoid of interest, and will be briefly examined in section A below. The second theory, in my opinion, is the one most naturally suggested by the mystical texts. But a third theory was widely accepted. According to this, the intellect, in the advanced stages of mystical contemplation, immediately perceives its object, but in doing so employs a quasi-sensible medium, viz, the love which God infuses in the soul of the mystic. I shall argue that this theory is unsound.

If theistic mystical consciousness really does involve knowledge of God (chapter 3), and if this knowledge is neither inferential nor similar to the types of perceptual knowledge which involved a quasi-sensible medium, then it seems reasonable to infer that theistic mystical consciousness beholds God ‘unveiled’. The argument which will be developed in the following sections thus provides an indirect defence of the claim that theistic mystics perceive God with the same immediacy with which they perceive sense data or their own mental contents.

The theories we are going to examine employ theological as well as philosophical considerations and are specifically designed to account for Christian mysticism. Nevertheless, they are of more than parochial interest. The accounts of mystical perception which are incorporated in some of these theories are primarily based on philosophical considerations, and could, with minor modifications, be adopted by non-Christian theists interested in providing a theoretical account of the cognitive aspect of any sort of theistic contemplation.

A

Henry Browne and Auguste Saudreau[38] maintained that theistic mystical experience does not normally involve an 'experimental' knowledge of divine things. There are reasons for taking their contention seriously. Both were intimately familiar with (Christian) mystical literature. Their books were not attacks upon mysticism's pretensions, but were designed to recommend the practice of contemplation. Finally, they shared the general theological assumptions and scholastic framework of the other parties to the dispute. This suggests, I think, that there is some feature of Christian contemplation which lends itself to the view that theistic mystical consciousness is not (normally) noetic. The implications of this view are significant, for if theistic mystical consciousness is not noetic, the question of its validity does not arise.

In the eleventh chapter of *Darkness or Light*, Browne argues that 'mystical vision' is a mode of faith. (He calls our attention to the fact that both faith and mystical contemplation have an 'infused and "passive" character', and that both are 'obscure'. (p 236)) What, then, differentiates mystical 'vision' from faith? Faith consists in believing something because God has said it. It thus has two objects. Faith's secondary object is the proposition which one accepts because one believes God, for example, that He will be our judge. Its primary object is the God whom one believes. Mystical prayer occurs when faith and love are, for the moment, directed only towards faith's primary object.

Saudreau's account is similar to Browne's but superior because it provides an explanation of the fact that mystics often speak of experiencing God's presence. The objects of the mystic's intellect are 'the truths known by faith: the greatness, perfections, amiability, incomprehensibility of God'. (p 57) Mystical contemplation normally involves nothing more than a 'general and confused' apprehension of God's greatness and perfection, but sometimes God 'acts powerfully in the intellect, presenting to it in a brilliant light certain distinct ideas' concerning His omnipotence, the mysteries of the Trinity, and so on. (p 149) In either case, what the mystic apprehends are *truths* or *propositions*. The only things which distinguish these 'infused' convictions from the convictions of ordinary faith are heightened certainty and deepened appreciation. (pp 57, 65–8, 148–50 and 160–1)

Why, then, do mystics speak as though they immediately perceived God's presence? First, because God's presence is easily inferred from the effects which He has produced in the contemplative's soul – its 'sense of well-being', its 'progress in virtue', sensations of 'sweetness', and 'feelings of love'. Second, because mystics sometimes enjoy an infused and irresistible *conviction* that God is present in their souls. Thus, even though contemplatives do not experimentally *perceive* God, it is natural for them to speak of feeling Him, or of enjoying His presence. (pp 67–70, 74–7, 83 and 86–7)[39]

What led Browne and Saudreau to adopt their theories? In part, they were motivated by doctrinal considerations. Thus, Browne argues that the beatific vision essentially consists in 'any direct and intuitive knowledge of His [God's] *existence* and Essence, *his Person and his attributes*' (p 164, my italics), that the beatific vision is impossible in this life, and that, therefore, contemplatives do not know God directly or by 'vision'. This argument is defective on at least two counts. That the beatific vision cannot be enjoyed in this life is a theological opinion which, while widely held, is not universally accepted. (See section D, below.) Browne also ignores the fact that the beatific vision is normally identified with a 'direct' and 'intuitive' knowledge of God's *essence* or inner life, not merely of His existence or (some of His) attributes. But even if this theological position were correct, doctrinal considerations cannot provide a philosophical reason for repudiating the possibility of a 'vision' of God.[40] And indeed both Browne and Saudreau admit that an experimental perception of God is not intrinsically impossible. (Saudreau even concedes that, although rare and exceptional, direct contact may sometimes occur in the experience of contemplatives who have passed through the dark night of the soul. (pp 95–6)[41]) Their case, therefore, must ultimately rest upon the strength of the textual evidence which they can muster on its behalf.

Some of their proof texts must be discounted. For example, in supporting his position, Sandreau appeals to passages in which mystics assert that during their experience they did not reflect upon God's presence, passages in which they maintain that they did not behold God within their hearts but at a distance, passages in which they describe periods of aridity where God was absent, and passages in which they express the conviction that their experiences could not have been delusive since the effects were joy, peace and love. (pp 71, 77–82, and 89) But (1) that mystics do not reflect upon God's presence does not imply that they do not experience God's presence. (2) That God is experienced as other or transcendent (rather than immanent) does not imply that God is not experienced as present. (Numinous experience, for example, has a transcendent object, but this transcendent object is *encountered*.) (3) While aridity is a 'mystical state', i.e. a state which typically occurs to mystics at certain stages in their careers, it is not clear that it should be regarded as a mystical experience. Indeed, it appears to be at least partly caused by the *absence* of mystical experience. Aridity is a state of depression, lassitude and spiritual languor which normally follows a period of intense mystical activity. At least one of its causes is the fact that mystical illuminations and consolations appear to be a thing of the past. (4) That mystics sometimes infer that their experiences are *veridical* from the effects which these experiences leave in their souls, does not imply that they infer *God's presence* from these effects. (Just as the fact that we sometimes infer that our visual experiences are veridical because they cohere with the experiences of others does not imply that visual experiences are not really perceptions but are instead inferences from this coherence to the reality of their alleged objects.)

Most of the passages cited by our authors are ambiguous, i.e. they are equally compatible with the view that the experiences which they describe involve an inference to God's presence or with the view that they involve an experimental perception of divine reality.

Most of their textual evidence is therefore inconclusive. Furthermore, the texts they cite must be taken in conjunction with the countless texts that speak of feeling, touching, or seeing God, of perceiving His presence, and so on. Our authors explain these expressions as metaphors, but this seems perverse in the absence of strong doctrinal, philosophical or textual grounds for doing so.

Is their theory, then, no more than an arbitrary and subjective interpretation of the facts of mystical experience? I think not. In the first place, a few texts clearly do support their position. For example, in his seventy-fourth sermon on the *Song of Solomon*, Bernard claims that he knew that God was present in his soul because He 'quickened my sleeping soul ... aroused and softened and goaded my heart, which was in a state of torpor and hard as stone ... It was ... *only* by the revived activity of my heart that I was enabled to recognise His presence; and to know the power of His sacred presence by the sudden departure of vices.'[42] In the second place an important aspect of the Christian contemplative tradition lends itself to our authors' interpretation.

Three closely related states typically occur in the lives of Christian mystics. (1) An active self-emptying in which the soul is focused on God or directed towards God. Since the firm and steady act of loving attention which is the heart of this prayer is 'unnatural', and since the exclusion of discursive thought, impressions and desires is very difficult, an effort of will is necessary.[43] (2) With practice, the act of loving regard or attention becomes easier until one is eventually able to enter into this state effortlessly, and sometimes without actively attempting to do so. In this state, the mind is empty except for 'stirrings of love', 'a naked intent, stretching unto God, not clothed in any special thought of God'.[44] The principle distinction between this state and the previous state is increased passivity, and feelings of sweetness, joy, and peace ('consolations'). (3) The third state is essentially identical with the second except for the fact that it involves an obscure sense of divine presence. 'The soul ... tastes him by a divine touch ... a supernatural motion by which the soul knows what God is, not because she has seen him, but because she has touched him.'[45]

Since these states are not sharply differentiated from one another, it is often difficult to determine which of them is being described. The situation is complicated by the fact that the meaning of the terms which were traditionally used to speak of these states varies from author to author. The first is often referred to as 'recollection', or 'acquired contemplation'; the second as the 'prayer of simplicity', the 'prayer of simple regard', or the 'prayer of loving attention'; and the third as the 'prayer of quiet'. But Teresa, for example, sometimes uses 'recollection' for discursive meditation, sometimes for the prayer of simplicity, and sometimes for the prayer of quiet. Some authors regard the prayer of simplicity as acquired (by the use of our faculties assisted only by the grace available to every redeemed soul), while others believe that it is (divinely) infused. 'Prayer of quiet' appears to be occasionally applied to the second state when the passivity is very marked, or the consolations are especially intense.[46] Nevertheless, in spite of these difficulties, it is possible to distinguish between these states in a rough and ready way.[47]

The first two states are not noetic. The third does involve an 'experimental perception' of divine reality, but it is 'dark' and 'obscure'. Browne and Saudreau concentrate almost exclusively upon these experiences,[48] and their theories derive what plausibility they have from this fact. Nevertheless, their conclusions are unwarranted. In spite of its obscurity, the third experience is noetic,[49] and the more advanced states referred to by terms like 'union', 'betrothal', and 'marriage', involve a vivid sense of God's presence. Furthermore, these experiences (quiet, union, betrothal, marriage, etc.) are precisely the ones which most writers have in mind when they speak of theistic mystical experiences. The theories of Browne and Saudreau are therefore defective.

B

Étienne Gilson has discovered the following theory of mysticism in Bernard and William of Saint Thierry.[50]

(1) Bernard asserts that divinely infused charity is the knowledge or vision of God. 'I speak of that vision which is in charity. For charity is that vision.' (Quoted, p 151.) More precisely, charity in an ecstasy in which 'the slumbering of the external senses is accompanied ... by an "abduction" of the internal sense' is (provides) the vision of God. (p 105) (Gilson and Bernard do not always distinguish carefully between charity and the ecstasy of charity, and this creates certain problems of interpretation. It should be remembered, however, that it is only love in ecstasy which can be equated with the experience of God.)

(2) Bernard believes that an intellectual vision of God is impossible in this life and, therefore, rejects the view that mystical contemplation literally involves some sort of immediate knowledge or perception of God. We cannot touch God with our intellects (cannot enjoy the beatific vision) as long as we are in the body (or more accurately, as long as we are in these sinful and corrupt bodies). But we can, in ecstasy, touch God with our wills or hearts, and this love by which we adhere to God provides a kind of immediate knowledge or vision, or is a substitute for knowledge and vision. (pp 91, 114 and 235)

(3) To understand this, we must see what Bernard and William mean by 'knowledge'.

(a) Consider sense knowledge. If perception of a sensible object is to occur, the mind must form to itself an image or copy, a 'similitudo' or phantasm of the sensible object which is suitable both to the sensible object and to the perceiving sense. When it has done so, the mind is said to know or perceive that sensible object. The essential (necessary and sufficient) condition of perception is the presence of this image in the mind by virtue of which the mind becomes in a certain way like the object, and thereby knows the object. (p 208)

(b) More generally, cognition 'is based entirely on a likeness of the subject knowing to the object known'. (p 148) Knowledge occurs when and if 'some action proceeding from the object has transformed the knowing subject to its likeness ... the likeness is the knowledge itself, at least in the sense that it is the indispensable and sufficient condition of the knowledge.' (p 149)

(c) There is a certain ambiguity in the claim that like knows like. It may mean that (i) one must become like x to know x. (For example, it has been said that one can understand love or humanity only in so far as one loves or is human.) Or it may mean that (ii) one knows x through a likeness or image or similitude of x.[51] As we shall see, both sorts of likeness are involved in contemplative knowledge. Since the mystic's will is conformed to God, he has become like God, and his loving will is an image or similitude by means of which God is apprehended.

(4) When we love God as we ought, we become an image of God. God loves Himself and everything else for His own sake. When we love God as He should be loved, we too love God for Himself and everything else, including ourselves, for His sake. Our love is then an image of the love by which He loves Himself.

(5) A properly ordered love in general, but ecstatic love in particular, thus involves 'the assimilation of the mind to the object which is the first condition of all knowledge'. (p 209) While this likeness is essentially a conformity of the will to God rather than a conformity of the intellect to God, it does (in ecstasy) involve a kind of knowing, for in ecstasy God becomes, as it were, 'sensible to the heart' and we 'know Him by feeling Him', (p 149) To perceive within oneself this divine love (which is a gift of God) 'is to perceive God in the sole manner' possible to us 'here below'. (p 149) Or again, the loving conformity of our will to God's will produces joy and 'this joy is a certain way of *feeling* God, an affective perception of His presence'. (p 210) The 'affection of love is [thus] the ... substitute here below for the vision of God which we lack, and love therefore in us stands for vision.' (p 149)

(6) Does mysticism involve an experimental perception of God's presence? There are two reasons for believing that it does.

(a) Mysticism involves an experimental contact because, when love is present in us, the Holy Spirit is present in us.

'The Holy Spirit is the love common to the Father and the Son, their Kiss, their Embrace.' (p 211) Our love of God is a gift of the Holy Spirit. Therefore, when we love God, God (the Holy Spirit) 'is present in the soul under the form of Gift'. (p 211) Since love is God's presence in our soul, to be aware of this love (this gift) is to be aware of God Himself. (cf pp 235–6)

One may object that the gift (our love) is a creature or work of God. Hence, to be aware of love is only to be aware of one of the things which God has made. It is not to be aware of God Himself. There is, therefore, no experimental contact.

It might be replied (though I am not certain that Gilson would wish to do so) that this creature (the gift of love) shares in, or participates in, or is an image of, the divine love (the Holy Spirit) which is its ground. Hence, to grasp the creature is to grasp the divine in which it is rooted. Whether this reply is adequate is unclear.

(b) When the soul is rapt in ecstasy and its love becomes for the moment immeasurably more perfect than it is ordinarily, it becomes 'a translucid mirror ... in which the soul now sees nought but God'. (p 152) The contact with God is like that which occurs when we see a face in a mirror. Our awareness of the face is indirect (mediated by something else). It nevertheless involves a real experimental contact with an object which is present to us via the mirror image (viz, the face). If the analogy is to be taken seriously then, given that the mystic sees God in himself as in a mirror, the fact that he is not immediately aware of God, but only of His image, should not lead us to conclude that there is no real contact or co-presence.

Nevertheless, if Gilson's interpretation of Bernard and William is correct, then it is clear that even though they believe that there is a sense in which the mystic feels or perceives God, they also think that what the mystic is immediately aware of is himself, i.e. his love of God and joy in God, which is God's image.

The theory which Gilson finds in Bernard and William is difficult to evaluate because it is incompletely developed.[52]

At its heart is the assertion that the divinised will is an image by means of which God is known. This can be understood in two ways. Understood in one way, mystical knowledge is assimilated to other sorts of knowledge in which God is grasped by means of a natural or revealed analogue or image. For example, the metaphysician grasps God through the analogue of created being or created goodness. Faith grasps God through the images of paternity, generation, spiration and so on.[53] Mystical knowledge differs from these other forms of knowledge only in so far as the divinised will provides a more perfect analogue or image than those employed by reason and faith. Several of Gilson's remarks suggest this interpretation.[54] But if this is what Gilson means to say, then the theory is inadequate for it does not account for the perception-like character of theistic mystical experience. Augustine Baker speaks for most Christian mystics when he says that contemplation involves 'a real experimental perception of His divine presence'.[55]

Other remarks[56] suggest that Gilson wishes to be understood in a different way. The divinised will is not one thing from which the mind passes (by inference) to another but is instead a medium *through* which the soul grasps God as present to it. (Thus, he says that the joy of love 'is a certain way of *feeling* God, an affective perception of His presence. Charity ... feels Him, through the joy in Him that it gives.' (p 210)) However, if this is Gilson's position[57] it is not developed by him in a clear or articulate way. For that we must turn to Maritain.

C

According to Maritain, mystical contemplation is a gift of grace. In the first place, the presence of sanctifying grace is a necessary presupposition of mystical experience. (Through sanctifying grace God becomes present to a subject as the object of its 'loving knowledge'.) In the second place, the presence in the soul of 'the infused gifts of understanding and wisdom'[58] are needed if contemplation is to be possible. These gifts of the Holy Spirit are habits of contemplation or dispositions to mystical prayer. In the third place, these habits and dispositions are brought to act by 'a special inspiration of God', (p 260)

It is because mystical contemplation is grounded in grace that Maritain can say that God is the principal agent in mystical contemplation. Souls are 'only instruments' (St John of the Cross), or more accurately secondary agents through which God acts. (pp 257, 263 and 342–4) (It is for this reason that mystics assert that passivity is a feature of their experiences. (p 263))

Mystical union involves a participation in the life of God. The creature cannot literally become God, and union with God does not involve any kind of entitative transformation. Nevertheless, through grace, man can become God intentionally, i.e. it is possible for the soul to have 'as the object of its understanding and love God Himself as He sees and loves Himself'. (p 254) Only those who enjoy the beatific vision can see God as He sees Himself. However, it is possible in this life to love God as He loves Himself.

But the heart of mystical experience is 'an experimental knowledge of the deep things of God'.[59] In virtue of His action upon the soul, God is known 'as present'. (p 263) The soul 'within the very depths of itself . . . feels the touch of divinity'. Mystical consciousness is thus an 'experience . . . of the Divine Reality present within us', a '*passion* of God suffered within the soul', a '*felt contact*' with God. (p 272)

Furthermore, the object of this experimental knowledge is God 'considered in His proper essence and inner life . . . His inwardness; God's Selfhood'. (p 249) In this respect mystical experience resembles both faith and the beatific vision and is unlike metaphysical knowledge which only apprehends God as the ground of creatures. It differs from faith in so far as the 'knowledge' of faith is indirect. Faith grasps God's inner life through certain revealed analogies (paternity, generation, spiration, etc.), but the realities which faith 'knows' are not 'seen' or immediately experienced. Mystical experience also differs from the beatific vision, for in the latter the divine essence is 'grasped just as it is' 'without the mediation of any creature or concept' (p 249) or '*species* or idea' (p 310). In mystical contemplation, the divine essence is indeed (obscurely) seen but through the mediation of the consciously experienced effects of divinely infused charity. (On this point, see pp 249–53 and p 310.)

What happens in contemplation is that the consciously experienced effects of supernaturally infused charity (the 'passion' of divine love) become 'an *objective medium* of knowledge (*objectum quo* in scholastic terminology)'. (p 261)

Objectum quo's are 'mental objects by which knowledge takes place', and are to be distinguished from the '*objectum quod*, the object *which* is known'. (p 121) Thus 'formal signs', such as the 'images' retained in memory or concepts, are *objectum quo*'s. 'A remembrance, or presentative form retained in memory and used by the memory *hic et nunc*, is not *that which* is known when we remember. Is is the *means* by which we know. And what we know by that means is the past itself.... The concept ... is not *that which* is known when our intellect is at work; it is the *means* whereby intellection takes place. And what we know by that means is ... an actually or possibly existing thing.' (p 120) In short, *objectum quo*'s are not themselves objects of knowledge from which we infer the existence or character of their non-mental counterparts. What is known through an 'objective medium' of this kind is not known inferentially but immediately 'in the sense that no *quod* mediates it'. (p 394)

Maritain's position, then, is that under the influence of grace, the intellect uses the feelings and affections associated with infused charity as a means (an *objectum quo*) through which it (obscurely) apprehends God Himself. 'God is still known *through His effects* ... but these effects are no longer things or objects that are first known and from which the mind is elevated to God'. (p 261) God is attained 'without passing from a created *quod*', and thus 'without reasoning'. (p 261) In short, the consciously experienced effects of infused charity play a role analogous to that which 'species' (concepts, images, sense impressions, etc.) play in more familiar sorts of knowledge. The 'passion' of infused charity, like other species, is a mental object through which the intellect apprehends (some aspect of) reality.

But God is not only attained non-inferentially. He is also 'touched and experienced in an obscure manner'. Contemplation involves a knowledge of the divine object 'as present, in which the soul undergoes an action exercised upon it by that object and perceives in virtue of this very passion'. (p 263) It follows that mystical knowledge is more like sense knowledge than like thinking of something through a concept.[60]

D

The claim that the consciously experienced effects of infused charity can serve as a medium through which God is touched, tasted or seen may seem implausible or even bizarre.[61] But the appearance of implausibility could be dissipated by introducing more familiar cases in which an affective experience, a feeling or mood, serves as an *objectum quo*. Alternatively, the appearance of implausibility could be legitimately dismissed as a minor consideration if there were good reasons for supposing the theory to be correct. We shall consider each of these responses in detail.

Maritain believes that there are at least four analogues of mystical knowledge. The first analogy is provided by instances of 'metaphysical experience'. For example, an 'obscure experimental perception' of our freedom and transcendence, or of the 'nothingness' or contingency of created being. Again, 'a truth of the natural order, such as ... the existence of the First Cause, will [sometimes] take on the intensity of an intuition or an immediate evidence under the influence of an actual grace.' (pp 278–9) However, this analogy is too remote to be helpful. What is apprehended in these 'metaphysical experiences or intuitions' (p 279) are propositions (for example, that we are free, or that there is a first cause) which 'come home' to us, impressing us with the force of self-evidence, not the immediate presence of some reality distinct from ourselves.

The second analogy can be dismissed for similar reasons. A virtuous man is able to judge accurately in particular cases because of his connaturality with virtue (because he possesses the virtue). Thus, 'the chaste man judges by inclination matters affecting chastity in consulting his own interior bent'. (p 281) If we possess chastity, we can determine what is demanded by the virtue 'in a way that is not that of science but of instinct, by referring to our inclination'. (p 260)

Maritain appears to be making several points. (1) A man who is virtuous understands what virtue is all about because he is virtuous. (Cf 'I did not realise what love was like until I fell in love.') (2) The virtuous man does not simply recognise that certain things are good. Their goodness comes home to him and 'reverberates in his appetite', (p 453)[62] (3) If one has a virtue, one is spontaneously inclined to those things which fall under it, and hence one's 'instinctive' value judgments tend to be correct. But, even if these points are well taken, it does not follow that virtue, or the effects which its possession produces in consciousness, is a medium through which something is apprehended. Hence, the analogy is at best remote.

'The most obvious and natural analogies of mystical contemplation,' are provided by 'human love ... with the dim though profound experience of another person which it produces.' (p 282) We must be very careful here. One can speak of one's experience of something wherever one is personally involved in it, or with it, or is related to it at first hand. (Thus I can speak of my experience of academe, but not of my experience of commerce.) Hence, we can legitimately speak of our experience of someone we love. Furthermore, intense love (or hate!) may lead to a special and intimate knowledge which others lack. (For one thing, if I love or hate another, I am more attentive to him than I would otherwise be.) Neither of these points supports the contention that love is a medium through which another person is known. Hence, we must again conclude that the analogy is remote.

Our awareness of beauty provides us with yet another analogy. (pp 281–82) While ideas and concepts may accompany the perception of beauty, their occurrence is incidental. The object of this perception is 'the splendour or radiance of the form glittering in the beautiful object', a 'radiant intelligibility'.[63] The medium of this perception is 'the sensible object intuitively grasped' or (and this appears to be rather different) 'the sensible intuition itself' not 'a concept or an idea'.[64] Three comments are in order. First, Maritain himself admits that the analogy is remote.[65] Second, to appeal to this analogy, in order to illuminate the nature of mystical contemplation, is to explain the obscure by the obscure. Or, if this seems unfair, one must at least admit that Maritain's account of our experience of beauty is as controversial as his account of mystical contemplation. But finally, even if we were to concede that this analogy helps us to see how a mediated experimental awareness of 'spiritual realities' is possible, it would still not help us to understand how the consciously experienced effects of infused charity can function as a medium through which we apprehend a divine reality. A sensible intuition, or a sensible object intuitively grasped, is very different from an affection or feeling. Unlike intuition, there is no *prima facie* reason to

suppose that feelings or affections are cognitive. I conclude
that Maritain's analogies fail to remove the aura of implausibility which surrounds his theory.

Nevertheless, we could legitimately dismiss the appearance
of implausibility if there were good reasons for supposing the
theory to be correct. Unfortunately, Maritain provides little
by way of explicit argument.

There is, of course, an implicit argument, viz, that his
theory fits the facts better than alternative theories. The facts
are provided by the texts of the paradigmatic Christian
mystics, most especially by John of the Cross.

How, then, does John of the Cross speak of the experimental
knowledge which is involved in mystical union? He says that
'God never grants mystical wisdom without love, since love
itself infuses it'. Again, mystical theology 'is science through
love, the which love is its master'. He speaks of 'the light,
which is the union of love', 'this wisdom of love', 'loving
knowledge and wisdom', 'loving awareness of God', 'this
simple, pure and loving awareness', and of 'the awareness of
love'. Again he asserts that 'God, in one act, is communicating
to the soul light and love together, which is loving and supernatural knowledge, and may be said to be like heat-giving
light, which gives out heat, for that light also enkindles the
soul in love; and this is confused and obscure to the understanding, since it is knowledge of contemplation which ... is a
ray of darkness to the understanding.'[66]

Of the many quotations from John of the Cross cited by
Maritain, these have the most direct bearing upon his theory.
It is obvious that they do not compel us to adopt it. The texts
imply that the experimental knowledge of God depends upon
the love of God, and that love and this obscure perception of
divinity are so intimately connected that they appear to be
aspects of one and the same unitary experience. But nothing in
these texts forces us to conclude that love, or the affections and
feelings associated with it, provides the medium of this knowledge. Furthermore, texts of this type are compatible with a
theory which sharply distinguishes mystical intuition from the
love that accompanies it.[67] Finally, the fact that the authors of
very different theories (for example, Saudreau) appeal to the
same texts, suggests that Maritain's implicit contention (viz,

that his theory best fits the facts set forth in those texts) needs much more support than he provides for it.[68]

Since Maritain's theory is not the only theory that fits the facts, we must ask why it is preferable. In particular we must ask why his theory is preferable to one which asserts that mystical perception involves no medium, or to a theory which asserts that it involves a different medium.

At least five reasons may be offered for the claim that a medium must be involved in mystical perception.

(1) It is only in the beatific vision that 'the Divine Selfhood will be grasped just as it is', 'without the mediation of any creature or concept'. (p 249) The beatific vision cannot be enjoyed before death; therefore, no unmediated knowledge of God is possible in this life. Hence, the contemplative's experimental awareness of God must involve the presence of some medium.

(2) God's nature, essence or inner life cannot be known by creatures. (This is usually supported by general references to the limitations of human faculties and to God's otherness.) Therefore, our knowledge of God cannot be direct or immediate, but must involve a medium.

(3) Mystical knowledge is obscure. Contemplatives more often speak of touching or tasting God than of seeing Him. While mystical experiences are sometimes clear and lucid, mystics usually assert that they perceive God through a 'cloud of unknowing'. This obscurity can be explained if we suppose that the soul apprehends God through a veil or medium which partly screens Him from it. (Farges compares infused impressed species to 'transparent veils which diminish the brightness of the divine light and obscure its [the soul's] direct vision.'[69])

(4) There is no such thing as immediate knowledge. (This position is usually supported by arguing that 'epistemological dualism' must be postulated to account for error, since error is best understood as a lack of correspondence between the medium of knowledge and its object, or by appealing to the fact that all familiar cognitive experiences involve interpretation or judgment.[70]) Therefore, it is impossible for the contemplative to enjoy an immediate (unmediated) knowledge of God.

(5) Maritain and Farges seem to suppose that 'A (experi-

mentally) perceives x' entails 'A is aware of x's presence through (by means of) effects which x produces in (the soul of) A.'[71] If this is true, then an experimental awareness of God is possible only in so far as the contemplative becomes aware of God's presence through effects which God produces in his soul. These effects constitute a medium through which God is known.[72]

Maritain does not use all of these arguments. (He employs the first, and, I think, the fourth and fifth. As we shall see, he cannot use the second argument and there is no particular reason to suppose that he has been influenced by the third.[73]) Nevertheless, with the possible exception of the second, each of these arguments has been used to support the conclusion that mystical perception involves the presence of some kind of medium and is, therefore, worth examining.

But even if mystical perception were to involve a medium, why should we identify it with the consciously experienced effects of infused charity? There are, I think, two closely related reasons.

(6) The first is the Christian insistence that mystical union is a union of charity. Given that union with God is attained through love, i.e. that love is the means of this attainment and that the attainment itself is a form of love, it is not altogether unnatural to suppose that, if the experimental knowledge which lies at the heart of the experience involves a medium, the medium is provided by love.

(7) The higher stages of contemplation are attained by burying all creatures beneath a 'cloud of forgetting'. Mystical consciousness involves an abandonment of images, clear concepts, and familiar feelings and volitions. The mind is emptied of its ordinary contents. All that remains is the mystic's loving awareness of God. If this awareness involves a medium, it would seem that we must identify it with love, for love is the only thing in addition to this awareness which has not been excluded from the mystic's consciousness.

In order to evaluate these arguments properly we must first become a bit clearer as to just what is meant by saying that a cognitive experience is or is not immediate. There are at least four possibilities.

(1) A cognitive experience may be regarded as immediate if

it is (at least consciously) non-inferential. Sense perception is immediate in this sense. Ordinary ratiocination is not.

(2) It is sometimes suggested that the only experiences which are truly immediate are those that are entirely free from conceptualisation. The sense experience of an infant might be immediate in this sense. Sense perception is not.

(3) Or one might say that a mediated experience of B occurs when an experience of an A, that is 'existentially distinct' from B, constitutes our experience of B in such a way that 'to experience A is to experience B'.[74] It has been argued that our experience of other minds is mediate in this sense. (The medium is the physical behaviour of other persons. This behaviour is 'seen as' the external expression of a mind or soul which it reveals or manifests.) On the other hand, if our awareness of sense data (as distinguished from our awareness of the objects they reveal) is a cognitive experience, it is immediate in the sense in question because it does not involve seeing one thing as another or regarding one thing as a manifestation of something else which lies behind it. (Nothing is 'seen as' a sense datum, nor is there anything distinct from a sense datum which is an expression of it.)

(4) A mediated experience may be regarded as one in which an object is grasped through a 'species' (for example, a concept or image or set of sense impressions). Sense perception and our conceptual apprehension of such things as triangularity are sometimes said to be mediated in this sense. An infant's awareness of its sense impressions is not.

There is more than a verbal difference between (3) and (4). In the third case there are two objects of experience, A and B, A being 'seen' or (without any conscious ratiocination) interpreted as B. In the fourth case, the medium (the species) is not an object of the experience at all though it can be made an object if one turns one's attention from the object of the experience (for example, triangularity) to the cognitive experience itself.

It is clear that contemplative experience is non-inferential. The mystic does not, during contemplation, consciously infer that God is present from the nature of his experience. (See section A above.) It is, then, immediate in the first sense. Furthermore, as we have seen (chapter 3, II*E*), a certain

amount of conceptualisation appears to be a necessary feature
of mystical experience. For example, the conviction that the
experience has a real object which is holy and life-giving would
seem to be an integral part of theistic mystical consciousness.
It is not an interpretation which the mystic places upon his experience in order to account for it, but is a constituent of it. It
follows that theistic mystical experience is not totally devoid of
judgment and conceptualisation, and is therefore not immediate in the second sense.

   Is there anything which is such that the experience of it constitutes an experience of God? Does mystical experience have
two objects which are related in such a way that an experience
of the first is an experience of the second? One might argue
that certain sorts of extrovertive mystical experience are
mediate in this sense. Thus, in what Otto calls 'the second
stage of the way of unifying vision', the mystic believes that he
perceives a One which lies behind the phenomenal world, supports it, and manifests itself through it. It is possible that, in
this case, the mystic's experience of phenomenal objects just is
an experience of God, and that this sort of extrovertive mystical consciousness is therefore mediate in the third sense. In
other types of extrovertive consciousness, the object of the
mystic's experience is nature itself. One might think that these
experiences too are mediate in the third sense. After all, the
nature mystic does not literally perceive everything. It might
therefore be argued that those parts of nature which the mystic
does perceive (the trees in front of him, the wind caressing his
cheek, the bubbling brook behind him, etc.) function as a
medium through which nature as a whole is apprehended, that
in the state of expansion, an experience of these things *is* an experience of nature as such. On the other hand, the objects
which the mystic perceives are not existentially distinct from
nature but parts of it. It is odd to regard the surface of the desk
which is presented to us as a medium through which we apprehend something different from it, viz, the desk. It may be
equally odd to regard nature's parts as mediums through
which we grasp something distinct from them, viz, the whole.
(Although this is not entirely clear since the parts of nature
seem to possess an independence which the parts of physical
objects or organisms lack.) Be this as it may, Maritain is con-

cerned with theistic mystical consciousness and theistic mystical consciousness is not mediate in the sense in question. The
third sort of mediation occurs only when an experience has
two objects the first of which manifests the second, whereas, at
the height of introversion, the theistic mystic ceases to be conscious of himself and his activity and is only conscious of the
object of his experience. In short, in fully developed theistic
consciousness, there is only one *object* of consciousness, and
hence the third sort of mediation is not involved.[75]

What remains to be considered is the possibility that the experience is mediate in the fourth sense, that there is some 'subjective content', some 'species', *through* which God is
experienced. Maritain thinks that there is. The consciously
experienced effects of infused charity are, he believes, a species
in the sense in which concepts, images and sense impressions
are species. Maritain usually speaks as if these effects played a
role similar to that played by concepts in our apprehension of
their objects. (cf p 261, n 3) And of course, if these effects *are*
species, they do play such a role. On the other hand, Maritain
does not always speak in this way[76] and, in any case, other
remarks indicate that the role played by the feelings and affections which are produced by charity is more like that played by
sensible species. According to Maritain, 'the object of external
sense ... is not grasped in a word [concept] or image, but just
as it exists outside the mind, in the very extramental action of
the thing on the sense... Sensation ... terminates in the sensible thing as it exists outside ... in the thing's very action
upon the sense. And the actual existence, outside the knowing
subject, of the thing present in it through its action, is one of
the constitutive conditions of the object of the sense as such.'
(p 118, n 1) It is reasonably clear that Maritain wishes to say
the same thing about the consciously experienced effects of
infused charity, viz, that through these effects the subject
grasps something 'just as it exists outside the mind' (viz, God)
'in the very extramental action of the thing on the' soul of the
mystic. (I would also point out that to say that the passion of
supernatural love is an analogue of intelligible species (concepts) is to say too little, since the apprehension of something
through a concept need not involve its felt presence, that particular kind of 'immediacy' which is associated with mystical

experience and which makes the analogy with sense perception so natural.)

Do the five arguments which were presented earlier succeed
in showing that mystical experience involves the presence of
something analogous to a sensible species? I believe they do
not.

(1) The first argument is unconvincing. (a) That the beatific vision cannot be enjoyed in this life is a theological opinion
which cannot be established by philosophical reason; nor do
there seem to be coercive theological considerations in its
favour. (b) Quite orthodox divines have held that the beatific
vision can be (briefly) enjoyed in this life. For example, Augustine
and Aquinas believed that both Moses and Paul had done
so.[77] (c) The principal difficulty consists in the fact that the
argument's premise (that a direct intellectual vision of God's
nature is possible only after death) does not entail its conclusion. The contemplative's knowledge of God can be understood in at least three ways. One may suppose that the divine
essence is immediately grasped as in the beatific vision. Or one
may assert that the mystic does not directly apprehend God's
nature but does immediately apprehend 'his being or presence' (Butler) or some of His attributes. Or one might maintain that God's nature is obscurely known through (something
analogous to) a sensible species (Maritain, Farges). While the
premise is not compatible with the first alternative, it is compatible with the others. Hence, it does not entail the third.[78]

(2) Maritain believes that the nature of physical objects
cannot be directly apprehended. While we possess an experimental and non-inferential knowledge of these objects, 'we are
unable to attain a perception of their intelligible structures
themselves, and so we are forced to have recourse to a knowledge inductively built on sensible effects alone, one that does
not provide us with the essence, but only with simple outward
signs of it.' (p 31) As we have seen, Maritain thinks that, in contemplation, the consciously experienced effects of infused
charity play a role similar to the role played by sensible species
in our knowledge of physical objects. One might therefore
expect Maritain to say that just as the essence of physical
objects cannot be grasped by sensible intuition, so the essence
of God cannot be grasped by mystical intuition. But he does

not. According to Maritain, God's nature is known by faith, in the beatific vision *and* in infused contemplation.[79]

The conclusion would follow if, as is sometimes assumed, a direct apprehension of God must involve a grasp of His essence or inner nature. (If a direct apprehension of God necessarily involves a grasp of His nature, and if His nature cannot be known, then our apprehension of God must be indirect.) However, there appear to be no compelling reasons for believing that the assumption is true.[80]

(3) The third argument is also unimpressive. It is by no means clear that the obscurity of an experience can only be accounted for by supposing that it involves the presence of a medium through which the object of the experience is dimly apprehended. In the first place, although our experience of inner states and moods is often obscure and inarticulate, this obscurity and lack of articulation cannot be ascribed to the presence of something like a sensible species through which we become aware of these states or moods. In the second place, the obscurity of an experience is more often due to its complexity, to a paucity of conceptual equipment, or to a lack of careful attention and reflection, than to the presence of a medium. Finally, we must avoid being misled by a metaphor. Veils (if they are not too thick) can be media through which something else is seen, but they do obscure our view of what lies behind them. Sensible species and their analogates are like veils in the first respect, for they function as media through which other things are apprehended. It does not follow that they are like veils in the second respect.

(4) The fourth argument depends upon the assumption that there is no immediate knowledge. This assumption is false if 'immediate' is understood in either the first or third sense. Some knowledge is non-inferential, and not all knowledge involves experiencing one thing as another. (Consider, for example, our awareness of sense data, pains and moods, our knowledge of the truth of simple mathematical propositions, and, in my opinion, our perceptions of the surfaces of physical objects.) If 'immediate' is understood in either the second or the fourth sense, then the premise is more plausible but it does not entail that mystical experience involves the employment of anything analogous to a *sensible* species. If every non-

controversial mode of knowledge involves conceptualisation, or the presence of media through which the object of knowledge is apprehended, then it is reasonable to suppose that the mystic's experimental knowledge involves conceptualisation or media through which God is apprehended. It does not follow that the mystic's experimental knowledge involves media which are similar to sensible species. Only concepts may be involved.[81] To assert that all *perceptual* experience involves the presence of a quasi-sensible medium begs the question, and is clearly false if we grant that our awareness of sense data and other mental contents is a kind of perception.

Nor do we have to postulate some sort of quasi-sensible medium to account for the possibility of error.

It is often assumed that sense perception is veridical when sense impressions correspond with objective reality, and that perceptual error occurs when this correspondence fails. Similarly, it is sometimes said that memory is accurate when memory 'images' correspond to the past but inaccurate when they do not.[82] Even if this is a correct account of these types of error, there are no compelling reasons for believing that delusive mystical experiences should be explained in the same way.

It is, of course, true that if the theistic mystic's experience were delusive, then the phenomenological object of his experience (an overwhelming loving presence) would have no objective reality and thus be a 'mere appearance', a mental content and not an independently existing reality. It does not follow that if the theistic mystic's experience is veridical, its immediate object too is only an appearance and not (an aspect of) God Himself. It is a mistake to assume that, whether it is delusive or veridical, theistic mystical experience must have the same immediate object and that, since a mere appearance would be its immediate object if it were delusive, an appearance is the immediate object of veridical theistic experience. As J L Austin has pointed out,[83] there is no clear reason why phenomenologically identical experiences cannot have different (immediate) objects. For example, John perceived from a certain point of view, and the mere appearance of John. Such diverse things as real rats and hallucinatory rats, or God and mere appearances of God, may just happen to 'look' alike.[84]

But if the possibility of error is not to be explained by postulating a kind of quasi-sensible medium which may or may not correspond with reality, then how is it to be explained?

The possibility of error is created by the fact that there are other experiences which are similar to theistic mystical consciousness, and by the fact that theistic mystical consciousness incorporates corrigible judgments.

Experiences that are similar in certain respects to those of the classical theistic mystics may induce those who have some idea of what a theistic mystical experience would be like to believe erroneously that they have experimentally perceived (an aspect of) God. Monistic experiences may have led some theists (perhaps Eckhart, and some of the later Sufis) to make this mistake. It would also be possible to confuse a state of introversion in which the will is lovingly directed towards God (the prayer of simplicity) with an experimental perception of divine presence.

Furthermore, we have seen that theistic mystical consciousness incorporates corrigible judgments (for example, that the experience's phenomenological object is not a mere appearance but really exists). Since the experience is not the only thing relevant to a determination of the truth or falsity of these judgments, it is theoretically possible that the judgments are false and the experience which incorporates them delusive.

Error, then, is possible because there are experiences with which theistic mystical consciousness might be confused, and because theistic mystical consciousness incorporates corrigible judgments. To account for the possibility of error we need not postulate a quasi-sensible medium which corresponds to reality when the experience is veridical but fails to correspond to it when it is not.

I therefore conclude that neither the fact that noncontroversial forms of human knowledge involve conceptualisation or the use of media, nor the need to account for the possibility of error, provide compelling reasons for concluding that theistic mystical consciousness involves something similar to sense impressions, or sense data, or sensible appearances that are somehow distinct from the objects they (re)present. The considerations to which the fourth argument appeals may be sufficient to show that mystical experience

includes conceptual media. They do not show that it incorporates a quasi-sensible species.[85]

(5) At least two things are wrong with the fifth argument.
Its premise entails that perception can only occur when the
perceived object causally acts upon the perceiver. I do not find
this self-evident.

Furthermore, there appear to be forms of 'experimental perception' in which the subject is not aware of the perceived
object *through* effects which that object produces in him. Our
awareness of sense data and of our own mental states provide
cases in point.[86]

All five arguments fail. There is therefore no reason to
suppose that mystical experience involves the presence of
something analogous to a sensible species, and thus no reason
to believe that the mystic experiences God through the consciously experienced effects of infused charity.

C

If we reject a theory like Saudreau's on the grounds that mystical consciousness is experimental and non-inferential and if, as
I have attempted to show, a theory such as Maritain's is both
intrinsically implausible and inadequately supported, then we
must either reject the notion of mystical knowledge altogether
or seriously entertain the notion of an experimental intuition
of God's substance or presence or attributes which is immediate in the sense that it involves no quasi-sensible medium.

Chapter 3 has provided reasons for believing that theistic
mystical consciousness is cognitively valid. I therefore conclude that the first alternative should be rejected, and that the
mystic's knowledge of God is best thought of as immediate in
the sense in question.

Notes

[1] For example, the first and second should be familiar to readers of D T Suzuki and Alan Watts. The third and fourth are at the heart of neo-Vedānta and Aldous Huxley's 'perennial philosophy'. All four are part of the popular lore about mysticism. The authors of several important recent studies of religious experience argue that the experience of God is mediated by other contents. (Cf George Mavrodes, *Belief in God, op cit*, pp 49–89; Robert A Oakes, '"God": An Observation Term?', *The Modern Schoolman*, LIV [1976], pp 43–56; John E Smith, *Experience and God*, New York, 1968.)

[2] W T Stace, *Mysticism and Philosophy (op cit)*. Page references in this section are to this work unless otherwise noted.

[3] That this is what Stace means is clear from his remarks on pp 143 and 144. Double vision is not objective because the duplication of objects which occurs when the eyes are crossed (as opposed to the *experience* of such duplication) is such that 'there is no law of nature under which that could be subsumed and explained'. Duplication is 'in conflict with nature and law, is disorderly, and is for that reason subjective'.

[4] Stace believes that similar considerations show that extrovertive mystical consciousness is neither subjective nor objective but his argument rests on the dubious assumption that the extrovertive mystic perceives 'the very same oneness as is perceived in the introvertive experience'. (p 146)

[5] I am almost certain that it is this version of the argument which Stace has in mind. The argument, as presented on p 139ff, can be interpreted in either way. However, his presentation of this argument on p 49 of *Man Against Darkness and Other Essays* (Pittsburgh, 1967) suggests that the first interpretation is correct. And we must not forget his insistence that the experience has no object. (p 86)

[6] As Stace admits. See, e.g. pp 163ff.

[7] If the argument of chapter 3 is sound, mystical experience is objective in senses (2') and (3'), in sense (4', a'), i.e. in the sense that it is causally and epistemically connected with the assertion of claims which are objective in sense (a'), and in senses (4', b'), (4', c') and (4', e'). It is neither subjective nor objective in senses (1) or (1'). Whether it is subjective or objective in senses (4, d) or (4', d') depends upon whether the truth or falsity of religious claims can only be discerned by persons meeting special conditions (faith, possession of a religious 'blik', etc.). I suspect that the requisite conditions are neither more special nor more onerous than those needed to judge works of art, moral conduct or philosophical systems, but this is uncertain.

[8] In the earlier sections of his book, Stace is reluctant to speak of propositions about the One or the experience as either true or false (a reluctance which is based on his reluctance to speak of the experience as subjective or objective, or of the One as existent or non–existent). (pp 182–3 and 185) But in later sections, he speaks of the mystic's (paradoxical) descriptions as 'successfully communicat[ing] the truth about a

part of his ... experience', as giving 'a true description of ... part of his experience'. (p 298) He speaks of 'correct descriptions' (pp 299 and 303), of the mystic's language being 'the literal truth about his experience' (p 305) etc.

9   Stace's notion is presumably that mistakes in description would occur randomly, i.e. that mystics would not systematically make the same mistake. But, first, it is not clear that this is true, and second, even if it is true, it is irrelevant because mystics do not systematically employ the *same* paradoxes. (For example, the Hīnayāna Buddhist may say that a person who has passed into Nibbāna is neither annihilated nor not annihilated nor both nor neither, while a Christian mystic may speak of losing himself in God while retaining his naked being. But the Buddhist does not employ the Christian paradox and the Christian does not employ the Buddhist paradox. Nor is there any compelling reason to believe that the Buddhist and Christian are attempting to describe the same fact.)

10 Stace actually discusses four strategies – the theory of misdescription, the theory of rhetorical exaggeration, the theory of ambiguity and the theory of double location. The metaphor theory is not discussed in this connection although it is examined in a subsequent chapter. I am therefore taking liberties with Stace's text. My justification for doing so is this: (1) The double location theory is a type of ambiguity theory. (See fn 16 below.) (2) The theory of misdescription is not a strategy for *resolving* mystical paradoxes. In dismissing a mystical paradox as a misdescription we do not eliminate the inconsistency, we merely deny that the (apparently) inconsistent statement is true. (3) Stace should have considered the metaphor theory at this point since one of the standard ways of removing an apparent contradiction is by interpreting one or more of its terms metaphorically. I believe that the reason why Stace did not do so was because he thought of the metaphor theory as a general theory about mystical language rather than as a strategy for removing apparent inconsistencies, and had reserved a later chapter for a discussion of general theories of this type. But I see no reason why Stace should deny that the metaphor theory is a strategy for removing apparent inconsistencies as well as a general theory of mystical language, and that it is therefore appropriate to discuss it at this point.

11 This seems to be Stace's point on p 293.

12 One can, for example, distinguish three shades of blue, B^1, B^2, and B^3, such that B^1 and B^2 are more like each other than either is like B^3. It is not clear that this similarity is constituted by the possession of a common property.

13 Two other observations may be worth making. (1) Non-mystics often seem to understand the mystic's metaphors. Either non-mystics possess some sort of literal understanding of the mystical experience and/or its object, or it is false that metaphors can only be understood by those who can either translate them into literal statements or are directly acquainted with their terms. (2) Metaphors can always be replaced by literal statements. For example, 'Achilles is a lion' can be replaced by 'Achilles is like a lion'. The latter may be vague or imprecise but it is not metaphorical,

analogical nor symbolic.

14 Though in fairness to Stace we should recall that he does not address himself to the fact that the metaphor theory can be used to resolve mystical paradoxes.

15 In fact, Stace thinks that ambiguation cannot resolve the paradox expressed by 'mystical consciousness is something and nothing', arguing that 'nothing' in its second occurrence means 'has no empirical content', not 'is nothing to the intellect'. Even if Stace is correct, this is an obvious non sequitur, for 'mystical consciousness exists but has no empirical content' is consistent. (Although Stace apparently believes it is not. On his view, a pure empty consciousness would be a unity devoid of multiplicity, i.e. a whole without parts! (pp 256–7) But contrary to Stace, there appears to be no more reason to describe a pure empty consciousness as a whole without parts than to describe an empty box as a whole without parts.)

16 Stace seems to think that ambiguity and double location are distinct. In fact, double location is a *type* of ambiguity in which the subject is ambiguous instead of the predicate. For example, 'God is both in rest and motion' is equivalent to 'God is in rest and God is in motion'. Eckhart preserves consistency by using 'God' in its first occurrence for the non-personal Godhead, and 'God' in its second occurrence for the triune God of Christian orthodoxy.

17 But doesn't this merely push the problem back one step? For the nirguṇa Brahman is the same as the saguṇa Brahman and yet somehow different from it. In fact, this paradox can be rather easily resolved by ambiguation. 'The nirguṇa Brahman and saguṇa Brahman are the same', means: '"Nirguṇa Brahman" and "saguṇa Brahman" refer to the same transcendent reality.' 'The nirguṇa Brahman and saguṇa Brahman are different' means (roughly) '"Nirguṇa Brahman" refers to the Brahman as it really is, while "saguṇa Brahman" refers to the same Brahman as apprehended by those infected by ignorance.'

18 This contradiction too is only apparent. The Buddhists' claim can be interpreted as '"reality" and "emptiness" can't be meaningfully combined'. The formula 'reality (Nirvāna, tathātā, etc.) is neither Ø nor not-Ø nor both Ø and not-Ø nor neither Ø nor not-Ø' is used to assert that all attempts to combine 'reality' and 'Ø' in meaningful sentences produce nonsense. This may be problematic but it is not self-contradictory.

19 On p 265, Stace asserts that attempts to dissolve these paradoxes 'are just so many attempts to reduce mysticism to common sense ... and ... the level of our everyday experience'. If Stace were correct, then Śaṁkara and Eckhart's double location theories are attempts to reduce 'mysticism to common sense' and the 'the level of our everyday experience'. This is unconvincing. The fact that the language which is used to describe and express mystical experience is not inherently inconsistent does not entail that mystical experience is an ordinary or everyday experience.

20 Stace asserts that 'mystical utterances are self-contradictory' is not self-contradictory, and that contradictory statements are not meaningless. This is true but irrelevant. The problem is not that one cannot consist-

ently say that certain statements are inconsistent (for one can), or that inconsistent statements are meaningless (for they are not). The problem is
that inconsistent statements are necessarily false.

[21] Though I speak of an inference rule applying to a set of statements in the
one case, and binding a speaker in the other case, I do not mean to suggest
either that an inference rule might apply to a set of statements and yet not
bind a person who makes those statements, or that an inference rule might
bind some speaker and yet not apply to the statements he makes.

[22] As Stace admits on p 297. Stace thinks that, in the highest stage, the
mystic manages to combine and integrate unitary (monistic) consciousness and ordinary consciousness. (See, e.g., his *The Teachings of the Mystics*,
New York and Scarborough, Ontario, 1960, p 87f.) Stace's idea may be
that from this dual perspective, premises (1) through (4) appear to be
false, or neither true nor false. But this will not do either, and for the same
reason. From the *first* perspective, nothing appears but the One. Hence it
is impossible to consider these propositions from the standpoint of *both*
perspectives. (But perhaps there is only *one* perspective, for Stace says that
the two are not merely integrated but 'coalesce, and become one'. (ibid p
87) However, Stace does not develop this point, nor is it clear that we
should take it seriously. A fusion (as distinguished from an integration) of
introvertive consciousness and ordinary experience seems to have no
textual support. Furthermore, it is difficult to see how it could be handled
by Stace's typology, since it would be neither extrovertive nor introvertive
in his sense. (It does not exclude all empirical content, so it is not introvertive. It cannot be extrovertive because Stace believes that extrovertive
consciousness is a relatively inferior and incomplete form of mystical experience.))

Stace does have one other move to make. He suggests that when the
extrovertive mystic says that all spatio-temporal things are one, he is
seeing '*through* the space-time world to the unity, the One, which lies
behind and beyond it ... [and which] is identical with the One of the
introvertive experience.' (pp 273–4) The point would appear to be that
the statement 'all distinct things are one' is really about a unitary component of extrovertive mystical consciousness (or a unitary component of its
object) and that, therefore, (3) is false. ((3) is false because at least one of
our two statements is not about an experience which involves multiplicity
or the multiple object of such an experience.) This will not do. (1) It is perfectly clear that the statement in question is (among other things) about
sticks and stones, blades of grass, etc., and not simply about some unitary
component of the experience or its object. It is equally clear that the relevant experience is (among other things) a complex experience of different
natural objects, and not merely a unitary experience of the One. (2) These
remarks do not dispose of the other statement ('The world is and is not
identical with God'). Therefore, even if (3) is false, nothing has been said
which would suggest that (3') is false, where (3') is the statement that 'the
world is and is not distinct from God' is about (the complex object of) an
experience which involves multiplicity. If we replace (3) with (3') we can
deduce (5'), namely, this statement is false. The problem remains.

²³ If monism were true, then God would be identical with the world, and each phenomenal item would be identical with every other phenomenal item, or God would be real and everything else would be an illusion. If this were the case, then one might argue that no statement is really about a multiplicity of items, for there is no multiplicity of items for statements to be about. Whether or not this line of argument is legitimate (and notice that it appears to employ the principle that if a statement is about something, then that thing must exist), Stace cannot use it, for he rejects monism. Nor can he resolve the problem by arguing that from the standpoint of mystical consciousness (3) is false, or neither true nor false for, as we have seen, this suggestion is incoherent.

²⁴ 'Empirical property' and 'empirical object' are being used vaguely – a vagueness which reflects the vagueness of Stace's 'empirical content'. What is intended is roughly those 'internal' or 'external' properties or objects which are accessible to ordinary consciousness. The meaning of (2b) is something like this: 'The Pure self has no properties which are accessible to ordinary introspection or that can be made out by science or common sense.' According to (2d), the Pure Self does not sense, dream, entertain images, think about or contemplate ordinary objects or properties, etc. This is not transparent, but it is clear enough for our purposes.

²⁵ It is not clear that even monistic mystics are aware of nothing (although their experience appears to have no *empirical* content). It is true that monistic mystics sometimes speak as if there were no object of their experience. On the other hand, they often speak as if there were such an object (e.g., the One, Brahman, etc.). Furthermore, if the reason for asserting (2i) is that introvertive mystical experience is free from distinctions and multiplicity, then (2i) is dubious, for it is not clear that introvertive mystical experience actually is distinctionless. (See Section A above. cf chapter 3, II*E*.)

²⁶ Stace equates 'content' and 'empirical content' in many places and often speaks as if freedom from empirical content involved freedom from all content. See, e.g., pp 86, 151 and 152; cf *Man Against Darkness* (*op cit*), pp 25 and 51–2.

²⁷ He says that 'minds are distinguished from one another by their empirical content and by nothing else'. (p 151) This would suggest that (2b) and/or (2d) implies (2a).

²⁸ The situation with respect to (2c) and (2d) is trickier. If the concept of the Pure Self is partly defined in terms of the monistic experience, then it may be the case that (2iii) and (2iv) entail (2c) and (2d), respectively.

²⁹ However, as I pointed out, Stace does believe that (2d) implies (2c) and he may believe that (2c) implies (2a) and/or that (2d) implies (2b), and/or that (2b) implies (2a). If all these implications hold, then, if any one of the propositions (2i) through (2iv) is both true and provides a good reason for any one of the propositions (2a) through (2d), we have a good reason for (2a). I have admitted that (2ii) and (2iv) are plausible and I am prepared to admit that (2iii) and (2iv) may be good reasons for (2c) and (2d) respectively. I would thus admit that, probably, (2iv) is true and a good reason for (2d). But if it is, and Stace's implications hold, then probably

(2a) is true. Indeed, given that his implications hold, there are two routes from (2iv) to (2a). One is: Since the mystic is aware of no empirical object, the Pure Self of the mystic is aware of no empirical object. But if the Pure Self is aware of no empirical object, then the Pure Self is aware of nothing at all, and in that case the Pure Self has no properties. Or alternatively: Since the mystic is aware of no empirical object, the Pure Self of the mystic is aware of no empirical object. But if the Pure Self is aware of no empirical object, the Pure Self has no empirical properties, and if it has no empirical properties, it has no properties at all. Neither of these arguments is particularly convincing, which is a reflection of the fact that Stace's implications are not compelling.

30 Stace uses these terms interchangeably.

31 Stace's position is articulated in the fourth chapter of *Mysticism and Philosophy*.

32 This argument is never clearly stated but is strongly suggested by Stace's remarks on p 241.

33 Whether Stace thinks that the experiences are successive is unclear. The situation is complicated by the fact that Stace recognises only one type of introvertive mysticism. Several of the mystics whom he cites as evidence for the experience of differentiation are *theistic* mystics who do not claim to experience identity (as distinguished from union). (Cf p 244) Stace never clearly distinguishes between (1) simultaneously experiencing differentiation and identity, (2) successively experiencing differentiation and identity, and (3) one mystic experiencing (only) differentiation while another experiences (only) identity.

34 Dualists typically construe the self's union with the One as a likeness or conformity of wills. Stace observes that it is absurd to construe the union of phenomenal objects (which is revealed in the extrovertive vision) as a likeness or union of wills. This is true, but irrelevant. There is no reason to suppose that dualists are committed to explaining extrovertive unity in this fashion.

35 Ignorance and delusion are real facts on this theory. (If they are not, then it is not true that we are deluded and ignorant.) But 'x is deluded or ignorant' entails 'x exists'. If x's existence is not real, then neither is x's delusion or ignorance.

36 According to Albert Farges, Anthony of the Holy Spirit, Phillip of the Trinity, Fr Lahousse, Fr Arintero, and Fr Montagne 'held that the vision of God by contemplatives always takes place without impressed species, and by means of direct informing by the divine essence'. (*Mystical Phenomena*, transl from the second French edition by S P Jacques, New York, 1925, p 285.)

3ʹ *Ibid* p 612.

38 Henry Browne, *Darkness or Light, An Essay in the Theory of Divine Contemplation*, St Louis and London, 1925; Auguste Saudreau, *The Mystical State, Its Nature and Phases*, transl by D M B, London, 1924. References in this section will be to these texts unless otherwise noted.

39 There is an interesting similarity to Leuba (*op cit*, chapters X and XI). As we have seen, Leuba thinks that mysticism tends towards complete

unconsciousness. However, in moving progressively closer to unconsciousness, mystics experience a number of unusual feelings, sensations
and emotions. These are the source of the experience's 'noetic' character.
The belief in 'the presence during the trance of a revelatory content' is
inferred from 'impressions of loftiness, of sublimity, of revelation, recalled
when they return to full consciousness'. (*Ibid* p 279) The essential difference between Leuba and Saudreau is that the latter regards these
inferences as legitimate! As we shall see, Saudreau seems to have arrived
at his theory by generalising from experiences which are not clearly
noetic. Leuba however did not. (Perception-like experiences are part of
his 'data base'.) It is therefore fair to accuse him of distorting the very
facts which he is trying to explain. The 'experimental perception' which is
an invariable feature of higher forms of mystical prayer may be delusive
but it is phenomenologically inaccurate to suggest that it is really an
inference.

[40] Saudreau does provide one philosophical reason. On pp 83–5, he argues
that an experimental perception of God's presence would involve a 'touching' of, or 'physical contact' between, (human) substance and (divine)
substance, and that this (miracle excepted) is impossible as long as the
soul remains in the body. The notion of the 'touching' of two spiritual substances (which derives from John of the Cross) is so obscure that it is difficult to evaluate·this argument.

[41] Cf Browne, chapter VII. Although he implies that it is not inherently impossible, Browne is reluctant to admit that it has *ever* occurred (except in
the case of Jesus).

[42] *On Loving God and Selections from Sermons by St Bernard of Clairvaux*, ed by
Hugh Martin, London, 1959, pp 123–4 (my italics). It should be noted,
however, that elsewhere, (the forty-first sermon on the *Song of Solomon*)
Bernard speaks of feeling God's being. See also section B below.

[43] Evelyn Underhill, *Mysticism*, 12th ed, New York, 1955, p 313.

[44] *The Cloud of Unknowing Together with the Epistle of Privy Counsel*, ed by Abbot
Justin McCann, London, 1964, p 105.

[45] Jean–Joseph Surin, quoted in Ludovic de Besse, *The Science of Prayer*,
London, 1925, p 41.

[46] For a discussion of the different uses of these terms, and the confusion
which has been generated, see the 'Afterthoughts' which Dom Cuthbert
Butler added to the second edition of *Western Mysticism* (New York, 1966).

[47] Theistic mystics may sometimes enjoy monistic states and ascribe the joy
and peace which they experience in those states to God. These experiences
may even (given the mystic's beliefs, expectations, hopes, etc.) have a
theistic hue or flavour. They should nevertheless be distinguished from
the states we are now discussing. An act of loving regard is an essential
feature of the latter, but is not part of monistic mystical consciousness.

[48] I suspect that their reason for doing so was connected with their desire to
show that contemplation is a possibility for most people. This is fairly
plausible with respect to these states, especially the first two, but is considerably less plausible with respect to other forms of mystical prayer.

49 Teresa and Francis de Sales occasionally speak of the prayer of quiet in a way which suggests that it does not involve an experimental perception of God's presence. But if their discussions of the prayer of quiet are taken in their entirety, it is clear that they do not really wish to say this. (For example, Teresa says that sometimes at this stage 'the will . . . is working without knowing how it does so', and that souls occasionally experience 'joy, without knowing whence it has come to them' (*The Way of Perfection*, transl and ed by E Allison Peers, Garden City, New York, 1964, pp 203 and 204), but a few pages later she clarifies her remarks by saying that the soul *realises 'that it is in His company'* but it does not 'understand *how* it is enjoying' God's favour or precisely '*what* it is enjoying' (p 206, my italics).)

50 Étienne Gilson, *The Mystical Theology of St Bernard*, transl by A H C Downes. London and New York, 1940. Reprinted in 1955. All page references in section B are to this edition, unless otherwise noted.

51 On either interpretation the claim involves considerable difficulty. It appears to be clearly false that one must be like x to know x. For example, a person can know mathematical objects without being like them. Again, if any epistemological view has been discredited, it is surely the view that knowing something involves the possession of a mental picture of that thing. But of course matters are not quite so simple. One can try to preserve (i) in the face of obvious counter examples by restricting its application to cases in which the object of knowledge (e.g. being, freedom, love, or hope) cannot be fully grasped by the techniques of logic and science, or by construing 'likeness' in an attenuated sense. For example, Maritain believes that the mind becomes like x in knowing x, but in the case of conceptual knowledge this appears to mean little more than that the mind apprehends the object through its concept of that object. (Or more accurately, that the object known (i.e. that aspect of the thing known which the intellect apprehends) is identical with the content of the concept by which it is known.) As for (ii), it is clear that by 'image', 'likeness' or 'similitude' Gilson does not mean a mental picture. (Cf pp 209–10)

52 For our purposes it is not important to determine whether Gilson provides an accurate account of Bernard and William. What is of interest is the theory itself, not whether Bernard and William held it in precisely the form in which Gilson presents it.

53 Faith believes that the Father eternally begets the Son, and that the Father and Son eternally 'breathe forth' the Holy Spirit.

54 For example, on p 116 Gilson says of the loving soul: 'she recognises in herself the God whose likeness she bears. Seeing herself, she sees Him. St Paul teaches that God may be known through His creatures. How much more easily then can He be known by way of this creature He has made to His own image and likeness.' That no direct perception of God is involved in the experience is suggested by his remark that 'the knowledge of God that it [love] brings amounts to the divine likeness it confers and to the joy we feel in it. To be like God is to see Him? No doubt, but to see Him is to be like Him, and to experience the joy of the likeness at last recovered. That is no small thing but it is that and no more.' (p 209)

55 Quoted in Butler, *op cit*, p 11.
56 Those in which he employs the mirror analogy. Again, on p 91, Gilson asserts that 'the term of the life of charity, even here below, is to reach God by direct contact, to see Him, in a certain sense, with an immediate sight; to taste Him or to touch Him.'
57 It is not clear that it is. On the very page where Gilson appears to adopt this position, he asserts that 'there exist neither species nor phantasms which, transforming the mind to the likeness of God, would enable us in this life to know Him; charity has power neither to create *nor to supply for them*'. (p 210, my italics) Taken at face value, this remark would suggest that he rejects the sort of view which he might otherwise appear to be adopting.
58 Jacques Maritain, *Distinguish to Unite, or The Degrees of Knowledge*, *op cit*, p 260. All quotations in sections C and D are taken from this book unless otherwise noted.
59 As Maritain says, 'Mystical contemplation which is not experimental to at least some degree would be nothing.' (p 448; cf p 450)
60 It should be noted that although I shall refer to the theory as Maritain's theory, Maritain would ascribe its principal elements to Thomas Aquinas, John of the Cross, John of St Thomas, etc.

Another thesis should perhaps be mentioned, though it does not play a central role in Maritain's theory. Mystical knowledge is knowledge by connaturality where connaturality is a 'kind of conformity and intimate proportion' between one thing and another. (Maritain, *Art and Scholasticism and the Frontiers of Poetry*, New York, 1962, p 12.) Knowledge by connaturality 'or, as one says today, existential knowledge' (*ibid*, p 195), occurs when one knows something, or knows something better, or knows in a special way, (partially) because one is somehow assimilated to that which is known. Thus the virtuous man knows virtue in a different way from the intelligent but immoral professor of moral philosophy. Again, we have a better understanding of those with whom we are intimately acquainted, and to whom we bear a certain likeness. In a similar way 'we are made connatural to God through charity', and it is in virtue of this connaturality that the mystic knows God. (p 260) It should be noticed that the sorts of assimilation we have mentioned constitute a rather mixed bag. In the first case appreciation (having certain values come home to us) is crucial. In the second case (which is not discussed by Maritain) my likeness to another person provides me with an analogue on the basis of which I can grasp the character of his actions and responses. (I know how he will act and feel because I know how I would act and feel in similar circumstances.) Furthermore, intimacy involves the ability to employ clues more or less consciously and spontaneously which would be unnoticed by a casual acquaintance or stranger. In the third case, the consciously experienced effects of the infused charity, by which the mystic is assimilated to God, functions as a species through which God is apprehended. These three cases are so different that it is unclear whether anything is gained by lumping them together under the heading 'knowledge by connaturality'. In any case, the claim that mystical knowledge is an instance of knowledge by connaturality adds little or nothing to what has already been said in section C.

61 Not only are we reluctant to assign a cognitive role to the affective side of our nature, but the proposed *objectum quo* seems radically unlike more familiar media (concepts, sense impressions, etc.).

62 (1) and (2) may come to the same thing.

63 *Art and Scholasticism and the Frontiers of Poetry, op cit*, p 163.

64 *Ibid* p 163.

65 The reason he gives is that love and affection are an *effect* of aesthetic perception rather than its medium. (*Ibid*, p 165; cf *Distinguish to Unite*, p 281, n 1)

66 All these quotations occur between pp 338 and 343.

67 'Doubtless love and knowledge give strength to one another ... but of itself ... love is a blind force, and if it enables us sometimes to know, it does so indirectly, by provoking the understanding to seek and know.' (Farges, *op cit*, p 296) Farges is following Poulain on this point.

68 There are one or two isolated passages in John of the Cross which might seem to support Maritain's theory. Thus, in the *Dark Night of the Soul*, (transl and ed by E Allison Peers, Garden City, New York, 1959, p 99), John speaks of 'the passions, desires and affections ... wherewith I had experienced and tasted God after a lowly manner' and, in the *Ascent of Mt Carmel* (*op cit*, pp 343–5), he speaks of 'spiritual feelings ... in the affection of the will', or 'substance of the soul' which are 'produced passively', and from which 'an apprehension of knowledge or intelligence ... overflows ... into the understanding'. However, in the first passage, John appears to be speaking of the lower stages of contemplation which can be obtained by human effort (assisted by grace). If this is the case then little can be inferred from this passage, since John does not seem to think that this kind of prayer involves an experimental perception of God. The second passage is, as far as I have been able to discover, the closest he ever comes to expressing the theory which Maritain attributes to him. But it is hardly clear that we should identify the feelings to which John refers with the 'impressed species' of Maritain or Farges. In any case, he is only speaking of one of four types of 'spiritual vision', not of mystical knowledge in general.

69 Farges, *op cit*, p 77.

70 Robert A Oakes ('Mediation, Encounter and God', *International Journal for Philosophy of Religion*, II (1971). pp 148–55) makes both of these moves in arguing for the more restricted thesis that no perceptual knowledge is immediate.

71 p 118. Cf Farges, pp 69–70.

72 Farges's view is very similar to Maritain's. (See, e.g., Farges, pp 58–86 and 272–8.) The crucial difference between them is that Farges does not specify the nature of the divinely infused 'impressed species'. He tells us that it is the 'passive effect' of God's action on the mystic's soul, and that through it 'the agent is apprehended at the same time as the action and without reasoning'. (p 275) but he does not tell us what this passive effect is. (it is *not* 'the outbursts of love' which the divine action 'may cause'.

(p 276))

[73] That Maritain would endorse the fourth argument is indicated by his discussion of monistic mysticism. ('The Natural Mystical Experience and the Void', *Ransoming the Time*, transl by Harry Lorin Binsse, New York, 1969.) Maritain argues that the monistic mystic grasps the naked being (but not the essence) of his soul *through the very act* by which he empties his mind of all contents. Behind this theory lie two assumptions – that the soul, while in the body, can only grasp itself through its operations, and that because of its inherent weakness, the human intellect (as distinguished, for example, from angelic intellects) must grasp things through a multiplicity of concepts, impressions and other media. Maritain thus endorses the premise of the fourth argument. However, his endorsement is not (primarily) based upon an induction from the nature of more familiar modes of knowledge, or the need to account for the possibility of error, but on a metaphysical doctrine concerning man's nature and abilities, and his position in the hierarchy of spiritual beings.

[74] Oakes, 'Mediation, Encounter and God', *op cit*, p 152.

[75] Similar remarks can be made with respect to other types of introvertive mystical experience; they do not have two objects. Other religious experiences may be mediate in the third sense. Visionary experiences are not mystical experiences although mystics frequently have them. It might be suggested that symbolic visions, i.e. visions with decipherable meanings, are mediate in the sense in question. For example, visions of the spiritual espousal in which Christ places a ring on the finger of His beloved. The visionary content expresses the union of Christ with the soul, and is experienced as such. Again, while some numinous experiences are not focused upon an empirical object, others are. It would not be implausible to regard the latter as mediate in the third sense. (For example, a contemporary might have said that his experience of Jesus *was* an experience of the Holy.)

[76] On p 450 he simply says that love 'play[s] ... a role analogous to' that which a species plays in ordinary knowledge, without specifying the speciies as either an intellectual species (e.g. a concept) or a sensible species (e.g. sense impressions).

[77] Butler, *op cit*, pp lv–lviii.

[78] The second and third alternatives are incompatible. Hence, if the premise entailed the third alternative, it would also entail the denial of the second alternative, which is contrary to the supposition that the premise is compatible with the second alternative.

[79] Maritain is not atypical. While they have usually insisted that God's nature or essence cannot be grasped by purely natural means, most mystical theologians have believed that God's essence can be grasped by supernatural means (faith, or infused contemplation, or the beatific vision); they have thus rejected the second argument's premise.

[80] For example, Farges distinguishes between the vision of God's essence which involves 'seeing' the whole of God synthetically (though perhaps obscurely) (Farges. *op cit*, e.g. p 286) and mystical contemplation which only involves 'partial manifestation[s]', 'aspects or points of view' (*ibid*,

pp 290 and 289), and assumes that the former is direct while the latter involves the presence of infused species through which the contemplative's apprehension of God is mediated. This assumption is never justified; nor is it particularly plausible. Even though the idea of directly apprehending God may be problematic, the assertion that we can directly apprehend God's being, or presence, or 'partial manifestations' appears to be no more problematic than the assertion that we can directly apprehend God's nature. Hence, if one admits, like Farges, that God's nature can be directly perceived, it is unclear why one should object to the notion that God's being, presence, or 'partial manifestations' can be directly perceived. Infused species are needed in both cases, or they are needed in neither.

[81] Of course Maritain must reject this possibility since he believes that mystical consciousness is non-conceptual. (See chapter 3, II*E*.)

[82] As usually presented (by Locke, for example, or by the critical realists), this medium is the mind's immediate *object*, and is thus an *objectum quod*. According to Maritain, sense impressions and memory images (as well as divinely infused species) are *objectum quo*'s. Although talk of correspondence may seem more natural when the medium is treated as an *objectum quod*, it is not clearly out of order when treated as an *objectum quo*.

[83] J L Austin, *Sense and Sensibilia*, Oxford, 1962, p 52.

[84] There appears to be no reason to suppose that the phenomenological object of theistic mystical experience is constituted out of some sort of raw data, in the way in which (on certain views) the phenomenological object of sense perception is constituted out of sense impressions. Whether it is a mere appearance or an aspect of God Himself, the phenomenological object of theistic mystical experience appears to be 'primitive' or 'given' (in somewhat the same way that dream contents are primitive or given). The phenomenological object of theistic mystical experience may be complex in the sense that it has a number of different features or properties, but there appear to be no mental contents which can be distinguished from it, through which it is grasped, or out of which it is constructed. (Cf chapter 1, III*C*.)

[85] Similarly, Maritain's doctrine concerning the metaphysical limitations of the human intellect may imply that media must be involved in all human knowledge, and thus in mystical knowledge. But it does not imply that the media involved in mystical perception are quasi-sensible rather than conceptual.

[86] There is a certain similarity between some of the things which I have said in the last few paragraphs and Gardeil's claim that the mystic's awareness of God, like the soul's experience of itself, is direct, and not dependent upon such things as 'sense–impressions, phantasmata, intelligible species, concepts', and so on. (Butler, *op cit*, pp xlix–1.) However, whereas Gardeil is comparing mystical perception with the soul's perception of itself, I have been comparing mystical perception with our awareness of our own mental contents. Hence, while our points are similar, they are not identical. Poulain (in passing) does make a point similar to mine. (*The Graces of Interior Prayer*, *op cit*, pp 88–9 fn.) I should perhaps add that I by

no means intend to imply that mystical perception is more like our awareness of sense data or subjective states, than it is like sense perception. I
only wish to imply that it may be like it in one respect, viz, that it involves
no quasi-sensible medium through which the object of the experience is
grasped. In other respects, mystical perception and our awareness of
sense data or subjective states are unlike each other. For example, it is not
possible to be conceptually clear and to believe mistakenly that one is in
pain, or is appeared to redly, or is despondent. It is possible for the mystic
to be conceptually clear and yet mistakenly believe that he perceives God.
(This is presumably a reflection of the fact that God is not an inner state or
mental content.)

CHAPTER 5

Mysticism and Morality

Most of those who have studied mysticism think that there is a significant relationship between mysticism and morality. They do not agree about its nature. For example, Henri Bergson, Aldous Huxley and Walter Stace believe that mystical consciousness supports an ethics of love and compassion, while Arthur Danto thinks that mystical consciousness and morality are incompatible.

Two questions must be distinguished. (1) Are there important empirical connections between mysticism and morality? In practice, does mysticism reinforce moral ideals and support moral activity, or does it undermine moral ideals and inhibit moral activity? (2) Are there logical or epistemic connections between mystical consciousness and morality? Does mystical consciousness provide a backing or warrant for or against moral claims?[1]

The first question is a question for historians of religion and social scientists: the second is philosophical.

The first section of this chapter will consider several ideals of conduct which are closely associated with mysticism; attempt to determine whether these ideals are moral ideals; and explore the relation of these ideals to mystical experience. The second section will examine attempts to show that mystical consciousness provides a backing or warrant for altruism, and arguments which purport to show that mysticism and morality are incompatible.

Although they are intimately connected, mystical experiences can be distinguished from the religious traditions within which they are incorporated. (See chapter 1.) If the argument of this chapter is sound, mystical experience itself is

198

compatible with morality, but provides considerably less support for it than has sometimes been supposed.

I

Ideals or models of human behaviour are an integral part of most mystical traditions. This section will examine several of the most important of these ideals. I shall argue that some of these models are non-moral, and that those which are moral may be expressions of beliefs and attitudes which .are not specifically mystical. A person's picture of life at its best is an important part of his general moral outlook. If I am correct, the types of mystical experience which we shall consider[2] support non-moral ideals, or reinforce moral ideals whose principal roots lie elsewhere.

A

In *Western Mysticism*, Butler examines the ideals of Augustine, Gregory and Bernard.

According to Augustine the contemplative life is to be preferred to the active life for three reasons. First, the contemplative life is the end of the active life. Moral action disciplines the soul and assists others, but its ultimate aim is salvation, and salvation consists in the beatific vision, i.e., in contemplation. Christ's words to Mary provide the second reason. Martha symbolises the active life and Mary the contemplative life, but Mary is said to have chosen the better part. The third reason is the conviction (perhaps ultimately inherited from Plato and Aristotle) that the life of theoretical reason is intrinsically the best life. Thus in *The Trinity* xii, 1, Augustine says that the most 'excellent function' of the mind is the contemplation of 'things eternal' which is 'completed in cognition alone', and, in *de Quantitate Animae*, he maintains that the intellectual grasp of 'those things which truly and supremely are' is the 'highest act' of the soul.[3]

Nevertheless, the demands of charity sometimes require one to abandon a purely contemplative life. Thus, those who are fit for the government of the church and the discharge of ecclesiastical affairs 'are often called upon, by the needs of the church, to undertake the works of the active life'. (*Contra Faustum*, xxii, 58) For, as Augustine says in the *City of God* (xix, 19), 'no one should be so at leisure as in his leisure not to think of his neighbour's welfare'.[4] (Plato speaks similarly of the return to the cave. The philosopher king turns his back on a life of pure contemplation – a life which is intrinsically better – in order to serve his community.)

There are similarities between Augustine's position and two positions which will be examined later, viz, the positions of Advaita Vedānta and Hīnayāna Buddhism. Augustine, too, maintains that morality is a means to an end. The Brahman-knower and Arhat may also teach and administer in order to aid others. But there are significant differences. (1) For Augustine, the essence of Christian virtue (morality) is 'caritas' – the love of God for His own sake, and oneself and others in God. 'Caritas' is also an integral and essential part of the beatific vision and thus of the contemplative life. There is a continuity between morality and contemplation which is absent in Advaita and Hīnayāna. (2) The obligation to renounce contemplation in order to meet the needs of others is a vital part of Augustine's teaching (as it is of Plato's). Far from being an afterthought, it is woven into the very fabric of Augustine's understanding of the best life. This does not appear to be true of either Advaita or Hīnayāna.

Although Gregory's position is essentially the same as Augustine's, he appears to place more weight on the active life.

The active life is defined as giving bread to the hungry, teaching the ignorant, correcting the erring, recalling 'to the path of humility our neighbour when he waxes proud', tending the sick, dispensing 'to all what they need', and providing 'those entrusted to us with the means of subsistence'. (*Homilies on Ezechiel* II, ii)[5] Gregory calls our attention to the fact that contemplation reinforces morality and that, in spite of its superiority, the contemplative life is 'by choice' whereas the active life is by necessity. (The active life is necessary and sufficient for salvation. The contemplative life is neither necessary nor sufficient.) More significantly, Gregory suggests that in this life contemplation is a gift which is at least partly given for the sake of others. 'Whoever reaps benefit by seeing spiritual things, is bound by speaking to lay them before others. For he sees in order that he may announce, who, by the fact that he reaps benefit for himself, by preaching has a care also for the advance of his neighbour.' (*Homilies on Ezechiel*, II, ii 4)[6] Again, in *The Book on Pastoral Care*, i, 5, he insists that contemplatives have received their gifts 'not for themselves only, but also for others'.[7] Finally, Gregory implies that while the contemplative life is superior to the active life, the life which combines contemplation and action is better than either. 'The excellence of preachers is far above that of the continent and silent, and the eminence of the continent outdistances greatly that of married people.' (*Homilies on Ezechiel* II, iv, 6)[8] The 'continent' are those who live a life of contemplation. As Butler points out, Gregory has already said that preachers must practise both lives. It would seem to follow that the 'mixed life' which combines contemplation and action is the most perfect life. I would suggest that this evaluation is also implicit in Gregory's claim that Christ provides the model of both lives.

Christ set forth in Himself patterns of both lives ... united together... For when he wrought miracles in the city, and yet continued all night in prayer on the mountain, He gave His faithful ones an example not to neglect, through love of contemplation, the care of their neighbours; nor again to abandon contemplative pursuits through being too immoderately engaged in the care of their neighbours ... [but so to comport themselves] that the love of their neighbour may not interfere with the love of God; nor again the love of God cast out, because it transcends, the love of their neighbours. (*Morals*, xxviii, 33)[9]

Or consider Bernard who argues that even though the contemplative life is intrinsically better, our lives must include contemplation *and* action. First, because one cannot in this life constantly maintain oneself in contemplation and should therefore engage in works of charity instead of being inactive in the intervals between contemplation. Second, because even contemplatives are obliged to respond to the demands of their neighbour. 'Who doubts that a man when he is in prayer is speaking to God? And yet how often are we withdrawn from prayer, and that at the very dictate of charity, because of those who are in need of our assistance or our advice!' (Sermon on the *Song of Solomon*, 50)[10] In short, given the conditions of this

life, where distractions and the weakness of the body make
continuous contemplation impossible, and the needs of others
make demands upon our charity, the 'mixed life' is the best
life.

The theme is echoed again and again. According to Richard
of St Victor, the soul, in the fourth and highest degree of love,
returns from the heights of contemplation and 'goes forth on
God's behalf and descends below herself ... she goes out by
compassion'.[11] In the last passage of the 'Sparkling Stone',
Ruysbroeck asserts that

> The man who is sent down by God from these heights into the world is full of
> truth and rich in all virtues. And he seeks not his own but the glory of Him
> Who has sent him. And hence he is just and truthful in all things, and he pos-
> sesses a rich and generous ground, which is set in the richness of God: and
> therefore he must always spend himself on those who have need of him ...
> And by this he possesses a universal life, for he is ready alike for contem-
> plation and for action, and is perfect in both of them.[12]

By the end of the middle ages, the mixed life was firmly
enthroned as the ideal of the great Christian mystics.[13]

B

(1) In chapter 7 of *Advaita Vedānta*,[14] Eliot Deutsch describes
'Advaitic ethics'. The good is what leads to mokṣa and the bad
is what hinders it. In general, truth and righteousness further
self-realisation while their opposites make self-realisation
more difficult. On the other hand, both the Brahman itself,
and the person who has recognised his identity with Brahman
are beyond moral distinctions. 'When the seer sees ... the
source of Brahmā, then the illumined one completely shakes
off both virtue and vice.' (*Mundaka Upanishad* III, 1, 3)[15] The
Brahman-knower has no reason to refrain from deceit, theft
and murder, presumably because 'conventional' moral
reasons only apply within the world of māyā and the
Brahman-knower no longer dwells in māyā, and because,
having already effectively attained mokṣa, righteousness need
no longer be cultivated as a *means* to mokṣa. However, even
though the person who has transcended all distinctions may
have no reason for refraining from deceit, theft and murder, he
is psychologically unable to engage in them, since unrighteous

deeds are expressions of egoism, and the Brahman-knower is free from egoism.

I C Sharma[16] maintains that, according to Śaṁkara, a person who has achieved enlightenment continues to work for the benefit of others, and as evidence appeals to Śaṁkara's commentary on the *Bhagavad-Gītā*. But Śaṁkara's comments are ambiguous. In iv, 20 Saṃkara speaks of a person who has found the truth, but 'who finding it impracticable to get away from action, engages in action as before with a view to set an example to the world or to avoid the displeasure of the ortho-dox'.[17] This person is 'a person who, having started with action, and having since obtained the right knowledge of the Self, really abandons action ... but' finds 'that for some reason he cannot abandon action'. (iv, 19)[18] Śaṁkara's remarks appear to be restricted to those who are committed to a social role *before* they achieve enlightenment, and cannot now divest themselves of it without failing in the duties which they have to others in virtue of that role. That this is what Śaṁkara has in mind is confirmed by another passage in which he says that a man who 'thinks he has achieved his ends and has re-alised the Self, even he should work for the welfare of others, though for himself he may have nothing to do'. (iii, 24)[19] The context of this passage makes it reasonably clear that Śaṁkara is referring to kṣatriyas, i.e. to men who, because of their in-herited role as rulers and warriors, have special obligations to others.

Śaṁkara's remarks may be usefully contrasted with the remarks of Augustine, Gregory and Bernard. According to the latter, the contemplative may be obliged to *assume* a role for the benefit of others (for example, that of bishop), and is often obliged (cf Bernard and Ruysbroeck) to perform acts of charity *irrespective* of his role. His obligations to others are not a function of commitments incurred prior to enlighten-ment.

In any case, the circumstances to which Śaṁkara alludes in these passages are clearly exceptional. The general thrust of his remarks is that action is only necesary for those who have not yet achieved enlightenment. 'For the man who knows the Self there is nothing to do.' 'For the man thus rejoicing in the Self no purpose is achieved by action.' 'No evil whatever, either by way of incurring sin, or by way of losing the Self, arises in this world from inaction.' (iii, 17, 18)[20] Not only are works unnecessary, they are not really appropriate. 'Since the man who has realised the Self is free from illusory knowledge, *karma-yoga* [the path of works] which is based upon illusion [the belief in 'an active self'] must be impossible for him.' (v, introd)[21]

Modern neo-Advaitins like Vivekānanda do preach the 'mixed life', the ideal of 'disinterested *sannyāsins*, bent on doing good to others ... disseminating education and seeking in various ways to better the condition of all, down to the *candāla* (untouchables)'.[22] But as Zæhner points out, it is important to remember that Vivekānanda had been educated at Calcutta's Mission College and was, prior to his encounter with Rāmakrishna, typical of a Westernised Indian middle class which had absorbed European social and ethical ideas.

Western thought has had relatively little impact upon Hindu metaphysics and spirituality. Only in the ethical and social sphere has the West had a significant impact upon Indian religious life and practice. This fusion of Western social and ethical ideals with Hindu thought and spirituality may be admirable. There may be elements within the Hindu tradition which lend themselves to this development. The fact remains that statements made by modern neo-Advaitin apologists concerning the desirability of the mixed life must be treated with caution. What is of interest for our purposes is not the view of modern neo-Advaitins, but the views of classical Advaita, i.e. of an Advaita as yet unfamiliar with Western ethical and social teachings. If the ideal of the mixed life is not found in classical Advaita, it is reasonable to infer that its inclusion in modern neo-Advaita is due to extraneous influences.[23]

(2) Because of its reluctance to speculate on the nature of ultimate reality or to draw metaphysical conclusions from its mystical experiences, Ninian Smart has suggested that Theravāda Buddhism may be the purest expression of introvertive (i.e., monistic) mystical consciousness.[24] Be this as it may, Hīnayāna Buddhism's attitude towards morality is in many ways similar to the attitude of a tradition in which monistic experiences clearly *are* central, viz, Advaita Vedānta. Three facts are especially significant.

First sīlā ('morality') consisting in right speech, right action and right occupation, constitutes the middle portion of the Noble Eight-Fold Path. 'Morality' is a means to a non-moral end, viz, the eradication of the avijjā (ignorance) and tanhā (craving) which bind us to a world characterised by anicca (impermanence) and dukkha ('unsatisfactoriness').[25]

Second, the brahma-vihāras, which are associated with the eighth stage of the Path (viz, right meditation or samādhi) have moral overtones. Mettā ('friendliness') consists in wishing well to all creatures, pervading every quarter of the world with friendly thoughts. According to Buddhaghosa, a person occupying this 'station' identifies 'all with his own self, without making the distinction that they are other beings'. Mettā involves 'bestowing benefits on others,[26] is based on the ability to see their pleasant side, and results in the stilling of ill-will and malice.'[27] Karunā (compassion) consists in sharing the pain of all sentient beings and cultivating the wish to remove it. Muditā (sympathetic joy) involves sharing the joy of all creatures. The fourth and highest station is upekkhā. One is impartial, free from aversion to others and from any desire to win their approval – serene, calm and unattached. This impartiality results from the recognition that all beings are 'non-existent' (empty of self), and that because of the law of karma each individual must work out his own salvation. Conze observes that 'on reaching its perfection the social attitude ... seems to become distinctly asocial'.[28] While this is true, it is misleading. The brahma-vihāras are not primarily instruments of moral discipline but a means of introducing order into our emotional life. Buddhaghosa's remark is significant. Their point is the elimination of malice and other disturbing emotions and feelings which make it difficult to achieve mental peace and equilibrium.[29] That is, their aim or point is not moral.

Third, the 'virtue' or excellence which is most highly prized in Hīnayāna Buddhism is not justice or compassion but pannā (wisdom), an insight into the 'emptiness' of samsāra (i.e. into its causal interrelatedness and lack of permanent substance) which has been so thoroughly appropriated that it pervades one's thought, feeling and conduct. A combination of pannā and samādhi lead to Nibbāna, but, of the two, pannā is by far the more important.[30]

These considerations suggest that, like the Advaitins, Hīnayāna Buddhists regard morality as a means to a private and
non-moral end, viz, their own enlightenment.

However, this may be something of an over-simplification.
Richard H Jones has argued[31] that even though those who are
not yet enlightened do regard morality as a mere means, those
who have achieved enlightenment do not. A person who has
eradicated thirst and illusion is no longer governed by egocen-
tric considerations and may, like the Buddha, elect to teach
others. If he does so, his actions can be regarded as altruistic
for they are designed to benefit others and they are not an
expression of self-interest.

Jones is correct, but it is important to notice that altruistic
behaviour is not an *intrinsic* feature of enlightenment. (Pacceka
Buddhas, for example, are solitary.) Nor are the enlightened
obliged to teach others. The ideal of enlightenment is thus not
essentially moral, though it is sometimes developed in a moral
direction. The principal model in Hīnayāna Buddhism is provided by the Arahant (Arhat), the 'saint' who has achieved
enlightenment by putting the Buddha's teachings into practice in his own life. But in so far as the Buddha too provides an
ideal which regulates Hīnayāna conduct (and enlightened
monks sometimes do teach and direct others), Hīnayāna
morality is not entirely egoistic.[32] Nevertheless, the Hīnayāna
ideal cannot be regarded as altruistic in any fully developed or
unqualified sense, for the enlightened are not obliged to act
altruistically nor is altruistic behaviour an intrinsic feature of
the best life. Morality is only binding in so far as it is a necessary condition for achieving one's own Nibbāna.

(3) Although the terms 'moral' and 'morality' are open-
textured, their meaning is not entirely indeterminate. For
example, it is clear that morality is concerned with actions.
While in evaluating an agent's actions we sometimes pay more
attention to his intentions and attitudes than to his behaviour,
the intentions are intentions to act, and the relevant attitudes
and dispositions are attitudes and dispositions which express
themselves in action. It is also clear that morality is concerned
with our relations to other people. Whether we have moral
obligations to ourselves is a moot question, but a code or way

of life which recognized no obligations to others would not normally be called 'moral'. Furthermore, moral action is typically characterised by conscientiousness or a sense of duty, by a desire for justice and equity, or by a concern for the well-being of others.

The fact that these features are part of what most people mean by 'morality' has an important implication. Ethical egoism is the position that an action is right or good or obligatory if and only if it (ultimately) promotes one's own well-being. There are different kinds of ethical egoism. In principle, an ethical egoist might argue that the claims of others should be ignored whenever it appears to one's advantage to do so, that benevolence and justice are expressions of weakness, etc. (Plato's Thrasymachus advocates a position of this sort.) Most people would regard this position as amoral or (more probably) immoral. In practice, most ethical egoists have acknowledged obligations to secure justice and promote the common good, although they have attempted to justify these obligations by showing how the promotion of justice and the common good ultimately serves one's own interests. Is this a moral position or not? It acknowledges that we have obligations to other persons, and enjoins us to be concerned about justice and the good of others. Nevertheless, these obligations and concerns are not ultimate since they are only a means to one's own private good. A position of this type is not clearly excluded by our second and third criteria but it is not clear that it meets them either. This seems to accord with common usage. We are, I think, hesitant to apply 'moral' to patterns of behaviour which we believe to be ultimately self-interested.

The situation is complicated by the fact that while most ethical egoists believe that virtue promotes one's own well-being, the relation between a virtue like justice and one's private good can be construed in different ways. Plato and Aristotle believe that justice and a concern for the public good are *part* of one's own private good. Epicurus and Hobbes think that the moral virtues have only an instrumental value, but concede that they are indispensable to human life. A third position is possible – that a person's private good can be secured at some point in his life, and that after he has secured it he can discard the moral virtues if he wishes to do so. I suggest that most of us would not hesitate to speak of the first position as 'moral', that we would probably regard the third position as non-moral or (possibly) immoral, and that we are unsure as to whether the second position should be called 'moral' or not.

The relevance of these considerations is obvious. Advaitans and Hīnayāna Buddhists are essentially ethical egoists although the private good which they seek is neither pleasure (Epicurus) nor security (Hobbes) but mokṣa or enlightenment.

But what type of ethical egoists are they? Moral behaviour is not _part_ of mokṣa or enlightenment nor is it obligatory once one has achieved these goals. For classical Advaita moral behaviour is obligatory only in so far as it furthers one's pursuit of mokṣa, or is demanded by a role which one had assumed before one was enlightened and cannot now escape. For Hīnayāna Buddhists, moral behaviour is only obligatory as a means to enlightenment. A person who is already enlightened may choose to aid others without attempting to further his own interests, but his behaviour is an act of superarrogation, it is not a duty. Classical Advaita and Hīnayāna Buddhism thus appear to be instances of the third type of ethical egoism. They are consequently non-moral or (possibly) immoral. (Although this judgment should be qualified by the recognition that social obligations are still thought to hold in some cases (Advaita), and to the extent to which selfless behaviour is either emulated (by some enlightened monks) or disinterestedly admired or praised (by those who have not yet achieved enlightenment).[33])

C

Mahāyāna Buddhism criticises Theravāda and the other Hīnayāna schools precisely because of their insistence upon the pursuit of a person's own 'private Nirvāna'. Although the richness and variety of Mahāyāna thought make generalisations difficult, I would like to comment upon certain aspects of Zen and the Bodhisattva ideal.

Arthur Koestler reports a Zen patriarch as saying, 'Zen is ... extremely flexible in adapting itself to almost any philosophy and moral doctrine as long as its intuitive teaching is not interfered with. It may be found wedded to anarchism or fascism, communism or democracy, atheism or idealism.'[34] Or consider Suzuki's remarks in Thomas Merton's *Zen and the Birds of Appetite*. According to Suzuki, even the 'Zen man' is a social being who 'cannot live outside society' or 'ignore ethical values'.[35] The 'field' is 'open' or 'empty' but the players on the field belong to a realm of distinctions which includes the distinction between good and evil. 'Our actual life consists [i.e. should consist] in the one supporting the other' or in their 'inseparable' cooperation.[36] Prajnā (wisdom) and virtues like dana (giving) reinforce each other. Giving 'means anything going out of oneself, disseminating knowledge, helping people in difficulties of all kinds, creating arts, promoting industry or social welfare, sacrificing one's life for a worthy cause and so on. But this ... is not enough as long as a man harbours the idea of giving ... in the giving there must not be any thought of a giver or a receiver, and of an object going through this transaction.' The giving must go 'on thus in Emptiness', dana 'flowing out of Prajnā.'[37]

Koestler has argued that Zen presupposes the existence of a rigorous social code or ethic, for example, Confucian ethics. Zen's emphasis upon spontaneity and relaxation can best be understood as a reaction to the anxiety and mental cramps which are induced by the restrictions and demands of a code of this type.[38] Whether this is true or not, it does seem to be the case that 'emptiness' and 'no-mind' are not, for Suzuki, a *source* of ethics or of ethical behaviour, but something which enables the 'Zen man' to engage in social and ethical action in a radically different manner from the rest of us. Its relation to ethics seems in principle no different from its relation to swordsmanship or archery or the tea ceremony. Familiar acts are performed in a new spirit or style.[39] Furthermore, Danto appears to be correct in asserting that this style is neither logically nor psychologically tied to any particular type of activity. This is less clearly true of the 'caritas' style, in which love for God and one's neighbour in God forms the ambience within which action takes place. Some attitudes are logically and psychologically tied to certain types of behaviour. Charity appears to be an attitude of this type. (Charity typically expresses itself in support, the relief of the needy, etc. not in theft, falsehood and murder.) Non-attachment, seeing into the 'emptiness' of things, on the other hand, does not, or at least not so clearly. If this is correct, then, even though the Zen ideal can be combined with moral activity, it is not intrinsically moral.

The Bodhisattva ideal seems more clearly moral. The Bodhisattva postpones his own final release until everyone has achieved enlightenment. Of the Bodhisattva, the *Prajnāparamitā* says 'they do not wish to obtain their own private Nirvāna ... they have set out for the benefit of the world, for the ease of the world, out of pity for the world. They have resolved: "we will become a shelter for the world, a refuge for the world, the world's place of rest, the final relief of the world, islands of the world, lights of the world, leaders of the world, the world's means of salvation".'[40]

The Bodhisattva ideal is contrasted with Hīnayāna's Arhat ideal. Since the Arhat is said to seek his own private Nirvāna, he is still affected by the distinction between mine and thine, and has thus not succeeded in freeing himself from all forms of self-attachment and egoism.

Whereas Theravāda and the other Hīnayāna schools place more value upon wisdom (prajnā) than compassion (karuna), Mahāyāna tends to place an equal emphasis upon both. They are, however, paradoxically related. In his compassion, the Bodhisattva is cognizant of persons and vows to save them, but in his wisdom he recognises that they are unreal. (Persons are nothing but collections of momentary 'dharmas' and, in the last analysis, the dharmas themselves have no reality.) According to the Diamond Sutra, 'a Bodhisattva should think thus: As many beings as there are in the universe of beings ... all these should be led by me into Nirvāna ... And yet, although innumerable beings have thus been led to Nirvāna, no being at all has been led to Nirvāna. And why? If in a Bodhisattva, the perception of "a being" should take place, he would not be called an "enlightenment-being" (=bodhi-sattva).'[41]

At first glance, the Bodhisattva ideal appears quite similar to the ideal of the mixed life. Just as the Christian mystic combines contemplation with active charity, so the Bodhisattva combines wisdom with compassion. Neither ideal is exclusively moral, but both contain an important moral component. This similarity, however, may be deceptive.

In the first place, it is not clear that Mahāyāna's criticism of the Arhat ideal is primarily moral. The Arhat believes that, because of the law of karma, each individual must work out his own salvation. All that a person *can* do is seek his own Nirvāna. If the Arhat were right, it would be as unreasonable to condemn him for failing to seek another person's Nirvāna as to condemn him for failing to resist another person's temptations. But according to Mahāyāna, the Arhat is mistaken, for persons are not really separate and distinct.

The Bodhisattva ideal appears in part to be a reflection of the Mahāyāna belief in the mutual indwelling of all things, the interpenetration of every aspect and level of reality. According to this view, there are no hard and fast lines between one thing and another. Reality is fluid, and distinctions are arbitrary and conventional. It follows that persons too indwell or inter-penetrate each other, and that the distinctions between them are purely conventional. Against this background, it makes a certain amount of sense to speak of the transfer of merit, bearing one another's burdens, and working for universal enlightenment.

I would suggest that Mahāyāna's criticism is only partly moral. The Arhat is not so much morally imperfect as spiritually imperfect. He still recognises distinctions, he retains a kind of belief in the reality of his own ātman or self, and he is not absolutely indifferent and non-attached. (He *distinguishes* between his *own* enlightenment and the enlightenment of others, and is *concerned* with his *own* well-being.) His basic flaw is not lack of compassion but lack of wisdom, for his self-concern is rooted in a distorted way of looking at reality.

In the second place, a 'love' or 'compassion' which refuses to recognise the independent reality of persons is somewhat removed from what we ordinarily regard as love or com-passion. The latter is a relation between independently real persons. Thus, it is odd to speak of having compassion for oneself, or for a character whom one knows to be fictional. Of course, I might say that when I look back on my adolescence I feel compassion for the boy I once was, but in doing so I dis-tinguish my present self from my past self, treating the latter as if he were another person. Again, while it is undoubtedly poss-ible to be moved by the misfortunes of fictional characters, an

impulse to relieve their distress or a wish to remove their dis-
comfort would indicate that one had forgotten that they *were*
fictional characters. Genuine love or compassion seems to
presuppose a belief in the independence and reality of its
object.

Similarly, it would seem that a moral attitude necessarily
includes a recognition of real obligations to other people. If it
does, the Bodhisattva's stance cannot be moral since it is impossible to have real obligations to non-existent people. (For
example, I cannot have real obligations to Mr Pickwick.)

The mixed life combines contemplation and moral activity.
Since there are reasons for doubting that Mahāyāna's repudiation of the Arhat's self-seeking is primarily based on moral
grounds, and since there are reasons for doubting that the Bodhisattva's behaviour is either compassionate or moral in any
standard sense, there are reasons for doubting that the Bodhisattva ideal provides a genuine analogue of the mixed life of
Bernard and other Christian mystics.

It should be noted that Mahāyāna incorporates what might
be called 'quasi-theistic elements'. For example, the Dharmakāya is the suchness of things thought of as an appropriate
object of devotional attitudes. While it is sometimes described
impersonally, it is typically said to be an intelligent mind and
a loving heart. Again, in Mahāyāna, Buddhas and Bodhisattvas assume the role of saviour gods. With the possible
exception of the Buddhism of Faith (Pure Land Buddhism)
Mahāyāna is not theistic; reality is ultimately 'emptiness'
(śūnyatā). Nevertheless, from a certain point of view it is
appropriate to think of reality as if it were personal.

It is difficult to believe that there is no connection between
an outlook which places compassion at the heart of things (if
only metaphorically) and an ideal or model of behaviour which
includes compassion as an essential ingredient. One might
suggest therefore that the presence of these quasi-theistic elements partly explains why compassion is a constituent of the
Bodhisattva ideal, while the fact that wisdom and emptiness
are basic or primary explains why that ideal is not fully moral.

These considerations lead to the following question: Does
the ideal of the mixed life ever *clearly* occur in contexts which
are essentially 'uncontaminated' by theistic notions and feel-

ings? The answer is uncertain, but our examination of the Bodhisattva ideal would suggest that it does not.

D

The ideal of the mixed life is closely associated with theistic mysticism, but it is apparently not peculiar to Christian mysticism. According to Reynold A Nicholson, 'to abide in God (*baqā*) after having passed away from selfhood (*fanā*) is the mark of the Perfect Man, who not only journeys *to* God, *i.e.* passes from plurality to unity, but *in* and *with* God, *i.e.* continuing in the unitive state, he returns with God to the phenomenal world... In this descent "He makes the Law his upper garment/And the mystic Path his inner garment".'[42] Afifuddīn al-Tilamsānī maintained that there are four 'journeys'. The first involves unitive states of consciousness. The fourth is 'associated with physical death'. The second and third involve turning back towards creatures. Thus, 'in the *third* journey, this Perfect Man turns his attention to God's creatures, either as an Apostle or as a Spiritual Director (Sheykh).'[43]

Theism cannot be identified with theistic mysticism. As Ninian Smart has suggested,[44] Jewish theism and the theism of primitive Islam are relatively pure expressions of numinous experience. Christian theism, Sufism and Indian theism weave the mystical and numinous strands together, but both Christian theism and Sufism have important non-mystical roots. Since the theism associated with the numinous strand tends to be preoccupied with questions of guilt, sin, righteousness and atonement, one must consider the possibility that the moral concern of theistic mystics is to be attributed to the fact that they are theists, and only incidentally to the fact that they are mystics.[45] On the other hand, theistic mysticism is a dualistic mysticism of love and grace. It incorporates the belief that souls are distinct from God, that God is love, and that God loves the unworthy. (Or perhaps more accurately, that one's own soul is distinct from the apparent object of the experience, and that that object loves one, and 'infinitely' surpasses one in worth and excellence.) But beliefs concerning the nature of what is religiously ultimate and thus most fundamental and valuable, tend to suggest patterns of behaviour; the idea that

human behaviour should imitate divine behaviour pervades
religious thought and practice. (For example, the Taoist sage
is himself an image of the Tao.) It would therefore be natural
for a theistic mystic to infer that he too should love others in
spite of their unworthiness. Thus, even though the ideal of the
mixed life undoubtedly has many roots, there is nothing *intrinsically* implausible in supposing that it was created by theistic
mystics on the basis of their own experience.

How could we test the hypothesis that theistic *mysticism* is
one important source of the ideal of the mixed life? One way of
doing so would be to examine the theisms of India, since these
appear to place relatively more weight on mystical consciousness than Western theisms, and relatively less weight on
numinous experience and the themes of sin, guilt, righteousness and atonement.

The *Bhagavad-Gītā* is, on the whole, a theistic work. One of
its central teachings is the doctrine of karma yoga. The practitioner of karma yoga rejects inactivity. Instead of withdrawing from the world, he continues to discharge his social and
moral obligations, but he does so in a spirit of non-attachment.
He acts, but without regard for the effects which his actions
have upon his own future. There is a certain similarity
between karma yoga and the ideal of the mixed life, for
in both cases 'contemplation' or 'union' is combined with
action.

Danto describes karma yoga in the following way. Suppose,
for example, that one is a doctor. As a doctor, one is concerned
with those consequences which are intrinsically connected
with the end of one's profession. The *Gītā* is not suggesting that
a doctor who has been informed that he had administered the
wrong medicine should reply that the consequences of his acts
mean nothing to him, for as a doctor he wishes to do those
things which produce health. On the other hand, he should
not be concerned with those consequences (wealth, repu-
tation, personal satisfaction, a fortunate rebirth) which are
only incidentally connected with the end of his profession. A
person acts properly when he discharges the duties of his role
well, but is not attached to the extrinsic consequences of his behaviour.[46]

Danto believes that this ideal is morally defective. By

merging with one's role in this manner one becomes impersonal, and 'we hold it against people who *are* utterly impersonal in their dealings, who identify with their offices: we say
they are not human, are mere machines, or have no heart.'[47]

Danto's objection is not entirely convincing. In the first
place, feelings, attitudes and deep commitments are built into
certain roles (citizen, priest, father, husband) but not others
(dustman, tennis player). I cannot perform my role as father
unless I love my children and am deeply committed to their
well-being. By contrast, no special feelings or attitudes are
needed to be a good dustman. Nor does the role involve
commitments which engage the depths of one's personality.
The accusation of impersonality is usually directed against
someone who identifies himself with the second type of role, or
routinely discharges the external obligations which are connected with the first type of role but gives no indication that he
possesses the feelings and attitudes, the cares and concerns,
which are also part of it. It is not clear that the accusation of
impersonality would be appropriate if it were directed against
a person who identified himself with *all* of his roles, displaying
not only the external behaviour but the inner attitudes and
commitments appropriate to each.

In the second place, no one who performs a function or role
for an ulterior end identifies himself with that function or role
since he has ends which do not belong to him in so far as he
serves that function or plays that role. Danto's point appears
to be that a person who practices karma yoga is unable to distinguish himself from his functions because karma yoga
involves the renunciation of every end except those defined by
the roles one plays. But this is false, for a person practises
karma yoga in order to achieve mokṣa and mokṣa is an end
which transcends all roles.[48]

But Danto has another objection which is potentially more
damaging. The acts performed by an agent who practises
karma yoga are not really his. First, because the acts are performed by his body, and he is distinct from his body. Second,
because the role with which he identifies is a kind of nature,
and people are not responsible for acts that are determined by
their nature. Since the acts which the agent performs are not
really his, he is not really functioning as a moral agent and is

therefore 'exempted from any moral penalties in the karmic order'.[49] But this detachment, according to Danto, is morally objectionable. 'There is something chilling in the image that the *Gītā* creates as we approach the end: Krishna ... and Arjuna .. move through the battle with that half-smile of the inturned face of Indian art as they slay their way dispassionately across the field of conflict.' Their stand 'is not a moral stand, but a stand outside morality'.[50]

This objection is also inconclusive. In the first place, as Danto recognises, the *Gītā* presupposes that an agent can refuse to perform the duties associated with his role and thus act against his 'nature'. The *Gītā* does not argue that because one's acts are 'determined' (i.e. defined) by one's 'nature' (i.e. one's role) they are unavoidable, and that one is therefore not responsible for them.

It is true that one's 'true self' or 'real I' is distinct from the psycho-physical organism (i.e., from the body together with sensation, vital forces (prāna), and ordinary empirical consciousness). Furthermore, the *Gītā* does tell us that it is not the Self but 'nature', i.e. 'the whole of one's past experience conjoined with the energies that constitute the natural orders of the world' which is the 'real doer'.[51] According to the *Gītā*, 'all actions are performed by the *gunas* of *prakriti*[52] alone. But he who is deluded by egoism thinks, "I am the doer".' (III, 27)[53] In reality, the true self is 'unaffected by empirical action and is a pure witness to this action'.[54]

But the *Gītā* also contains another theme. Ultimately the practitioner of karma yoga must achieve a higher bhakti (loving devotion) in which, united with the Lord, 'he acts in the knowledge that all action is essentially the Divine's action. He becomes an instrument of the divine.'[55]

Nevertheless, these considerations do not get to the heart of Danto's objection. Suppose that someone wholeheartedly discharges the duties of his various roles but is otherwise detached from the consequences of his behaviour, including its consequences for other people. Suppose, in particular, that as a soldier or policeman, he has correctly determined that he has an obligation to kill someone and does so in a spirit of detachment. Danto maintains that this is 'chilling' and he may be correct. But is it morally objectionable? It would be morally objectionable if (1) empathy or compassion, a sympathetic participation in other people's joys and sufferings, is necessary if our acts are to have moral value, and if (2) these attitudes are psychologically incompatible with detachment, a spiritual distance from one's own ordinary preoccupations and from the ordinary preoccupations of others. However, (1) is not clearly true (Kant denied it) and (2) seems to be falsified by the lives of some of the great mystics, for example Bernard or Eckhart. (To a certain extent we can, I think, understand this paradoxical combination of compassion and detachment. Consider, for example, the way in which we are able to share in the joys and sorrows of a small child while at the same time recognising their vanity.)

I conclude, then, that Danto has not shown that karma yoga is non-moral.[56]

E

If the argument of this section has been sound, we are entitled to draw the following conclusions. First, the ideal of the mixed life incorporates moral values. Second, Danto's moral objections to karma yoga are inconclusive. Third, the ideals of Advaita Vedānta and Hīnayāna Buddhism are non-moral. Since the ideal of the mixed life and karma yoga tend to be closely associated with theistic mysticism while Advaita Vedānta and (possibly) Hīnayāna Buddhism appear to be relatively pure expressions of monistic mystical consciousness, it seems reasonable to infer that theistic mysticism is implicitly moral, whereas monistic mysticism is not. What is not clear is whether the theistic mystic's attitude towards moral values is determined by his theism or by his mystical experiences. I suspect that the former is the principal determinant, and that the theistic mystic's experiences affect his attitudes primarily by reinforcing his commitment to theism.

The force of these considerations would be diminished if it could be shown that the ideal of the mixed life is an important feature of one or more non-theistic traditions, and that there are no reasonable grounds for supposing that its incorporation in those traditions is due to theistic influences. (Further study of the Bodhisattva ideal is needed in this connection.) To destroy the force of these considerations one would have to show that the ideal of the mixed life occurs as frequently within non-theistic mystical traditions as within theistic mystical traditions, and that its non-moral alternatives occur as frequently within theistic mystical traditions as within non-theistic mystical traditions. This is manifestly not the case.

II

There are often said to be important logical or epistemic connections between mystical experience and morality.[57] I shall first examine two attempts to show that mystical consciousness provides a backing or warrant for altruistic behaviour, and then consider two arguments which have been offered to support the contention that mysticism and morality are mutually incompatible. These arguments are paradigmatic. Most of the arguments which attempt to establish a logical or epistemic connection between mysticism and morality are variants of the arguments discussed in this section. My conclusion is that all four arguments are unsound, and that there is therefore reason to suspect that there are no significant logical or epistemic connections between mystical consciousness and morality.

A

(1) Walter Stace believes that mystical consciousness provides a foundation for altruism.[58] It does this in two quite different ways.

In the first place, mystical consciousness causally induces loving behaviour by eliminating the major obstacle to altruism, viz, the egoism of ordinary consciousness. This thesis is empirical and some evidence supports it. Nevertheless, its truth is irrelevant to our present purposes. The existence of psychological connections between mystical consciousness and morality has no tendency to establish the existence of logical or epistemic connections between them.

In the second place, mystical consciousness provides a justification or warrant for loving behavior. Consider the following argument.

(1) We are all one – identical with each other or part of one another. There are no separate selves. (This proposition is directly warranted by mystical consciousness.) Therefore,

(2) I should treat others as I (either do or should) treat myself, i.e. I ought to care tenderly for them, benefit them, and so on.

I find this argument suspect on at least three counts.

First, the premise is not clearly true and, in any case, it does not seem to be directly warranted by mystical consciousness. If the proposition that we are fundamentally identical or part of one another was directly warranted by mystical consciousness, it would be difficult to account for the fact that it is rejected by theistic mystics, by Theravādins, and by mystics adhering to the Sāmkhya-Yoga system. This fact suggests that the proposition in question is an interpretation of mystical experience and not a contention which is directly warranted by it. The most that could be claimed is that Stace's unitary experiences (cosmic consciousness and monistic consciousness) incorporate the belief that all selves are one. But even this is not clear. The impressions of intimate union and of the dissolution of boundaries which are part of nature mysticism are one thing, a belief that we are literally one entity is quite another. Only the latter entitles me to conclude that I should treat others as I treat myself because they *are* myself.

One might think that the premise immediately follows from a conviction which is directly warranted by monistic experience, viz, all distinctions are unreal. However, while it is not entirely implausible to suppose that a belief in the unreality of all distinctions is an intrinsic feature of monistic consciousness, I believe that it is a mistake to do so. Monistic mystics (frequently) distinguish aspects within (the object of) their experience. Furthermore, even if these experiences are cognitively valid, and even if the experience or its object is distinctionless, it does not follow that all distinctions are unreal, for the experience and/or its object may be something less than the whole of reality. The monistic experience, for example, might be an experience of the depth of one's own soul.

Second, the argument suggests that we should care for

others because they are identical with us. Altruism is grounded in egoism and is, therefore, not genuine.

Third, it has been argued (by Paul Tillich, Martin Buber, D H Lawrence, and others) that love should involve distance and difference as well as union. If this is the case, and if Stace's premise is true, then it would appear that real love is impossible. His premise, far from supporting the claim that we should care for others, makes love impossible.[59]

Since the premise of Stace's argument is not directly warranted by the types of mystical experience which he considers, we are not entitled to conclude that they justify altruism. We are at most entitled to conclude that a certain interpretation of these types of mystical consciousness justifies altruism. Unfortunately even this conclusion proves to be unwarranted, for the premise not only fails to justify altruism, but would, if true, make altruism impossible.

(2) Browning has called our attention to the fact that in addition to the argument from union, there is an argument from 'mysticisms of emptiness and void . . . Since in the final experience of nirvana, norodh ['stopping'] or "no mind" all vestiges of ego and self are abolished, it is argued by some that all egoism, selfishness, and self-centeredness vanish and only altruism and love remain.'[60]

Up to a point, this makes a certain rough sense. The unreality of the self implies the unreality of its interests and concerns. 'I am interested in (desire, hate, etc.) x' entails or presupposes 'I exist'. Hence, if the latter is false, the former is false.[61] Whether the experience of 'emptiness' can be used to justify altruistic behaviour is another matter.

The argument would presumably go like this:

(1) Reasons for acting egoistically are provided by one's interests, needs, concerns and desires.

(2) These interests, needs, concerns and desires are real only if the self is real.

(3) The self is unreal. (The backing for this premise is provided by the experience of 'emptiness'.) Therefore,

(4) A person's interests, needs, concerns and desires are unreal. (From 2 and 3.) Therefore,

(5) There are no good reasons for acting egoistically. (From 1 and 4, and the assumption that if an interest or need is

unreal, it cannot provide a good reason for action.)
Therefore,

(6) There are good reasons for acting altruistically. (From 5.)

Several things are wrong with this argument. In the first place, (5) does not entail (6). Even if there were no good reasons *for* acting egoistically, it would not follow that there were good reasons *against* acting egoistically. And even if there were good reasons against acting egoistically, it would not follow that there were good reasons for acting altruistically. The wisest thing to do might be to withdraw from society, and it is not clear that this course of action is either egoistic or altruistic. (Those who withdraw from society have been accused of egoism. For example, Mahāyāna accuses Hīnayāna of a subtle self-seeking. But this is controversial. The Hīnayāna Arhat has succeeded in rooting out what we ordinarily regard as selfishness. He has extinguished thirst and neither injures others nor harbours ill-will towards them. He no longer competes with them or sacrifices their real interests to his own.)

In the second place, (3) is a statement of the Buddhist no-ātman doctrine, and this doctrine appears to rest as much upon metaphysical analysis as upon mystical experience. (Remember that we are looking for epistemic connections between mystical consciousness and moral claims, not between metaphysical claims which are more or less loosely based upon mystical consciousness and moral claims.)

There is a third objection. While insisting that the Ātman-Brahman alone is truly real, Advaita Vedānta does ascribe a certain provisional validity to ordinary practical reasoning. Familiar reasons are valid at the level of mundane spatio-temporal reality. In so far as the mystic continues to be part of this world, he has the same reasons as anyone else for eating bread instead of iron filings, leaving by the stairs instead of the upper window, or predicting rain when the sky looks threatening. The Buddhist school which developed the doctrine of emptiness with the most sophistication (viz, Mādhyamika) rejected the belief in an underlying substance such as the Ātman-Brahman, but it did distinguish between paramārtha satya, or absolute truth, the intuitive non-conceptual insight into the emptiness of reality, and saṃvṛti satya, or conventional truth.[62] And this creates a problem, for, on the conventional level, the self is real and there is hence no reason to suppose that ordinary motives for acting self-interestedly are suspended. Ordinary prudential reasons may only apply at the level of mundane reality, but at that level there is no reason to believe they are invalid. (3) and (4) are only true at the level of absolute truth and hence (5) is only true at the level of absolute truth. Therefore, unless we can assert that the mystic no longer dwells in the conventional world at all, it is a mistake to conclude that prudential considerations provide him with no reason for acting self-interestedly.

B

In this section we will turn our attention to arguments which purport to show that mysticism and morality are incompatible. Consider the following two arguments:

(i) (1) The divine (the absolute, the One, that which is truly real) embraces opposites, or opposites coincide in the divine. (The backing for this statement is provided by mystical consciousness.)

(2) These opposites include moral good and moral evil. Therefore,

(3) The distinction between moral good and moral evil is unimportant or unreal. (It is unimportant if both moral good and moral evil manifest the divine. It is unreal if moral good and moral evil coincide.)[63]

(ii) (4) The divine altogether transcends the phenomenal world and/or the phenomenal world is unreal or totally lacking in value. (The backing for this statement is provided by mystical consciousness.) Hence,

(5) The categories which apply within the phenomenal world, and the distinctions which can be drawn between things within it, are infected by illusion (or are at least unimportant).

(6) Moral categories apply within the phenomenal world, and the distinction between moral good and moral evil is a distinction between phenomenal realities. Therefore,

(7) Moral categories are infected by illusion (or are at least

unimportant).[64]

Several comments are in order:

(1) Certain types of mystical consciousness do seem to imply that moral values are not the most important values. One may respond to this fact in two quite different ways. (a) One may argue that moral values are by definition the most important ones, that the best life must include an unqualified respect for the moral law, and that if mysticism assigns a secondary role to moral values then mysticism undercuts morality. (b) One may, on the other hand, argue that moral values are instrumental and are, therefore, logically posterior to those values (for example, blessedness, happiness, self-realisation) to which morally good things are means. If mystical consciousness is one of the ends (or part of an end) to which moral values are means, then mystical consciousness is not necessarily incompatible with morality even if it does relegate moral values to a secondary position.

But the contention that moral values are not the most important values should not be confused with the conclusions of the two arguments we are now discussing. If these arguments are sound, moral values are not merely assigned a secondary or instrumental role but either collapse altogether or are reduced to insignificance.

(2) Proposition (1) is based on cosmic consciousness and (4) is based on monistic consciousness. Since there are other types of mystical consciousness, we cannot conclude that mysticism as such is incompatible with morality. The most we can conclude is that cosmic consciousness and monistic consciousness are incompatible with morality.

(3) I have suggested that the first argument appeals to cosmic consciousness, and that the second argument appeals to monistic consciousness. Do these modes of consciousness really support the conclusion that moral values are either illusory or unimportant? They would support that conclusion if (a) the relevant experiences were veridical and if (b) the convictions articulated in (1) and (4) were directly warranted by those experiences. The second assumption seems to be false.

Nature mysticism includes a sense of the radical unity of all things, and nature mystics do sometimes speak of the identity of phenomenal objects. Nevertheless, it is not clear that cosmic consciousness includes a sense of the coincidence of *all* distinctions or that it normally involves a sense of the divinity of specifically moral evil. However, if either of these two intuitions *is* an intrinsic feature of cosmic consciousness, it is possible to argue (with Zæhner) that cosmic consciousness, for that very reason, cannot be veridical and that therefore, if the second assumption is true, the first assumption is false.

If the conviction that all distinctions are unreal were indeed built into monistic mystical consciousness, then the unreality of the phenomenal world would follow from monistic experience. But as we have seen, a belief in the unreality of *all* distinctions does not appear to be a structural feature of monistic consciousness. Nor do monistic mystics always conclude that the phenomenal world is unreal or lacking in value. (Monistic mystics like Plotinus and the adherents of Sāṁkhya-Yoga believe in real distinctions and a real space-time world. Furthermore, Plotinus believes that the world is good in so far as it reflects the One, and Sāṁkhya-Yoga ascribes value to it in so far as it serves the purposes of puruṣa.)

These considerations suggest that (1) and (4) are interpretations of cosmic consciousness and monistic consciousness respectively rather than propositions which are directly warranted by those modes of consciousness, and that we are, therefore, only entitled to conclude that certain (extreme) *interpretations* of cosmic consciousness and monistic consciousness are incompatible with morality but not that cosmic consciousness and monistic consciousness themselves are incompatible with it.

(4) The experience of 'emptiness' would be incompatible with morality if it incorporated the conviction that *all* distinctions are equally invalid, for this would entail that all moral distinctions are equally invalid. It is not clear that it does include this conviction. (See chapter 3, IIF.) If it does, then one can argue that because moral distinctions are valid, the experience is delusive. While it may not be clear precisely where the burden of proof lies, our moral experience is at least as compelling as our religious experience.

(5) Theistic mystical consciousness provides no support for the conclusion that moral values are illusory or unimportant. In some contexts 'x is more real than y' is equivalent to 'x is

more valuable than y, and y is dependent upon x.'[65] Given that a sense of dependence and comparative worthlessness (the dependence and comparative worthlessness of oneself and of creatures generally) is built into theistic consciousness,[66] that the world is less real, or only relatively real, or comparatively unreal, *does* follow from theistic mystical consciousness. What does *not* follow is that *moral values* are less real, or only relatively real, or comparatively unreal. This does not follow because, for theistic consciousness, the transcendent order itself is a realm of moral value. Indeed, the moral value which is exhibited in the phenomenal world is considered to be no more than an image or reflection of God's archetypal moral goodness.

III

Mysticism sometimes affects morality adversely. It does so when it makes a person indifferent to moral values and the importance of moral distinctions. On the other hand, mysticism often appears to have a positive and beneficial effect upon the moral lives of those who are touched by it. Mysticism strengthens morality both by strengthening those attitudes and dispositions which are moral or which have moral consequences (such as charity, equanimity and detachment), and by bringing certain truths home to us (such as, for example, the truth of the reality of the transcendent order and the fact that persons belong to that order as well as to nature). What is not clear is that mysticism teaches any morally relevant truths which are not available to us apart from mystical experience,[67] or that any moral ideal or norm depends upon mystical consciousness for its validity. If the argument of section II is correct, then neither cosmic consciousness, monistic consciousness nor the experience of emptiness is a necessary or sufficient condition of the truth or falsity of any moral proposition. Theistic mystical consciousness may include a positive evaluation of love and holiness and a belief that these play an important part in the scheme of things. But there is no reason to believe that the conviction that human love and holiness are morally valuable cannot be adequately supported without appealing to mystical consciousness, or even that mystical consciousness provides the most compelling grounds for this conviction. I therefore conclude that while there may be significant psychological or social connections between mysticism and morality, there are few significant logical or epistemic connections.

Notes

[1] The two questions are not unrelated. As Stace has observed (*Mysticism and Philosophy, op cit*, p 333), it is not particularly plausible to suppose that mystical consciousness provides a warrant for morality if it inhibits morality in practice. The reason, I believe, is this. Other things being equal, we expect people who are in a good epistemic position to perceive the grounds of morality to act at least as morally as those who are not. If the mystic's conduct and his ideals are either immoral or amoral, then there is a presumption that mystical consciousness provides no logical support for morality. For similar reasons, if the mystic's conduct and ideals are exemplary, there is indirect evidence that mysticism does not justify immoral or amoral activity.

[2] I shall not discuss nature mysticism. The moral effects of cosmic consciousness are ambiguous. They may occasionally be good, are sometimes bad, but are usually neither good nor bad. (There is little hard evidence that the feelings of empathy which are part of cosmic consciousness have significant effects upon a person's moral *behaviour*.) In so far as cosmic consciousness is associated with a specific ideal, it is an ideal which embraces good and evil. Cosmic consciousness often expresses itself in 'pantheism', the belief that nature, or the spirit which permeates it or animates it, is holy or divine. Because nature indifferently embraces good and evil, the ideals which are associated with this outlook tend to be amoral. (Though this should not be over-stated. While the nature mystic or 'pantheist' may say that everything is holy, the evil which he celebrates is usually natural evil such as suffering and destruction, unconventional social behaviour, or deviant sexual behaviour – not theft, murder or betrayal.) There is therefore even less reason to believe that cosmic consciousness provides independent support for moral ideals, than to believe that other types of mystical experience do so.

[3] Quoted in *Western Mysticism, op cit*, pp 162 and 163.

[4] Quoted, *ibid*, pp 160 and 165.

[5] Quoted, *ibid*, p 171.

[6] Quoted, *ibid*, p 176.

[7] Quoted, *ibid*, p 180.

[8] Quoted, *ibid*, p 184.

[9] Quoted, *ibid*, p 176.

[10] Quoted, *ibid*, p 192.

[11] 'Four Degrees of Passionate Charity', *Selected Writings on Contemplation, op cit*, p 224.

[12] *The Adornment of the Spiritual Marriage, etc., op cit*, pp 220–21.

[13] Butler maintains (*op cit*, pp 211–12) that John of the Cross departs from this tradition, and quotes from the prefatory remarks to stanza xxix of the *Spiritual Canticle*:

> Here it is to be noted that, for so long as the soul has not reached this estate of union of love, it must needs practise love, both in the active life and in the contemplative; but when it reaches that estate it befits it not to be occupied in other outward acts and exercises which might keep it back, however little, from that abiding in love with God, although they may greatly conduce to the service of God; for a very little of this pure love is more precious in the sight of God and the soul, and of greater profit to the Church, even though the soul appear to be doing nothing, than all these other works together... Therefore if any soul should have aught of this degree of solitary love, great wrong would be done to it, and to the Church, if, even for a brief space, one should endeavour to busy it in active or outward affairs, of however great moment. (*Spiritual Canticle*, 3rd rev ed, transl and ed by E Allison Peers, Garden City, New York, 1961, pp 416–17.)

It should be noted however that this passage is only found in the second redaction of the *Spiritual Canticle*, and that the second redaction may be spurious. (See Peers' introduction, *ibid*, pp 36–7.)

[14] *Op cit*.

[15] Quoted, *ibid*, p 100.

[16] I C Sharma, *Ethical Philosophies of India*, New York and Evanston, 1970.

[17] *The Bhagavad-Gītā with the commentary of Śrī Śankarachāryā*, transl by A Mahādeva Śāstri, Madras, 1961, p 136.

[18] *Ibid*, p 135.

[19] *Ibid*, p 107.

[20] *Ibid*, p 103f.

[21] Eliot Deutsch and J A B van Buitenen, *A Source Book of Advaita Vedānta*, Honolulu, 1971, p 219.

[22] Quoted by R C Zæhner in *Hinduism*, New York, 1966, p 167.

[23] One might object that classical Advaita assumes that, normally, one already will have fulfilled one's social obligations. (Ideally, one becomes a sannyāsin (an ascetic who has severed all ties with society) only after one has been a householder and discharged the duties of that stage.) But this misses the point, viz, that in classical Advaita, the *highest* stage of life does not itself involve any social obligations. By contrast, the mixed life *combines* contemplation and action in the highest stage.

[24] See, e.g., *A Dialogue of Religions*, London, 1960.

[25] Anatta (no soul or self) is the third 'mark of existence'. But the non-existence of a persisting ego or soul, or of any other permanent substance, is a logical consequence of the belief that samsāra (the space-time world) is nothing but a flow of momentary constituents (dhammas).

[26] Since the brahma vihāras are a method for disciplining our emotions, Buddhaghosa is presumably referring to the *wish* or *desire* to confer benefits, and not (except perhaps incidentally) to external behaviour.

27 Quoted in Edward Conze, *Buddhist Thought in India, op cit*, p 82.

28 *Ibid*, p 90.

29 The other tool which is closely associated with the eighth stage is the jhānas. The jhānas culminate in monistic mystical consciousness (the stage of 'neither perception nor non-perception' or, in some versions, 'the attainment of cessation'). There are usually said to be eight (or nine) jhānas but there is some reason to believe that the fourth jhāna – the state of equanimity, calm, or 'even-mindedness' – is valued more highly than the last four (or five). For example, it is said that the Buddha, as he approached death, passed through all the jhānas but came to rest in the fourth. The brahma vihāras and the jhānas ultimately appear to have the same aim, viz, even-mindedness.

30 According to Rune E A Johansson (*The Psychology of Nirvana*, Garden City, New York, 1970, p 83ff), a few texts suggest that pannā alone may sometimes be sufficient.

31 Richard H Jones, 'Theravāda Buddhism and Morality', *Journal of the American Academy of Religion* XLVIII (1979), pp 371–87.

32 How widely spread is this ideal? The fact that the Buddha's compassion is prized by those who are not yet enlightened is inconclusive since one may prize it for self-regarding reasons. That a person values the Buddha's compassionate behaviour because of its benefit to him is no evidence that he cherishes an altruistic ideal.

33 The latter applies to Advaita as well as to Hīnayāna. Śaṃkara, for example, attempted to 'pass the torch' to others. I have the impression, however, that admiration and emulation of selfless behaviour is more pronounced in Hīnayāna than in classical Advaita. If this is correct, it is probably due to the fact that Advaita lacks anything comparable to the Buddha story. (The Buddha's selfless history lies at the core of Buddhism. Advaita has nothing quite like this.)

34 Arthur Koestler, *The Lotus and the Robot*, London, 1960, p 270f.

35 Thomas Merton, *Zen and the Birds of Appetite*, New York, 1968, p 104. (Part II consists of a dialogue between Merton and Suzuki.)

36 *Ibid*, pp 105–106.

37 *Ibid*, p 112.

38 *Op cit*, pp 271–2. Cf Arthur Danto on Taoism (*Mysticism and Morality*, New York and London, 1973, p 112f.)

39 *Ibid*, pp 80–2.

40 Quoted in Edward Conze, *Buddhism: Its Essence and Development*, New York, 1959, p 128.

41 Quoted, *ibid*, p 130.

42 Reynold A Nicholson, *The Mystics of Islam*, London, 1963, p 163.

43 *Ibid*, p 165.

44 *A Dialogue of Religions, op cit*.

45 This hypothesis is confirmed by the following consideration. Although it strongly emphasised the affective side of religion, The Great Awakening was not a mystical movement. (The regenerate underwent a change of heart, but they were not extrovertive or introvertive mystics.) Nevertheless, in his *Religious Affections* (New Haven, 1959) Jonathan Edwards

maintained that genuine conversion involves a sense and relish of 'the transcendently excellent and amiable nature of divine things, as they are in themselves' (p 240), 'a love to divine things for the beauty and sweetness of their moral excellency' (p 253f), an understanding of divine things and a conviction of their reality and certainty, 'evangelical humiliation' (p 311), the 'the lamblike, dovelike spirit and temper of Jesus Christ' (p 344), and holy practice consisting 'very much' in 'all the duties of the second table of the law', i.e., in moral behaviour (p 396). This ideal which combines 'experimental' insight and practical activity is not that different from the ideal of the mixed life subscribed to by Christian mystics. This suggests that the primary source of both ideals is the (Christian?) theism which these evangelicals and mystics have in common (and/or their emotionally involved commitment to it), and not the specific nature of their different experiences.

[46] *Op cit*, pp 92–3.
[47] *Ibid*, p 93.
[48] One might argue that mokṣa is an end associated with the role of sannyāsin or wanderer. There is a sense in which this is true. The sannyāsin, having discharged his obligations as citizen and father, is now in a position to devote himself exclusively to the achievement of mokṣa. In a more fundamental sense, it is false. Mokṣa, with its release from life's ills, is the ultimate though often unrecognised aim of every conscious being *qua* conscious being; it is not an aim one has only in so far as one assumes a special role.
[49] *Ibid*, p 98.
[50] *Ibid*, pp 94–5.
[51] Eliot Deutsch, *The Bhagavad Gītā*, New York, 1968, p 165.
[52] Prakrti, which is composed of the guṇas, is the 'stuff' of which nature is constructed. Nature comprises (ordinary) psychological realities and transactions as well as physical realities and transactions. It is distinct from the true self, and distinct from the Lord.
[53] *Ibid*, p 50.
[54] *Ibid*, p 166.
[55] *Ibid*, p 169. However, Zæhner argues that, in the *Gītā*, the purified soul is essentially inactive. It recognises that its acts are not the expression of its own inner being but of the motions of prakṛti which is activated by, or in some way identical with, God's power and activity. It acquiesces in God's action, so to speak, but does not participate in it. (*Concordant Discord, op cit*, p 134). It may be significant that in at least one important theistic development of the themes of the *Gītā* and *Upanishads* (viz, Viśiṣṭādvaita Vedānta), the Pure Self is regarded as a doer. According to Rāmānuja, the Pure Self is the agent in every action, and not merely (as it is for Śaṃkara) the consciousness in every act of awareness.
[56] Whether we have anything which precisely corresponds to the mixed life is less clear. We would if karma yoga were an essential component of the most perfect life. I have already alluded to Viśiṣṭādvaita Vedānta. P N Srinivasachari (*The Philosophy of Viśiṣṭādvaita*, Adyar, 1946) describes its ethical position in the following way. After karma yoga has been described

as 'duty for duty's sake irrespective of inclination within and utility without' (p 330), Srinivasachari concludes by asserting that it 'is not really an end in itself, but is a means to mukti through self-purification and self-knowledge': (p 333) This would imply that it is not part of the most perfect life. On the other hand, Srinivasachari maintains that 'the *jñānī* [the knower] realises the kinship of all *jīvas* [souls] and regards the joys and sorrows of others as his own. Sympathy is not merely a feeling that impels the *yogin*, but is a spiritual motive that induces him to action... The monistic theory that abolishes individuality [Advaita Vedānta] affords no scope for such social love'. (p 345) 'The mystic realises that he is only an instrument of the divine will... His life is supramoral in the sense that it is the crown and completion of the moral life. God is absolutely good and is not morally indifferent, and the chief quality of God is transmitting His godliness to His *other* and making him perfect. Saintliness and unrighteousness can never co-exist.' (p 443) Mysticism is only amoral in the sense that 'morality is at best a struggle to reach the ideal of goodness,' whereas the saint 'has no longer to seek the good but becomes goodness itself.' 'Spirituality is perfected in service.' (p 444) The Viśiṣṭādvaita ideal thus appears to be the mixed life.
Nevertheless these passages must be handled carefully. In the first place, Srinivasachari is a modern Viśiṣṭādvaitin, a professor of philosophy familiar with Western thought. Its influence therefore cannot be excluded. In the second place, Srinivasachari fails to cite classical texts that clearly take the position which he has articulated. We are thus not entitled to conclude that the mixed life was unambiguously recommended by premodern Viśiṣṭādvaita Vedānta. In spite of these reservations, however, it seems reasonable to conclude that the emphasis placed upon action in the *Gītā* and theistic Vedānta reflects a greater concern for moral and social values than is found in either Advaita or Hīnayāna Buddhism.

[57] Or more accurately, between propositions which are directly warranted by mystical consciousness and moral propositions.
[58] *Mysticism and Philosophy, op cit*, chapter 8.
[59] Although I suppose that one could argue that, in spite of our real unity, the difference between our empirical egos is sufficient to create the requisite distance.
[60] Don Browning, 'William James' Philosophy of Mysticism', *The Journal of Religion* 59 (1979), p 58.
[61] Or neither true nor false.
[62] Candrakīrti gives three definitions of 'saṃvṛti satya' – (1) 'views', (2) the phenomenal world, (3) 'views in conformity with conventional ideas'. False statements (e.g., the statement of the man who, mistaking a rope for a snake, says 'that's a snake') are subsumed under saṃvṛti satya, and in this respect Mādhyamika does admit differences and degrees with the realm of saṃvṛti satya. (Some claims are more deeply infected with falsehood than others.) See T R V Murti, *The Central Philosophy of Buddhism, op cit*, pp 243–55.
[63] For an argument of this type see R C Zæhner, *Our Savage God (op cit)*. Zæhner is critical of non-theistic mysticism precisely because he believes

that it implicitly incorporates this type of reasoning.

[64] Arthur Danto (*op cit*) argues that the 'logic of mysticism' forces mystics to draw this conclusion.

[65] This usage may be contrasted with that of Advaita Vedānta in which 'less real' is interpreted with the help of the notion of sublation (one perception or insight sublates another if it supersedes it and shows it to be in error), and with that of Mādhyamka in which 'unreal' is interpreted as 'self-contradictory or incoherent'.

[66] It is clearly built into numinous consciousness. I believe that it is also built into theistic mystical consciousness.

[67] Mystical experience might have been the fountainhead of some of these insights (without mysticism they might never have occurred to anyone) but, once discovered, we need not be mystics to discern their truth.

Conclusion

In the preceding chapters I have argued for a number of controversial conclusions. Among the more important of these are the following:

(1) There are no good reasons for believing that interpretations of mystical consciousness cannot be distinguished from descriptions of mystical consciousness, or for believing that it is impossible to construct a cross-cultural typology of mystical experience. Furthermore, there are rough criteria which can be used to distinguish interpretations from descriptions, and to determine whether we are dealing with several types of experience or a single experience. (chapter 1)

(2) Zæhner is correct and Stace is wrong. There are at least two distinct types of introvertive mystical experience – monistic mystical consciousness and theistic mystical consciousness. (chapter 1)

(3) Mystical experience is not non-conceptual; in so far as it is noetic, it incorporates concepts. (chapter 3)

(4) Mystical experience is not alogical, and it does not transcend subjectivity and objectivity. (chapter 4)

(5) Introvertive mystical experience is immediate and direct, its apprehension of its object is not mediated through other contents in the way in which our awareness of physical objects is mediated through sense impressions. (chapter 4)

(6) The analogy between sense experience and mystical consciousness is sufficiently close to provide a good reason for believing that mystical experiences are veridical. (chapter 3)

(7) The standard objections to mysticism's cognitive validity are inconclusive. (chapter 3)

(8) The existence of an adequate scientific explanation of religious experience would be compatible with its cognitive

232

validity. (chapter 2)

(9) Mystical experience in general has no direct logical or epistemic bearing upon morality. (chapter 5)

Throughout the book, I have attempted to make a case for the uniqueness and validity of theistic mystical consciousness.[1] But this is not its main purpose. Its main purpose is to show that there are good reasons for crediting at least some mystical intuitions, and thus for believing that there are realms of being or types of reality hidden from ordinary consciousness.

An interesting philosophical argument seldom convinces everyone. This is a reflection of the nature of philosophy's subject matter (knowledge, reality, truth, significance, meaning), and of the absence of a mechanical decision procedure for settling philosophical disputes. Nevertheless, even if they are not conclusive, some philosophical arguments are better or more convincing than others. It is my hope that the reader who has not been convinced by the arguments of this book will have at least achieved a better understanding of the philosophical issues, and that he will be forced to concede that the case for the validity of mystical experience is stronger than he had previously believed.

Notes

[1] It is important to note that the validity of theistic mystical consciousness does not preclude the validity of other types of mystical consciousness, though it may preclude the validity of some of the interpretations which have been placed upon them.

Works Cited

Alston, William P, 'Psychoanalytic Theory and Theistic Belief', *Faith and the Philosophers*, ed by John Hick, London: Macmillan & Co, New York: St Martin's Press, Inc, 1964, pp 63–102.

Religious Belief and Philosophical Thought: Readings in the Philosophy of Religion, New York and Burlingame: Harcourt Brace & World Inc 1963.

Austin, J L, *Sense and Sensibilia*, Oxford: The Clarendon Press, 1962; New York: Oxford University Press, 1964.

Bernard of Clairvaux, *On Loving God and Selections from Sermons by St Bernard of Clairvaux*, ed by Hugh Martin, London: SCM Press, 1959.

Browne, Henry, *Darkness or Light, An Essay in the Theory of Divine Contemplation*, London and St Louis: B Herder Book Co, 1925.

Browning, Don, 'William James' Philosophy of Mysticism'. *The Journal of Religion* 59 (1979), pp 56–70.

Bucke, Richard M, *Cosmic Consciousness*, New York: E P Dutton and Co Inc, 1956.

Burr, Ronald, 'Wittgenstein's Later Language Philosophy and Some Issues in Philosophy of Mysticism', *International Journal for Philosophy of Religion* VII (1976), pp 261–87.

Butler, Edward Cuthbert, *Western Mysticism, The Teaching of Augustine, Gregory and Bernard on Contemplation and the Contemplative Life, 2nd ed with Afterthoughts*, New York: Harper Torchbooks, Harper & Row, 1966; London: Constable, 1967.

Carstairs, G M, 'Daru and Bhang', *Quarterly Journal of Studies on Alcohol* 15 (1954), pp 220–37.

Clark, Walter H, *Chemical Ecstasy, Psychedelic Drugs and Religion*,

New York: Sheed & Ward, 1969.

The Cloud of Unknowing Together with the Epistle of Privy Counsel, ed by Abbot Justin McCann, London: Burns & Oates, 1964.

Conze, Edward, *Buddhism: Its Essence and Development*, New York: Harper Torchbooks, Harper and Brothers, Publishers, 1959; London: Faber & Faber, 1963.

Buddhist Meditation, London: George Allen & Unwin Ltd, 1956; New York and Evanston: Harper Torchbooks, Harper & Row, Publishers, 1969.

Buddhist Thought in India, Three Phases of Buddhist Philosophy, London: George Allen & Unwin Ltd, 1962; Ann Arbor: The University of Michigan Press, 1967.

Copleston, Frederick, *Aquinas*, Harmondsworth, Middlesex: Penguin Books, 1955.

Custance, John, *Wisdom, Madness and Folly: The Philosophy of a Lunatic,* London: Victor Gollancz, 1951; New York: Pellegrini & Cudahy, c 1952.

Danto, Arthur C, *Mysticism and Morality, Oriental Thought and Moral Philosophy*, New York and London: arper Torchbooks, Harper and Row, 1973.

Deikman, Arthur, 'Implications of Experimentally Induced Contemplative Meditation', *Journal of Nervous and Mental Disease* 142 (1966), pp 101–16. Reprinted in *Psychedelics*, (ed by Bernard Aaronson and Humphrey Osmond, Garden City, New York: Anchor Books, Doubleday and Co Inc, 1970; London: Hogarth Press, 1971).

Deutsch, Eliot, *Advaita Vedānta, A Philosophical Reconstruction*, Honolulu: The University Press of Hawaii, 1973.

The Bhagavad-Gītā, transl with introd and critical essays, New York: Holt, Rinehart and Winston, 1968.

Deutsch, Eliot and J A B van Buitenen, *A Source Book of Advaita Vedānta*, Honolulu: The University Press of Hawaii, 1971.

Dhavamony, Mariasusai, *Love of God According to Śaiva Siddhānta*, Oxford: Oxford University Press, 1971.

Donovan, Peter, *Interpreting Religious Experience*, London: Sheldon Press, 1979.

Edwards, Jonathan, *A Treatise Concerning Religious Affections*, (*The Works of Jonathan Edwards*, vol 2), New Haven: Yale University Press, 1959.

Eliade, Mircea, *The Two and the One*, London: Harvill Press, New York: Harper Torchbooks, Harper and Row, 1965.

Emerson, Victor F, 'Research on Meditation', *What is Meditation?* ed by John White, Garden City, New York: Anchor Books, Doubleday & Co Inc, 1974, pp 225–43.

Farges, Albert, *Mystical Phenomena Compared with their Human and Diabolical Counterfeits, A Treatise on Mystical Theology in Agreement with the Principles of St Teresa*, transl from the 2nd French ed by S P Jacques, New York, etc.: Benziger Brothers, 1925; London: Burns, Oates & Co, 1926.

Flew, Antony, *God and Philosophy*, London: Hutchinson, New York: Harcourt, Brace & World, 1966.

Gale, R M, 'Mysticism and Philosophy', *The Journal of Philosophy* LVII (1960), pp 471–81.

Garside, Bruce, 'Language and the Interpretation of Mystical Experience', *International Journal for Philosophy of Religion* III (1972), pp 93–102.

Gilson, Étienne, *The Mystical Theology of St Bernard*, transl by A H C Downes, London and New York: Sheed and Ward, first published in Feb 1940. Reprinted in 1955.

Hepburn, Ronald, *Christianity and Paradox: Critical Studies in Twentieth-Century Theology*, London: C A Watts & Co Ltd, 1958.

Hospers, John, *An Introduction to Philosophical Analysis*, 2nd ed Englewood Cliffs, New Jersey: Prentice-Hall, Inc, 1967; London: Routledge & Kegan Paul, 1970.

Huxley, Aldous, *The Doors of Perception and Heaven and Hell*, Harmondsworth: Penguin Books, 1959; New York and Evanston: Harper Colophon Books, Harper and Row, Publishers, 1963.
The Perennial Philosophy, New York and London: Harper Bros, 1945.

James, William, *Varieties of Religious Experience*, New York: Modern Library, Random House, 1936; London: Longmans, Green & Co, 1952.

Jan van Ruysbroeck, *The Adornment of the Spiritual Marriage, etc.*, transl by C A Wynschenk Dom, ed by Evelyn Underhill, London: John M Watkins, 1951.

Jefferies, Richard, *The Story of My Heart*, London: Constable,

1947.

Johansson, Rune E A, *The Psychology of Nirvana*, London: George Allen & Unwin Ltd, 1969; Garden City, New York: Anchor Books, Doubleday and Co, Inc, 1970.

John of the Cross, *Ascent of Mt Carmel*, transl and ed with a general introd by E Allison Peers, Garden City, New York: Image Books, Doubleday and Co Inc, 1958.
Dark Night of the Soul, transl and ed by E Allison Peers, Garden City, New York: Image Books, Doubleday and Co Inc, 1959.
Living Flame of Love, transl and ed with an introd by E Allison Peers. Garden City, New York: Image Books, Doubleday and Co Inc, 1962.
Spiritual Canticle, 3rd rev ed, transl and ed by E Allison Peers, Garden City, New York: Image Books, Doubleday and Co Inc, 1961.

Jones, Richard H 'Theravāda Buddhism and Morality'. *Journal of the American Academy of Religion* XLVIII (1979), pp 371–87.

Jung, Carl, *Psychology of the Unconscious*, New York: Dodd, Mead and Co, 1947; London: Routledge & Kegan Paul, 1951.

Kalupahana, David, *Buddhist Philosophy: An Historical Analysis*, Honolulu: The University Press of Hawaii, 1976.

Katz, Steven T (ed), *Mysticism and Philosophical Analysis*, (Studies in Philosophy and Religion 5), London: Sheldon Press, New York: Oxford University Press, 1978.

Koestler, Arthur, *The Lotus and the Robot*, London: Hutchinson, 1960; New York: The Macmillan Co, 1961.

Knowles, David, *The English Mystical Tradition*, London: Burns & Oates, 1960; New York and Evanston: Harper Torchbooks, Harper and Row Publishers, 1965.

Landis, Carney, *Varieties of Psychopathological Experience*, ed by Fred A Mettler, New York, etc: Holt, Rinehart and Winston, 1964.

Leuba, James H, *The Psychology of Religious Mysticism*, London: K Paul, Trench, Trubner & Co Ltd, New York: Harcourt Brace & Co Inc, 1925.

Ludovic de Besse, *The Science of Prayer*, London: Burns, Oates and Washbourne Ltd, 1925.

Maréchal, Joseph, *Studies in the Psychology of the Mystics*, transl by Algar Thorold, London: Burns, Oates & Washbourne, Ltd, 1927. Reprinted by Magi Books (Albany, New York, 1964).

Maritain, Jacques, *Art and Scholasticism and the Frontiers of Poetry*, transl by Joseph W Evans, New York: Charles Scribner's Sons, 1962.

Distinguish to Unite, or the Degrees of Knowledge, transl from the 4th French ed under the supervision of Gerald B Phelan. London: Geoffrey Bles, New York: Charles Scribner's Sons, 1959.

Ransoming the Time, transl by Harry Lorin Binsse, New York: Charles Scribner's Sons, 1941. Reprinted by Gordian Press, (New York, 1969). Published in Great Britain as *Redeeming the Time*, (London: Geoffrey Bles, 1943).

Martin, C B, *Religious Belief*, Ithaca, New York: Cornell University Press, 1959.

Masters, R E L and Jean Houston, *The Varieties of Psychedelic Experience*, New York: Dell Publishing Co, 1967.

Mavrodes, George, *Belief in God, A Study in the Epistemology of Religion*, New York: Random House Inc, 1970.

Merton, Thomas, *Zen and the Birds of Appetite*, New York: New Directions, 1968.

Metzner, Ralph (ed), *The Ecstatic Adventure*, New York: Macmillan, 1968.

Moore, Peter, 'Recent Studies of Mysticism: A Critical Survey', *Religion* 3 (1973), pp 146–56.

Murti, T R V, *The Central Philosophy of Buddhism, a Study of the Madhyamika System*, London: George Allen and Unwin, 1955.

Nicholson, Reynold A, *The Mystics of Islam*, London: Routledge and Kegan Paul Ltd, 1963.

Oakes, Robert A, 'Biochemistry and Theistic Mysticism', *Sophia* XV (July 1976), pp 10–16.

'"God": An Observation Term?', *The Modern Schoolman* LIV (1976), pp 43–56.

'Mediation, Encounter and God', *International Journal for Philosophy of Religion* II (1971), pp 148–55.

Otto, Rudolf, *The Idea of the Holy: An Inquiry into the Non-Rational Factor in the Idea of the Divine and its Relation to the Rational*, (with additions), transl by John W Harvey, New York: Oxford University Press, 1958; Harmondsworth: Penguin Books, 1959.

Mysticism East and West, A Comparative Analysis of the Nature of Mysticism, transl. by Bertha L Bracey and Richenda C Payne, New York: Meridian Books, 1957.

Owens, H P, *The Christian Knowledge of God*, London: University of London, the Athlone Press, 1960.

Pahnke, Walter N, 'The Contribution of the Psychology of Religion to the Therapeutic Use of the Psychedelic Substances', *The Uses of LSD in Psychotherapy and Alcoholism*, ed by Harold Abramson, Indianapolis: Bobbs-Merrill Co, 1967.

'Drugs and Mysticism', *International Journal of Parapsychology* VIII (1966), pp 295–320. Reprinted with some minor excisions in John White, *The Highest State of Consciousness*, (see below).

'Drugs and Mysticism: An Analysis of the Relationship between Psychedelic Drugs and the Mystical Consciousness', Doctoral Dissertation: Harvard University, 1964.

'LSD and Religious Experience', *LSD, Man and Society*, ed. by R C Debold and R C Leaf, Middletown, Connecticut: Wesleyan University Press, 1967; London: Faber & Faber, 1969.

Pahnke, Walter N and William A Richards, 'Implications of LSD and Experimental Mysticism', *Journal of Religion and Health* 5 (1966), pp 175–208.

Pensa, Corrado, 'On the Purification Concept in Indian Tradition, with Special Regard to Yoga', *East and West* 19 (1969), pp 194–228.

Poulain, Auguste, *The Graces of Interior Prayer (Des Graces d'Oraison). A Treatise on Mystical Theology*, transl from the 6th ed by Leonora L Yorke Smith and corrected to accord with the 10th French ed with an introd by J V Bainvel, St Louis: B. Herder Book Co, 1950.

Prince, Raymond and Charles Savage, 'Mystical States and the Concept of Regression', *Psychedelic Review* 8 (1966), pp 59–75. Reprinted in John White, *The Highest State of Consciousness*, (see below).

Rāmānuja, *The Gitabhashya of Ramanuja*, transl by M R Sampatkumaran, Madras: Professor M Rangacharya Memorial

Trust, 1969.

Richard of St Victor, *Selected Writings on Contemplation*, transl by Clare Kirchberger, London: Faber & Faber, New York: Harper, 1957.

Saṁkara, *The Bhagavad-Gītā with the Commentary of Śrī Śankarachāryā*, transl by A Mahādeva Śāstri, Madras: V Ramaswamy Sastrulu and Sons, 1961.

Shankara's Crest-Jewel of Discrimination (Viveka Chudamani) with a Garland of Questions and Answers (Prasnottara Malika), transl and with an introd to Shankara's philosophy by Swami Prabhavananda and Christopher Isherwood, London: The New English Library Ltd, New York: New American Library, 1970.

Saudreau, Auguste, *The Mystical State, its Nature and Phases*, transl by D M B London: Burns, Oates & Washbourne, Ltd, 1924.

Scharfstein, Ben-Ami, *Mystical Experience*, Oxford: Basil Blackwell, New York: Bobbs-Merrill, 1973.

Schimmel, Annemarie, *Mystical Dimensions of Islam*, Chapel Hill: The University of North Carolina Press, 1975.

Schleiermacher, Friedrich, *The Christian Faith*, Edinburgh: T & T Clark, 1928.

Schmidt, Paul, *Religious Knowledge*, Glencoe, Illinois: The Free Press of Glencoe Inc, 1961.

Scholem, Gershom G, *Major Trends in Jewish Mysticism*, London: Thomas & Hudson, 1955; New York: Schocken Books, 1961.

Sharma, I C, *Ethical Philosophies of India*, New York and Evanston: Harper Torchbooks, Harper and Row, 1970.

Slotkin, James S, *Peyote Religion: A Study in Indian-White Relations*, Glencoe, Illinois: The Free Press, 1956. Reprinted by Octagon Books, (New York, 1975).

Smart, Ninian, *A Dialogue of Religions*, London: SCM Press, 1960. Reissued as *World Religions, A Dialogue*, (Harmondsworth and Baltimore: Penguin Books, 1966).

Doctrine and Argument in Indian Philosophy, London: George Allen and Unwin Ltd, 1964.

Interpretation and Mystical Experience'. *Religious Studies* 1 (1965), pp 75–87.

'Mystical Experience'. *Sophia* I (April, 1962), pp 19–26.

Smith, Huston, 'Do Drugs Have Religious Import?', *The Journal of Philosophy* LXI (1964), pp 517–30.

Smith, John E, *Experience and God*, New York: Oxford University Press, 1968.

Srinivasachari P N, *The Philosophy of Viśiṣṭādvaita*, Adyar: The Adyar Library, 1946.

Stace, Walter T, *Man Against Darkness and Other Essays*, Pittsburgh: University of Pittsburgh Press, 1967.

Mysticism and Philosophy, London and Basingstoke: Macmillan, Philadelphia and New York: J B Lippincott, 1960.

The Teachings of the Mystics, New York and Scarborough, Ontario: New American Library, c 1960.

Streng, Frederick, *Emptiness: A Study in Religious Meaning*, Nashville and New York: Abingdon Press, 1967.

Suzuki, D T, *Manual of Zen Buddhism*, New York: Grove Press, 1960.

Teresa of Avila, *Interior Castle*, transl and ed by E Allison Peers, Garden City, New York: Image Books, Doubleday & Co Inc, 1961.

The Life of Teresa of Jesus, transl and ed by E Allison Peers, Garden City, New York: Image Books, Doubleday & Co Inc, 1960.

The Way of Perfection, transl and ed by E Allison Peers, Garden City, New York: Image Books, Doubleday and Co Inc, 1964.

Tillich, Paul, *Theology of Culture*, ed by Robert C Kimbell, New York: Oxford University Press, 1959.

Underhill, Evelyn, *Mysticism, A Study in the Nature and Development of Man's Spiritual Consciousness*, 12th ed, revised, London: Methuen & Co, 1930; Cleveland & New York: Meridian Books, The World Publishing Co, 1955.

Wapnick, Kenneth, 'Mysticism and Schizophrenia', *Journal of Transpersonal Psychology* 1 (1969), pp 49–67. Reprinted in John White, *The Highest State of Consciousness*, (see below).

Watts, Alan, *The Way of Zen*, London: Thames & Hudson, New York: Pantheon Books, 1957.

White, John (ed), *The Highest State of Consciousness*, Garden City, New York: Anchor Books, Doubleday and Co, Inc, 1972.

Wilson, John, *Language and Christian Belief*, London: Macmillan & Co Ltd, New York: St Martin's Press, 1958.

Philosophy of Religion, the Logic of Religious Belief, London and New York: Oxford University Press, 1961.

Zæhner, R C, *The Comparison of Religions*, Boston: Beacon Press, 1962. Originally published as *At Sundry Times, an Essay in the Comparison of Religions* (London: Faber & Faber Ltd, 1958).

Concordant Discord, the Interdependence of Faiths, Being the Gifford Lectures on Natural Religion. Delivered at St Andrews in 1967–1969 by R C Zæhner, Oxford: The Clarendon Press, 1970.

Drugs, Mysticism and Make Believe, London: Wm Collins Ltd, 1972. Published in the United States as *Zen, Drugs and Mysticism*, (New York: Pantheon Books, 1973).

Hindu and Muslim Mysticism, London: University of London, The Athlone Press, 1960, New York: Schocken Books, 1969.

Hinduism, London: Oxford University Press, 1962, New York: Oxford University Press, 1966.

Mysticism. Sacred and Profane, an Inquiry into Some Varieties of Praeternatural Experience, New York and London: Oxford University Press, 1961.

Our Savage God, London: W Collins Ltd, 1974, New York: Sheed & Ward, 1975.

Index of Proper Names